D0915594

ARRESTING ABUSE

ARRESTING
ABUSE

Mandatory Legal Interventions,

Power, and Intimate Abusers

Keith Guzik

Northern Illinois University Press

DeKalb

© 2009 by Northern Illinois University Press

Published by the Northern Illinois University Press, DeKalb, Illinois 60115

Manufactured in the United States using postconsumer-recycled, acid-free paper.

All Rights Reserved

Library of Congress Cataloging-in-Publication Data

Design by Shaun Allshouse

Guzik, Keith.

Arresting abuse: mandatory legal interventions, power, and intimate abusers /
Keith Guzik.

   p.   cm.

Includes bibliographical references and index.

ISBN 978-0-87580-403-3 (clothbound : acid-free paper)

1. Family violence—Law and legislation—United States. 2. Family violence—
United States. I. Title.

KF9322.G89 2009

345.73'0255—dc22

2009009090

To Dick and Flora,
For the Wisdom and Work Ethic

Contents

Acknowledgments

A work of this type is, of course, not possible without the support of various individuals and organizations. And I want to apologize from the outset for the names I overlook. But of those I haven't, I would first and foremost like to thank the offenders and criminal justice organizations and workers in "Centralia County" who allowed me to poke and prod around their life experiences and day-to-day workplaces to better understand the practice and effects of mandatory legal interventions against domestic violence. I hope this book repays in some measure the immense trust you showed me as a researcher.

A number of other groups provided me the material support necessary to complete this project. I would especially like to thank the Law and Social Science Program of the National Science Foundation for the Dissertation Improvement Grant that provided me the funds to complete my research and have my interviews transcribed; the Department of Sociology at the University of Illinois for graciously providing me graduate assistantships throughout my time there; the Center for Latin American and Caribbean Studies (CLACS) at the University of Illinois for a Tinker Field Research Grant that allowed me to begin researching and thinking more earnestly about legal interventions against domestic violence; the University of Illinois Graduate College for travel grants that allowed me to attend academic conferences in order to discuss this research; and the Law and Society Association for selecting and supporting me to attend its Graduate Student Workshop, which put me into contact with a talented group of scholars who helped me further refine my work. I would also like to express my gratitude to Bloomfield College for providing me a work environment where I could bring this book to completion, and to Northern Illinois University Press, and Melody Herr and Sara Hoerdeman in particular, for having faith in me as an author.

This book also required the critical input of a number of minds much sharper than my own. I am indebted to the anonymous readers who reviewed earlier versions of this manuscript as well as my related work for invaluable feedback that shaped the trajectory of the ideas presented here. Non-anonymously, I need thank Catherine Kenney and Jennifer Hardesty for their careful reading of and wonderful input to my dissertation, on which this book is based. I thank Elizabeth Pleck as well, not only for her excellent comments on the dissertation, but for first pushing me to understand and remain sensitive to the different types of abuse subsumed under the generic term of "domestic violence." Various scholars I had the good fortune to meet at different Law and Society Annual Meetings also influenced my work in positive ways. I am grateful to Donna Coker, Sally Engle, Holly Maguigan, James Ptacek, Jinney Smith, and Deborah Tuerkheimer for insightful discussions and their positive reception of my research. The work of getting the manuscript into something approaching publishable form was aided greatly by Evan Stark. His careful review of my work and encyclopedic knowledge of domestic violence and the law impelled me to think more carefully about many of the ideas in the book, especially those concerning abuser types. Though not directly influencing the ideas appearing here, a special mention is also owed to Marie Butler, whose precise transcriptions of my interviews made the work of analyzing hours of dialogue considerably easier.

Finally, I would like to give special thanks to three people who have served as my mentors over the years. I thank Juan Carlos Gorlier for having taken the extraordinary amounts of time and energy to put me under his wing and develop my research interests and academic skills. Our intellectual explorations at Storrs and on the streets of Boston will always remain dear to me. I am equally obliged to Andrew Pickering for introducing me to a world of ideas I could not have imagined existed—never mind becoming taken with—before stepping foot in central Illinois. Wherever our future paths might lead, I sincerely hope they continue to cross. Lastly, this book does not exist without Anna-Maria Marshall, who nurtured my interest in the law, introduced me to the Law and Society community, was generous with her research funds, encouraged me to circulate my work and the proposal for this book, and always covered the tab. Much more than being a great mentor, you have been a great friend. Thank you.

ARRESTING ABUSE

Introduction

We have to find creative ways to prosecute these cases to try to generate pleas of guilty to domestic battery other than the classic, "We have a good case, and if you don't plead guilty, we'll go to trial. And we'll win and you might go to jail or get a harsh sentence." One thing we do is we find ways, and I want to be careful in the way I say this, because, what we're not doing is overprosecuting or overcharging cases. There's a fine line between being aggressive and abusing your powers as a prosecutor. We consciously make an effort to not abuse our powers. But there's a lot of ways to generate pleas to a case that you know the victim will not prosecute. (Matt, Centralia County Assistant State's Attorney)

This black officer was telling me, "Hey, I understand, just go ahead and get your clothes and all and leave." But this white officer came, he said, "No." He said, "Put those handcuffs back on him," just like that. . . . I knew the white officer who told him to put that handcuffs back on me. The only reason I knew him . . . I don't know him, I just knew of him because I'd seen his picture on the TV, and I heard a lot of conflict about what he help did. (Henry)

Once we go through that with the police situation and all, then this relationship ain't gonna be no more good 'cause I'm not gonna trust you no way. If you tell the police this little lie to try to hurt me, then what's gonna be the next lie? That's pretty much how I look at it now. If you're gonna call the police on me, then it's not gonna stop. It's not gonna stop, and I choose not to deal with them type of women. In every relationship, you're supposed to trust, you're supposed to have faith in people, and you're supposed to be able to count on them. So, if you do that, I'm gonna do this, and that's walk away from you. There's too many other women out there that's gonna treat me a lot better. (Walter)

An Overview

This book examines the power of the criminal justice system to stop domestic abusers. Over the last decade, police departments and state's attorney's offices across the country have adopted mandatory arrest and no-drop prosecution policies to handle domestic violence cases.[1] Mandatory arrest policies require the police to arrest abusive partners,[2] while no-drop prosecution policies commit state's attorney's offices to pursue charges against abusers,[3] even if victims do not cooperate (Schneider 2000:92–95). In addition to protecting victims from future violence by ensuring state action (Dawson 2004), these policies are intended to change the behavior of abusers by punishing them for their violent behavior (Buzawa & Buzawa 1996a:178; Herrell & Hofford 1990).

The embrace of the criminal justice system as the primary weapon in the fight against domestic violence comes at a time when various dimensions of U.S. society are being "governed through crime" (Simon 2007). On the heels of reductions in social welfare spending spearheaded by the Reagan administration and continued under the Clinton and Bush administrations, the criminal justice system in general and punishment in particular have become principal means for conducting social policy. Most famously, the 1980s witnessed the emergence of a new assemblage of specialized criminal statutes, administrative bodies, and policing procedures to combat drug use (Massing 2000; Nolan 2001). Similar processes have occurred with respect to juvenile misconduct (Kupchick 2004) and mental illness (Goldkamp & Irons-Guynn 2000) as well.

Controversial from the start, mandatory arrest and no-drop prosecution have been the subjects of increasingly vigorous debate among battered women's advocates and legal scholars. Critics charge that mandatory policies disempower women by removing decision making from them (Ford 1991, 2003; Mills 2003) and aggravate the negative consequences of criminal justice interventions in poor and minority communities (Dasgupta 2003; Coker 2001; Ferraro & Boychuk 1992). As a result, some have called upon the women's antiviolence movement to "divest" from the criminal justice system and centralize "the ownership for ending violence against women" within community-based groups and procedures (Dasgupta 2003). Proponents generally maintain that the measures are needed to provide battered women the same legal protections afforded other victims of violent crime (Flemming 2003; Hanna 1996; Klein 1996). Moreover, the criminal justice response has been hindered by a faulty view of domestic violence that misses both the nature and the harms of abusers' controlling behavior (Stark 2007). Thus, what is needed is not a retreat from the state, but rather an intensification of the alliance based on the criminalization of "coercive control" (Stark 2005).

Despite this attention, little is known about how mandatory arrest and no-drop prosecution actually work in practice and how they affect abusers. Few studies have examined how the police and courts implement these policies, and fewer still have interviewed perpetrators to explore how they change as a result. Without such an understanding, it is difficult to know the true impact of this approach to combating intimate partner abuse. This book represents an effort to answer these fundamental questions.

The quotes that begin the introduction provide a glimpse into the central themes of the book. I hope that they might serve as general lessons for studying the application of punishment and criminal legal interventions in other contexts as well. The first theme is that practice matters. That is, *the power of the criminal justice system is exercised through specific tactics* by which law enforcement and criminal court officers are able to gain control over abusers. For those already familiar with policing and prosecution practice in other settings, many of the tactics described in this book—such as the packaging of criminal charges hinted at by Matt, the assistant state's attorney—will appear familiar. Others, as we will see, represent legal innovations designed to accommodate the requirement to aggressively pursue domestic violence cases. Whatever their provenance, such tactics figure prominently in the fight against intimate abuse. Not only do they represent the means by which legal authorities are able to realize arrests and win convictions, but they also structure the significance of punishment for offenders. As such, remaining aware of the practices through which power is actualized is critical for understanding the impact that punishment produces.

Second, *the fight for gender equality through the criminal justice system is not easily separated from the processes of racial and class inequality that the same system engenders.* This basic lesson is only partly demonstrated in arrest and conviction numbers, which evidence disproportionate numbers of African Americans arrested and prosecuted for domestic violence.[4] More importantly, as the quote from Henry demonstrates, the meanings that offenders attach to their experiences of being arrested and prosecuted are shaded by race and class. While advocates hope that punishment teaches abusers a lesson, often the lesson they learn is that they are the victims of an unjust legal system that discriminates against the poor and persons of color. Thus, to understand the impact of punishment, we must also remain cognizant of the broader social context in which such policies are deployed and consider the possibility of unintended consequences.

Finally, *the power of the criminal justice system is continuously opposed by the agency of abusers.*[5] While mandatory arrest and no-drop prosecution are intended to give the state control over offenders, throughout their contact with the police and courts, abusers maintain their capacity for meaningful action. Even behind bars, they are able to invent and implement new forms of control that allow them to exert influence over their partners. And as Walter's words demonstrate, in the face of the multiple forces coercing them to change, abusers are able to define their experiences in ways that preserve their sense of self and the patterns of abusive behavior that accompany such definitions. Being sensitive to individuals' capacity to resist power, then, is critical for understanding the impact of punishment upon those deemed criminal.

From the outset, it must be noted that this is not and cannot be a definitive tally of the value of the criminal legal system in the fight against domestic violence. Most significantly, it lacks the views of victims, making it impossible to know both the full nature of change that perpetrators experienced and the benefits that victims derive from these policies, regardless of their impact on abusers. However, in terms of the criminal justice system's power to change offenders, this work provides a critical assessment. While mandatory arrest and no-drop prosecution allow the state to extend formal legal supervision over an increasing number of violent men and women, thus seemingly increasing its power over them, offenders prove resistant to change. They see themselves as victims of injustice, continue to view their violence as justified, and devise new strategies to preserve their definition and enactment of self. The reasons for these outcomes rest in the nature of power itself, in the state tactics, structures of social inequality, and modes of individual agency through which mandatory arrest and no-drop prosecution are realized. While the rest of the book is dedicated to explaining these processes of power, it is not too early to state here my belief that the promise for defeating intimate partner abuse lies in better matching the tactics of power used against abuse to the antiviolence movement's goals for gender change and to exercise such force through mechanisms and institutions that do not exacerbate social inequality.

The Feminist Fight against Domestic Violence and Mandating Legal Action

Men's violence against their intimate partners has emerged as a concern in the public conscience at different times in American history (Pleck 1987). In the 1970s, it was second-wave feminists who spearheaded efforts to eliminate intimate partner abuse. Challenging prevailing understandings of domestic violence as a "private" problem for couples to work out on their own or as the consequence of a psychological disorder affecting women who stay with abusive partners (Roy 1977), feminists defined domestic violence as a "public" problem embedded in a web of social relations that enabled men's violence against their partners (Schneider 2000:5–6). The gendered division of labor in society, for instance, rendered many women dependent on their partners for economic survival and thus prevented them from leaving abusive relationships (Martin 1976:39–43). Similarly, cultural norms dictated that violence against women was permissible in certain contexts (Martin 1976:61–66).

The law, meanwhile, reinforced the definition of domestic violence as a private problem. Prior to the 1980s, police officers would seldom arrest men who battered their wives, and prosecutors rarely filed criminal charges against abusers (Binder & Meeker 1992). The police instead pursued a policy of mediation (Bard 1970). In mediation, the goal of officers responding to domestic violence calls was to defuse the situation and restore peace in the home, which they attempted by separating the couple, perhaps "walking the husband around the block," before allowing both partners to reenter the home (Jaffe et al. 1993).[6] In the rare instances in which arrests were made, prosecutors often dismissed the cases, since victims, whether for fear of retaliation or emotional and financial attachment to their partners, were unwilling to testify against their partners (Ferraro & Boychuk 1992:219–20).

Mobilizing on the tenet that "the personal is political," feminists premised the struggle against domestic violence on challenging the socially constructed boundaries between "public" and "private." To counter the impact of the gendered division of labor that relegated many women to the "private" sphere of the home, shelters were founded to provide victims a safe space away from their abusers (Schechter 1982).[7] In place of popular "public" images reinforcing detrimental cultural attitudes toward domestic violence (think Rhett Butler slapping and then bedding a "hysterical" Scarlett O'Hara in *Gone With The Wind*), feminists offered images and stories drawn from women's "private" lives (think *The Burning Bed*, the network television film based on the story of Francine Hughes, a survivor of domestic violence who resisted the physical and emotional abuse of her husband by burning him to death as he lay drunk and passed out in bed [Rapping 2000]).

In the legal arena, feminists embraced different strategies to extend protections guaranteed citizens in "public" life to women enduring violence in the "privacy" of their homes. Orders of protection, also referred to as "restraining orders" or "no-contact orders," allowed abused women to access courts independent of police action and have judges issue injunctions barring their abusive partners from contacting them. Lobbying efforts resulted in a number of local-level experiments, such as the well-known Domestic Abuse Intervention Project (DAIP) in Duluth, MN, which combined mandatory arrest policies, advocacy work by battered-women's activists, and educational campaigns in schools and the media (Shepard & Pence 1999; Kurz 1998). Activists also launched a score of successful lawsuits against police departments for denying domestic violence victims the same "equal protection" of the law provided to other victims of violent crime (Buzawa & Buzawa 1996:102–3; Zorza 1992:53–60). On the heels of these expensive lawsuits, and under pressure from insurance companies to prevent future litigation, municipalities began requiring police departments to draw up specific guidelines for handling domestic violence cases more aggressively, which proved to be a major force in the spread of mandatory policies.

However, the impetus for change in the criminal justice system's handling of domestic violence cases came from other directions as well. As Schechter's (1982) authoritative history of the early battered women's movement shows, the government, nearly coterminous with the rise of the movement, demonstrated an interest in criminalizing domestic violence. Already in 1979, President Carter announced the creation of the Interdepartmental Committee on Domestic Violence (Schechter 1982:192; see also Zorza 1992:62). Academic research evaluating the efficacy of projects such as DAIP followed as well, the foremost of which was Sherman and Berk's (1984) landmark study, which found that the use of arrest in domestic violence cases led to a significant decrease in repeat violence in Minneapolis. Finally, the publication of the Attorney General's Task Force on Family Violence's Final Report in 1984 helped formally usher in the new criminal legal approach to domestic violence. Following on Sherman and Berk's research, the Task Force endorsed a policy of deterrence, recommending that arrest "is the appropriate response" to domestic violence cases, that "special units to process family violence cases" be organized for the prosecution of these cases, and that states enact "laws to permit law enforcement officers to make warrantless arrests for misdemeanor offenses involving family violence" (U.S. Attorney General's Task Force on Family Violence 1984).

As a result of these diverse forces, a new regime of domestic violence "governmentality" had taken shape by the 1990s, weighted on the pillars of protection orders, mandatory arrest, no-drop prosecution, and batterer intervention programs. Reconfiguring the boundaries between "public" and "private" space, this new regime endeavored to transform the subjectivities of violent men and victimized women (Merry 1995, 2002). Aggressive arrest and prosecution would disrupt masculine entitlement and power (Merry 1995) and "send a clear social message that battering is impermissible" (Schneider 2000:94). Mandatory action against abusers, in turn, would push women to become independent subjects separated from their abusive partners (Merry 1995). In a similar fashion, orders of protection would function as a spatial technology to control domestic violence by mandating the physical separation of the abusive partner from his victim (Merry 2001). Finally, punishment would be augmented by efforts to reform abusers in court-mandated batterer intervention programs designed to instill "new forms of masculinity" in offenders (Merry 2001:16).

Assessing the Impact of Mandatory Legal Interventions

As noted above, the mandatory elements of this regime have proven contentious for battered-women's advocates. Supporters of the policies contend that they provide battered women the same legal protections afforded other victims of violent crime (Flemming 2003; Hanna 1996; Klein 1996), send a clear message to both batterers and society that intimate abuse is intolerable (Schneider 2000:94), and relieve battered women of the burden of having to make difficult decisions regarding the arrest and prosecution of abusive partners (Wanless 1996; Hanna 1996; Cahn & Lerman 1991; Buel 1988). Recent research has underscored the potential benefits of these policies for victims. Studies have found a lower probability of domestic violence in states possessing more aggressive domestic violence legislation (Dugan 2003), greater victim satisfaction with police than in the past (Stephens & Sinden 2000; Ptacek 1999), high levels of satisfaction with the additional services, such as victim advocates, accompanying more aggressive policing and prosecution (Fleury 2002; Hoyle & Sanders 2000; Buzawa et al. 1999), increased levels of intimate violence reporting to the police (Felson et al. 1999), lower rates of recidivism among men completing sentencing (Murphy et al. 1998), and general support from women for these measures (Smith 2003).

Conversely, critics argue that mandatory policies disempower women by removing decision making from them (Ford 2003, 1991; Mills 2003, 1999) and ignore the grave problems associated with criminal justice administration in the United States, especially for minority populations and the poor (Maguigan 2003; Coker 2001; Welch 1994; Ruttenberg 1994; Ferraro & Pope 1993; Ferraro & Boychuk 1992). These concerns are underscored by studies demonstrating increased numbers of women arrested for domestic violence (Miller 2001), lower rates of intimate violence arrests than stranger violence arrests, when controlling for situational factors such as the presence of weapons (Avakame & Fyfe 2001), increased levels of abuse accompanying higher levels of intimate-violence reporting (Hirschel & Hutchinson 2003; Coulter et al. 1999), prolonged time required for processing cases (Davis et al. 2003), legal authorities' insensitivity to victims of abuse and ignorance of different types of intimate abuse (Ferraro & Pope 1993; George 1998), victim dissatisfaction with prosecutors and what they perceive to be overly harsh treatment of their partners (Davis et al. 2003), aggressive defense strategies that revictimize survivors of violence during criminal trials, and survivors' own fears that they will be forced to testify against their partners and lose their financial support (Hartley 2003).

Implicated in this debate are competing visions of the appropriate role for the state in women's fight for gender equality. Supporters of mandatory policies adhere to a *liberal feminist* perspective (see Smart 1995:70) that sees women's equality tied to extending rights to women. Critics of the mandatory policies argue that a rights-based perspective does not go far enough. As Schneider (2000) writes, "although women's rights have been perhaps 'too much' for society, in a sense they have been 'too little' for the women's movement" (41). Highlighting the intersection of race, class, and gender, feminists adhering to a *social justice* perspective (Smart 1995:180–83) argue that criminal legal measures must be accompanied by other forms of assistance (Merry 1995; Coker 2004), such as public funding for women's economic needs, that would allow women to better manage their situations of abuse. A *critical feminist* perspective (Brown 1995), meanwhile, opposes the social justice and liberal projects altogether, contending that state-based strategies of gender emancipation simply render women colonized subjects of masculinist state power (193–96).

While the dilemmas and difficulties accompanying the implementation of mandatory measures have led some in the past to conclude that women and the law belong to cultures with "irreconcilable differences" (Ferraro & Pope 1993:97), a view that evokes a *critical feminist* perspective, most researchers today take a more pragmatic approach, attempting to identify those elements of criminal justice practice that women find beneficial and amplify them in legal interventions. For instance, studies have noted that women find control over the process of pressing charges or seeking restraining orders "empowering," as it provides them control over legal resources which they can use to manage their violent relationships (Ford 1991; Chaudhuri & Daly 1992). In the same vein, having "attorneys listen to battered women, giving them time and attention" and having "judges understand their situations, giving them support and courage" validate women's claims to abuse and fortify their capacity for managing violence (Chaudhuri & Daly 1992:246). Ptacek's (1999) superb ethnography of women obtaining restraining orders describes not only the different demeanors judges display in their interactions with women and their assailants, but also the positive influence this "emotion labor" provides in having women perceive courts as a space in which they can challenge men's coercive control over them (158, 166).

Responding to these experiences, advocates have worked to train legal authorities to be more responsive and sensitive to the needs of victims (Epstein 1999; Buzawa & Buzawa 2003:157). As well, others have suggested offering women "mandatory action" alternatives to arrest and prosecution that increase their control over the state response to violence. Such alternatives include transporting offenders to detoxification centers (Sherman 1992), restorative justice (Coker 2002; Strang & Braithwaite 2002), and therapeutic justice (Rottman & Casey 1999; Fritzler & Simon 2000).

While this body of literature illuminates the dilemmas of mandatory arrest and no-drop prosecution for victims of intimate partner abuse, less attention has been given to their effects on abusers themselves. Punishing abusers is intended to make them decrease their violence (Hanna 1996:1895) and demonstrate to society that domestic violence will not be tolerated (Schneider 2000). However, studies investigating whether the policies live up to this promise have been few and narrow in their methodological approach.

What we know about the efficacy of aggressive policing strategies stems largely from a series of controlled experiments conducted by criminologists and sponsored by the U.S. National Institute of Justice (NIJ).[8] Couched in rational choice thinking, the experiments tested the hypothesis that arrest would deter batterers from future abuse. To complete the experiments, researchers compared the impact of arrest on future reports of batterer behavior relative to that of other possible interventions, including no arrest, police mediation, or the issuance of citations.

Sherman and Berk's (1984) influential Minneapolis study found that arrest "manifested significantly less subsequent violence" than either advice or orders to leave (Sherman & Berk 1984:261). Subsequent studies placed the deterrent effect of arrest in doubt, however, with three of the five replication studies sponsored by the NIJ actually finding that arrest escalated abuse (Sherman 1992). Further analysis of the arrest experiment data revealed that the deterrent effects of arrest varied for different types of batterers. While it deterred white, employed, married men, it escalated violence among black, unemployed, single men. Criminologists have come to explain these differences through a "stake in conformity" thesis: arrest deters those individuals who have something to lose—whether a job or marriage—while it fails to deter those with nothing to lose (Pate & Hamilton 1992; Sherman 1992; Sherman et al. 1992a; Sherman et al. 1992b).[9]

A more recent reexamination of the arrest experiment data by Maxwell et al. (2002) amends the "stake in conformity" thesis. Importantly, the analysis of these researchers makes use of the victim reports on offender behavior that the arrest experiments collected but were unable to use due to gaps in the data. Correcting for these gaps, the authors find that arrest reduced both the prevalence and incidence of new victimizations (Maxwell et al. 2002:64). And while the deterrent effects diminished over time, the authors found no evidence of an escalation effect from arrest. Additionally, the study's findings do not support the idea that marriage promotes deterrence, but they do confirm the impact of job status, with employment demonstrating "15% to 21% decreases in the odds of new incidents" (Maxwell et al. 2002:68). Thus, this study lends added weight to the view that arrest deters domestic batterers and that offenders' employment status is crucial to its efficacy.

Conversely, the ability of no-drop prosecution to alter the behavior of violent men has been placed in considerable doubt by a handful of statistical studies. The best-known work reports that the chances of new violence are less when victims have the opportunity to drop charges against their abusers (Ford & Regoli 1993). More recently, Davis et al. (2003) find the "proportion of defendants committing new misdemeanors doubled from 12% to 25%" in a Milwaukee court instituting an aggressive prosecution approach. Along the same line, Dugan et al. (2003) discover that "increases in the willingness of prosecutors' offices to take cases of protection order violation are associated with increases in the homicide of white females" (194). Meanwhile, in a study of a Massachusetts court pursuing a no-drop policy, Buzawa et al. (1999) report that a majority of offenders who were not prosecuted or were prosecuted without court supervision do not reoffend.

While these studies provide needed estimates of the outcomes produced by mandatory arrest and evidence-based prosecution, they possess limitations that restrict our understanding of the policies' efficacy. First, the studies do not examine the operation of policing and/or courts. The arrest and prosecution experiments were designed simply to measure the outcomes experienced by batterers exposed to these interventions. Without an understanding of what happens to batterers during arrest and prosecution, we know very little about "the mechanisms by which change in achieved" (Dobash & Dobash 2000).[10]

Second, these studies do not include batterers as sources of data. Nor do they consult research on batterers in their research design or interpretation of findings. They thus ignore the contributions of a whole field of research on intimate abusers. Researchers working in this field have found that batterers represent a distinct type of criminal subject (Johnson 1995; Holtzworth-Munroe & Stuart 1994; Ptacek 1988). Though not examining the effects of mandatory criminal legal interventions, interviews with abusive men have found that police encounters often bring about stories of victimization from men (Eisikovits & Buchbinder 2000:135–37) and serve as the basis for reformulating abusive, masculine identities (Anderson & Umberson 2001:370). As such, the idea that the arrest and prosecution experiments hold that batterers are mere rational, cost-analysis actors who can simply be punished away from violence is overly simplistic.

It is in response to such limitations that some researchers have called for research that examines "how assailants experience the criminal legal system" (Fleury 2002:203; see also Maxwell et al. 2002:72–73; Fagan 1996:33). By understanding how domestic batterers experience mandatory arrest and no-drop prosecution and what outcomes these experiences produce in their lives, we would better understand the efficacy of mandatory policies in the fight against intimate abuse.

Studying the Impact of Mandatory Legal Interventions on Abusers

In examining the impact of mandatory arrest and no-drop prosecution on abusers, this study begins by taking seriously the claims of Sally Engle Merry (2001, 2002) that these policies represent elements of a new regime of domestic violence governmentality. Inspired by Foucault's studies of the "micro-physics of power" and the creation of subjectivities within institutional sites such as the prison (1977) and insane asylum (1965), post-structuralist "governmentality" scholars (Rose 1999; Dean 1999; Valverde 1998; Burchell et al. 1991) understand institutions not as monolithic actors who repress individual subjects, but as assemblages of actors, strategies, and techniques that actively engage individuals in order to shape their subjectivities.

Governmentality has been growing in popularity within the social sciences as a theoretical framework for understanding and analyzing the operation of power in modern and postmodern society. This popularity owes in good measure to this framework's sensitivity to the intersections of structure and agency, two core concerns of the social sciences. Expanding upon Foucault's descriptions of power, studies of governmentality understand that individuals take shape through their participation in different programs of governmentality, or "endeavours to shape, guide, and direct the conduct of others" (Rose 1999:3). As such, governmentality offers a deeper and more dynamic understanding of power than do the structural perspectives handed down from Marxist scholars.

Especially enlightening in this field is the work of Mitchell Dean (1998) and Marianne Valverde (1998), both of whom study problem or "targeted" populations, the unemployed and the alcoholic, respectively. These authors provide detailed accounts of the operations utilized by authorities to produce ethical, self-governing subjects. For Dean, by establishing a new unemployment benefits program that required the unemployed to not only acquire marketable job skills, but choose an employment placement enterprise (ECE) to manage their cases and the provision of those skills, the Australian government placed the unemployed person in an operation whereby he or she was transformed from a client of the state, protected from the workings and demands of the market, to an "active entrepreneur of his or her own self" on the job market. For Valverde (1998), by having alcoholics complete each of "the twelve steps," Alcoholics Anonymous places their members in a series of pragmatic operations, from the admission of powerlessness over alcohol to carrying the message and practices to other alcoholics, whereby they come to be not recovered alcoholics, but alcoholics able to control their disease. Following these researchers, I conceptualize the new regime of domestic violence governmentality as a unique constellation of institutional practices that work individuals in particular ways to reshape their subjectivities. At the most basic level, then, this work looks to uncover how mandatory arrest and no-drop prosecution engage domestic batterers and what outcomes batterers experience as a result.

This investigation of mandatory legal interventions is also informed by law and society research, a rapidly growing area in the social sciences. The field offers two major contributions that guide this study. The first is past research detailing the operation of policing and criminal courts. Ethnographic studies of policing, conducted by criminologists in the late sixties, seventies, and early eighties (LaFave 1965; Wilson 1968; Bittner 1970; Reiss 1971; Rubinstein 1973; Muir 1977; Black 1980; Brown 1981), describe in detail the specific strategies (law enforcement, order maintenance, and service provision), stages (contact, processing, and exit), and practices (questioning, commands, and threats or actual use of physical coercion) comprising policing in general and domestic violence policing in particular. Ethnographic descriptions of court practice by law and society scholars, meanwhile, provide a continually evolving view of the different operations of power in the court setting, including procedural rules (Packer 1968), the authority of the prosecutor's office (Packer 1968), the organizational interests of courtroom workgroups (Eisenstein & Jacob 1977; Blumberg 1967; Casper 1972), the punitive aspects of pretrial proceedings (Feeley 1977), and the discursive nature of attorney–client interactions (Sarat & Felstiner 1995; Felstiner 1998).

These thick descriptions provide an invaluable resource for understanding observations of the police and court practice. Of course, mandatory arrest and no-drop prosecution are intended to modify usual law enforcement practice by curtailing the discretionary power of the police and prosecutors. As such, what batterers experience as they come into contact with the police and courts differs from what other criminal suspects experience. This book explains that change in criminal justice practice in order to answer the question of what happens to intimate abusers when they are arrested and prosecuted under mandatory policies.

The second contribution of law and society research is insights into the "common place of law" (Ewick & Silbey 1998), or people's everyday experience of the law. Challenging traditional instrumental, or deterrence, approaches to criminal justice, studies of people's experience of criminal law have found that the manner in which criminal justice procedures are administered is more meaningful to defendants' subsequent law-abiding behavior than are the substantive outcomes the procedures yield. Jonathan Casper's (1972) seminal study researching policing and the courts from the perspective of felons found that offenders' encounters with the police and criminal courts did little to affect their relation to crime. "When they do violate the law and happen to get caught," offenders "do not find morality or principle guiding the behavior of those who are supposed to be enforcing the law" (Casper 1972:96). A similar conclusion is reached in the research on restorative and procedural justice, pioneered by John Braithwaite (1989) and Tom Tyler (1990), respectively. Tyler (1990), for instance, finds that defendants are more likely to abide by the decisions of legal authorities when they perceive those decisions to be procedurally just, meaning that authorities sought their "participation" and were "neutral," "respectful," and "fair" when making them.

Outside criminal law, other socio-legal studies emphasize legal encounters as dynamic performances that unfold through the interaction of authorities *and* citizens in time. For instance, observing attorney–client interactions in divorce cases, Sarat and Felstiner (1995) find that neither the client nor the attorney is able to control their meetings, despite the latter's intimate knowledge of the law. Rather, the meetings are interactive sessions in which the definition of goals and strategies are "bound up with the strategies and tactical efforts of both lawyer and client to 'control' and direct their interaction" (Sarat & Felstiner 1995:7). Ewick and Silbey (1998) expand upon these ideas in examining legal consciousness. They find that the meaning of law for people is bound together with the ideologies they hold about legal rules, institutions, and authorities and the specific performances through which they enact these ideologies. Understanding the outcomes of law thus depends on comprehending the dexterity of its players. The lesson to be drawn from these studies is that if one wishes to know the impact of mandatory policies upon abusers, one needs consider not only the actions of the police and courts, but also those of offenders, as well as the meanings that these legal encounters produce.

Finally, this book is also informed by more recent work on the nature of intimate partner abuse and domestic batterers. In recent years, this field of investigation has advanced in two significant directions. These are research on batterer types and research on the intersection of masculinity and intimate abuse.

For years, many domestic violence researchers have argued that not all batterers and types of abuse are alike. Holtzworth-Munroe and Stuart

(1994), for instance, identify three major subtypes of batterers: "family-only batterers," who engage in the least severe violence, are unlikely to engage in sexual and/or psychological abuse, and restrict their violence to family members; "dysphoric/borderline batterers," who engage in moderate to severe marital violence, including psychological and sexual abuse, and who demonstrate deep emotional dependence on their intimate partners; and "generally violent/antisocial batterers," who engage in moderate to severe marital violence, including psychological and sexual abuse, and who display antisocial personality disorders (477–82). Michael Johnson (2006a, 1995), meanwhile, draws from the work of feminist researchers and classifies domestic violence according to two central dimensions—violence *and* control. Using these criteria, Johnson (2006a) distinguishes among four types of intimate abuse: 1. *intimate terrorism,* in which the "individual is violent and controlling"; 2. *violent resistance,* in which the "individual is violent but not controlling, the partner is the violent and controlling one"; 3. *situational couple violence,* in which the "individual is violent," but "neither the individual nor the partner is violent and controlling"; and 4. *mutual violence control,* in which "both the individual and partner are violent and controlling" (1). Most recently, Evan Stark (2007) forcefully argues that domestic violence consists of three basic types: "*fights* in which one or both partners use force to address situationally specific conflicts"; "*partner assaults* . . . where violence and threats are used to hurt, subjugate, and exert power over a partner"; and "*coercive control,*" in which men use violence, intimidation, isolation, and/or control to "inhibit women's self-direction, compromise their liberty, and cause a range of harms that are not easily subsumed under safety concerns" (234–42, 219).

These findings on batterer and abuse types are critical to domestic violence research and policy. First, they offer a way to resolve the divisive symmetry debates that have plagued this field of research. Since the 1970s, domestic violence research in the social sciences has been divided between family violence researchers (Straus et al. 1980; Straus & Gelles 1990), who insist that women are as violent as men in intimate relationships, and feminist researchers (Dobash & Dobash 1979; Martin 1976), who contend that domestic violence involves men's violence against women in intimate relationships. In his research, Johnson claims that each group of researchers has relied on different samples of batterers that have simply captured the different types of abuse. Family violence researchers, relying on general population surveys that only asked about and recorded violent conduct, overwhelmingly captured situational couple violence, while feminist researchers, listening to victims' stories of abuse gathered from shelter and court samples, largely captured intimate terrorism (Johnson 1995:288–91).

Second, these categories also promise a more practical conceptualization of the problem for service providers to work with. For example, in "fights" or situational couple violence, "both partners view the use of force as a legitimate (if not necessarily desirable) form of conflict resolution, and injury is very rare" (Stark 2007:234). "Assaults" and "coercive control," on the other hand, involve both violent and nonviolent tactics that work to subjugate women (Stark 2007:236–41). As a consequence, one practical step for improving legal interventions against intimate abuse, if women's equality is indeed a concern, would be to "exclude fights from interdiction" and calibrate assessments to better detect and intervene against coercive control (see Stark 2007:378–82).

Despite their obvious importance, the research community has been slow to embrace these typologies (Johnson 2006a:1014–15). Agreeing with Johnson's argument that we must use such distinctions if we are "to make useful policy recommendations," this book implements them to classify the abusive behavior of the research participants. As a consequence, this study also explores whether mandatory arrest and no-drop prosecution policies affect different types of abusers differently.

The second key development in domestic violence research has been studies further elaborating the links between masculinity and intimate partner abuse (Eisikovits & Buchbinder 2000; Dobash et al. 2000; Hearn 1998; Ptacek 1988). This research, based on interviews with violent men, finds not only that batterers explain their violence by minimizing its severity, excusing themselves from responsibility, and/or justifying its use, but that the performance and telling of violence hangs together with men's construction of masculine subjectivities. Men present their violence as rational and effective, as opposed to the hysterical, irrational violence of women (Anderson & Umberson 2001), and use it as a means for confirming a "masculine identity" not "'subordinated' to a woman" (Dobash & Dobash 1998:167). Significantly then, men's performance of violence helps them realize key elements of a masculine self: rationality, family order, power over women. This book also makes use of this line of research to address how mandatory arrest and no-drop prosecution affect the violent, masculine subjectivities of abusers.

To pursue these diverse lines of inquiry, I conducted field research in Centralia County,[11] a Midwestern county home to a large state university and three small cities. Some 180,860 people reside in the county, 79% of whom are white, 11% African American, 7% Asian, and 3% Latino (see Table 1). Economically, the standing of these groups varies widely, with white households earning a median income of $41,707 and black, Asian, and Latino households earning between $20,000–25,000. The similarity between the household incomes of blacks, Asians, and Latinos owes largely to college enrollment. While 59.1% of Asians and 42.9% of Latinos in the county are enrolled in college, just 17.7% of blacks are (U.S. Census 2000).

In sum, African Americans in Centralia County, as in many other parts of the United States, represent a marginalized group in terms of both household income and educational attainment. As might be expected, this disparity plays a role in the administration of domestic violence law in the county, a point I will return to at various places in the book.

Centralia proved an ideal site for the study, since each of the major police departments in the county follows a mandatory arrest policy and the county's state's attorney's office pursues a no-drop prosecution policy. To collect data for this project, I employed different qualitative methods to study mandatory interventions across multiple sites and sources of data. To study what happens to intimate abusers when they are arrested under mandatory policies, I completed ride-alongs with police officers in Plainsville, one of the three cities in Centralia County, in order to observe mandatory arrest in action and to question officers about the specific tactics and strategies they use in policing domestic violence.[12] To study what happens to intimate abusers when they are prosecuted under no-drop prosecution, I conducted field observations at the Centralia County Court, sitting in at the courtroom to observe arraignment, pretrial, plea bargains, and trial proceedings, and interviewed local defense attorneys and members of the state's attorney's office to better understand the practices used in handling partner abuse cases. Finally, to study how mandatory arrest and no-drop prosecution affect the abuse of violent masculine subjects, I conducted interviews with 30 domestic violence suspects, in which I asked respondents to describe their interactions with the police and the courts, the events that led to their arrest, and the changes that they had experienced in their lives as a result of their legal encounters.[13]

Chapter Summaries

The results of this research are presented over six chapters. The first chapter provides an ethnographic description of mandatory arrest policing, paying specific attention to the practices that comprise officers' response to domestic violence calls. The chapter finds that the performance of domestic violence policing is significantly different than it was in the past. More than having undergone a mere change of attitude, the police have refined old as well as developed new policing tactics to respond to the particular characteristics of domestic violence calls and the agency of domestic batterers. Tracing these practices in time, the chapter describes how these tactics allow law enforcement officers to gradually dislodge abusers from their interpersonal and material relations of violence and socialize them into new social relations as subordinates to state power. Interestingly, in terms of thinking about the meaning of these practices for men as well as the intersec-

TABLE 1—Population, Household Income, and College Enrollment in
Centralia County

VARIABLE	VALUE
Population	186,800
White	78.8%
Black	11.2%
Asian	6.5%
Latino	2.9%
Median Household Income	
White	$41,707
Black	$23,372
Asian	$20,170
Latino	$25,127
Enrollment in College	
White	22.3% (30,659)
Black	17.7% (3,378)
Asian	59.1% (6,645)
Latino	42.9% (2,054)

Source—2000 United States Census

tion of gender and the law, officers are trained in and rely upon discursive techniques that resemble and play upon men's own masculine discourses of abuse. In this sense, the police gain power over domestic battery suspects by turning their own discourses and relations of abuse against them.

In the second chapter, I describe the different practices that batterers are exposed to under no-drop prosecution. The chapter explains that mandatory prosecution brings about numerous tactical changes in the court's handling of domestic battery cases that shape the agency of suspected batterers in specific ways. While many of these tactics coalesce in an effort to have the defendant plead guilty, no-drop prosecution engenders its own resistance from defense attorneys who regard it as a flawed, overly aggressive use of prosecutorial power. Regardless of whether suspected abusers plead or not, their violence is redefined as they are processed through the court setting. If the police look to make batterers speak about their violence in order to gather evidence against them, the courts generally silence them, as the state already possesses the documented story of violence it needs to prosecute the case. In attorney–client meetings, however, defense attorneys actively shape men's stories of abuse into legally viable accounts. In this sense, the courts strengthen men's evasions of violence, even as they work to have men plead guilty to domestic battery.

The third chapter introduces the participants taking part in this study and the violence they are reported to have committed. To accomplish the first task, I use three different sources of data (police reports, criminal histories, and batterer narratives) to construct a measure for classifying respondents according to Michael Johnson's categories of abuser types. To accomplish the second, I use the police reports again to classify participants' abusive conduct according to measures taken from both the Revised Conflict Tactics Scale and feminist research on intimate conflicts. This chapter finds that the respondents participating in this study represent a diverse group in terms of social background, batterer type, and severity of violence committed, thereby evidencing that mandatory arrest and no-drop prosecution policies in Centralia County net different types of batterers and domestic violence.

The fourth chapter describes domestic violence suspects' experiences with mandatory arrest and no-drop prosecution. It highlights their agency in responding to the operations of power by the police, jail, and criminal court against them, which is manifested in legal performances that fluctuate between compliance with and defiance of the law. These legal performances are central to both the substantive outcomes intimate abusers experience and the interpretive meanings these experiences hold. On the one hand, the police and courts are able to regularly secure arrests and convictions against them, which leaves abusers under the state's administrative authority. Importantly, arrests and plea bargain convictions disrupt many abusers' attempts to explain away their violence during police investigations and to reestablish control over their victimized partners during plea negotiations. However, these actions do not deliver strong messages about abuse. Nearly all the respondents in this study understand their punishments as unjust sanctions meted out by an unjust local legal system rather than the consequences of their own actions. These injustice claims emerge from abusers' group (gender, race, and class) identities as well as the very practices through which the police and courts gain authority over them.

In the fifth chapter, I examine men's descriptions of both the events that led to their arrest and their intimate relationships. This chapter finds that intimate abusers continue to evade responsibility for violence following arrest and prosecution. In addition to denying, minimizing, excusing, and justifying their violence, they also avoid responsibility through a new type of story not identified in past research: self-defense. In resonance with past research, this chapter finds that respondents construct and affirm masculine identities as strong, powerful men when describing their violence. Significantly, however, it also finds that men frequently neglect to affirm masculine identities through their violence and simply edit themselves from the stories. Respondents' descriptions of their intimate relationships deepen their constructions of gendered subjectivities, with men noting their capacity for accommodation and caring while emphasizing their partners' controlling, promiscuous, crazed, and manipulative nature. Through their stories of violence and construction of gendered subjects both within and outside the violent event, men distance themselves from their violence while laying claim to a victim identity. In comparing these stories with those told the police at the time of arrest, this chapter finds that men's descriptions of violence are durable discursive constructs that change little through time. Those who do change more often demonstrate negative, lateral movements between stories of evasion rather than positive, progressive assumptions of responsibility.

The sixth chapter examines the changes that respondents experienced following their contact with mandatory arrest and no-drop prosecution. This chapter shows that criminal legal encounters carry greater consequences for domestic violence suspects than previously noted. These include not only the loss of jobs and trust in marriages, which affect those with "high stakes in conformity," but also the loss of the assurance that their abuse will be kept private by their partners. Public exposure of private violence costs batterers their social recognition as normal, nonviolent citizens and intimate partners, a stigmatization that affects various aspects of their lives, from the ability to secure employment to the ability to realize intimacy with new partners. To mitigate these costs, batterers attempt to reprivatize their violence by keeping their abusive histories secret and defining their selves as nonviolent. The consequences of their violent pasts continue to weigh on them as they discuss their futures. Most express a will to avoid renewed contact with the criminal justice system. In addition, they describe particular plans for governing the self to realize this goal. Involving different configurations between the self, intimate other, and social forces such as religion and employment, these programs of self-governance carry different implications for abusers' careers in intimate abuse. While some evidence deterred batterer subjectivities, others carry little hope for change in their performance of violence.

In the conclusion, I reflect on the significance of these findings. Returning to the beginning, I discuss what this research means for thinking about domestic violence policy and, by extension, the deployment of the criminal legal mechanisms for conducting social policy. Building from the central themes of the book—the tactics of criminal justice, the interconnectivity of structures of inequality, and the agency of abusers—I consider the possibilities offered by different proposals for reforming the social response to intimate abuse, proposals that range from intensifying the current approach to bypassing the state altogether. Ultimately, I contend, the promise for defeating domestic violence lies in implementing victim-centered justice procedures that better match the tactics of state power to the goals of victim empowerment and offender responsibility. The book finishes with a specific set of proposals that could be implemented to realize this vision.

1   The Practice of Mandatory Arrest

On June 10, 1983, Tracey Thurman called the Torrington Police Department to report that her estranged husband, Buck, who had physically abused and threatened to kill her on numerous occasions, and against whom she had a restraining order, was standing outside her house. It was not the first time Tracey had contacted the Torrington police. In fact, she had notified them on at least 10 previous occasions about his physical abuse and threats. Some 25 minutes after Tracey's call, a single officer arrived on the scene. By that time, Buck Thurman had dragged Tracey by the hair to the backyard and stabbed her 13 times. When the officer reached the backyard, Buck was still holding the bloody knife. In the officer's presence, Buck dropped the knife and stomped on Tracey's head until her neck broke. He then ran into the house, grabbed their son, returned to the scene, and dropped the child on the wounded woman, telling him that he "had killed your fucking mother." He then kicked Tracey in the head a second time before three additional officers responded to the scene. After the arrival of the other officers, Buck continued to wander around the backyard, where a crowd had gathered, and continued to threaten his wife. When approaching to attack Tracey, who was now lying on a stretcher, a last time, Buck was finally arrested and taken into custody (*Thurman vs. Torrington* 1984; Brennan 1989).

Tracey Thurman's story has come to represent domestic violence policing at its worst. The officers were slow to respond, giving Buck Thurman the time to nearly kill his wife. Once an officer was on the scene, he failed to detain Buck in any way, allowing him to break her neck in his presence. Though additional officers finally did respond to the call, they too failed to detain Buck, letting him to continue menacing Tracey. That Tracey survived the attack is a miracle, which owes nothing to the response of the police.

For battered-women's advocates, Tracey Thurman's story provided further evidence of what they had been claiming for years, that the police failed to take domestic violence seriously, and that this indifference contributed directly to men's violence against their partners. Feminists saw the inactivity of the police, like the abuse of batterers, embedded in a larger network of social relations that turned domestic violence into a private matter undeserving of police attention. Legal statutes in most states, for instance, allowed the police to make arrests in misdemeanor cases only if the crime was committed in their presence or if a warrant had been issued (Martin 1976:90). Ordering the world into a "public" space patrolled by officers and a "private" space that could only be pierced by an arrest warrant, this definition of police authority gave the police de facto legal backing to do nothing in domestic violence cases.

The view of domestic violence as a private problem was also reinforced by police culture. As noted in the introduction, the police, who were and still are predominantly male, believed like batterers that domestic disputes were "a family matter" that should be "mediated" rather than punished. Thus, rather than arresting a violent offender, officers would simply look to cool him down by "walking him around the block or joking with him about the violence" (Schechter 1982:158). In addition, officers commonly engaged in "victim-blaming," believing that the woman provoked the abuse or that she was "unworthy" of assistance if she expressed ambivalence about taking legal action against her abuser (Hart 1996). "The thinking that prevailed at the time," as explained to me by the chief of the Plainsville Police Department, "was that if the woman didn't do anything after she was hit, then why should we do anything." This standard for police action did not, of course, apply to victims of other types of violent crimes, evidencing, then, the boundaries by which officers distinguished domestic violence from other cases. Finally, police reticence to respond to domestic violence calls stemmed from the belief that such calls were especially dangerous. Interpretations of FBI data, for instance, found that 22% of officer deaths involved disturbance calls, giving credence to the view that domestic violence calls were particularly dangerous (Berk & Loseke 1980–81).[1]

Mandatory arrest policies were implemented to change this state of affairs. And as data from the Plainsville Police Department suggest, the policies have helped bring change. The city has experienced a dramatic increase in the number of domestic battery arrests since the implementation of the department's mandatory arrest policy. As seen in Table 2, the police department reports some 800 incidents of domestic battery each year. In 1996, the year before the department adopted its current arrest policy,[2] the department made just 40 arrests from these incidents. In each year since, however, the department has made some 300 arrests, a ninefold increase.

And this transformation extends beyond Plainsville. Despite some resistance to the adoption of mandatory arrest policies (see Ferraro & Pope 1993; Buzawa et al. 1996; George 1998), statistics show the number of persons arrested for family violence in the United States has risen 16.4% from 1993 to 2002, a period roughly corresponding to the time that mandatory arrest policing has become entrenched across the country (Federal Bureau of Investigation 2002). Hoyle (1998), in her authoritative look at police decision making in domestic violence cases, finds that officers now commonly make domestic violence arrests. Similarly, Jones and Belknap (1999) report "high compliance with the formal presumptive arrest policy" in Boulder, Colorado, where the police jailed the defendant in nearly three-fifths of the reported intimate partner abuse incidents (269).[3]

It is important to consider why this change has happened. Researchers have found that the increased compliance with mandatory arrest appears tied to changes in police organization and society in general. "Changes in policy and training," Hoyle (1998) explains, "along with the changes in wider societal attitudes which led to policy reform, seem to have altered

TABLE 2—Total Number of Domestic Battery Occurrences and Arrests in Plainsville, 1996–2002

Year	Occurrences	Arrests
1996	819	40
1997	748	327
1998	752	387
1999	773	357
2000	794	352
2001	772	349
2002	787	317

Source—Plainsville Police Department

the attitudes and values of new recruits and, to a lesser extent, older or established officers" (89). George (1998), researching officer attitudes toward domestic violence in the same Centralia County where I conducted my re-search, makes a similar observation, noting that "rookie cops" tend to follow departmental procedures and policies more closely than do their elders (86).

As important a question as *why* this change has happened is *how* this change happens on a daily, case-by-case basis. In this chapter, I argue that mandatory arrest policies, by requiring police action in domestic violence cases, have forced officers to refine and otherwise innovate their policing tactics. These tactics target specific attributes of batterer agency, including the material settings in which domestic violence occurs as well as batterers' influence over their partners. These tactics facilitate officers' crossing from the "public" into the "private." When encountering situations of domestic violence, the police deploy these tactics to ensnare the suspected batterer into different relations of power that progressively dislodge him from his position of authority in the "private" home and recast him as subject to the authority of the "public" state. These tactics are critical to understanding officer–batterer interactions, not only because they represent the means by which the police come to exercise power over batterers, but also because they represent points of contact between abusers and the criminal legal system that shape their experience with the system.

Mandatory Arrest Policing in Action

1

It's October 19th, and I am "riding along" with Officer Lambert from the Plainsville Police Department in response to a domestic battery call. We arrive to the address, an apartment complex. Two other cruisers are already at the scene. I follow Officer Lambert as he walks up to the complex. He takes a few moments to orient himself to the unfamiliar site and to determine where the reported apartment should be located. He then enters one of the apartment buildings, and I follow him up a tight staircase. Arriving at the apartment, I see that the doorjamb has been broken, indicating a forced entry. Officer Lambert makes his way into the apartment, while I wait outside.

He reappears a few moments later, escorting a large, middle-aged black male in handcuffs to the hallway. He leads him to a brief opening in the nar-row hallway, where there is a washer and dryer. Officer Lambert removes the handcuffs from the man, whose back is to the washer and dryer. I stand off to the side, keeping an eye on their interaction while trying not to be intrusive.

The man is slightly short of breath. His clothes are a bit disheveled, and he is barefoot. He has an open cut on his ear. Officer Lambert, standing in front of him with a notepad in his hand, explains that the police received a call about a domestic disturbance. The man, speaking calmly, and with his face down, explains that he understands and that he had asked Amber, his 13-year-old stepdaughter, to make the call.

"So, James, why were you guys fighting?" the officer asks, watching the man attentively.

Speaking softly and matter-of-factly, James responds, "My wife's upset because she caught me 'cattin' around. You know, she's the jealous type. She's always accusing me of having affairs. So today, the phone bill comes and she starts going through it, looking for numbers she don't recognize. There's one number there, from this girl I had met at the carwash a few weeks ago. My wife is asking about it, and I tell her it's just a friend of mine. You know, I call her sometimes to talk things over and whatnot. So, tonight, she goes and calls this number and starts asking the woman there if she's having an affair with me and if she knows I'm married. The woman hangs up on my wife, and then she gets even more upset and hits me with the picture frame with our marriage license in it." The man pauses to reveals the cut he has on his ear.

"Then what happened?"

"Well, she kept coming at me, trying to punch me and all, so I just wrestled her down and tried to calm her down. Then Amber came over and tried to get between us. My wife was still swinging, trying to hit me. I let her go, because I didn't want Amber getting hit. But she kept trying to hit me, so I got her down again on the couch. And that's when I told Amber to call the police."

The two men continued their quiet conversation, with Officer Lambert asking James about his marriage and his employment status. He explained that he and his wife had been married for four years now and that he considered Amber, his step-daughter, to be his own daughter. He worked at a local factory not far from the apartment complex.

Once they finished talking, Officer Lambert walked back down the hall and toward the apartment, with James and me behind him. When he noticed James walking behind him, Officer Lambert told him to wait outside. I remained outside the apartment as well.

With the door to the apartment left slightly open, I could hear a girl crying inside. I concluded that this was Amber. Inside, Officer Lambert conferred with Officer McBride, the first officer on the scene. Officer Lambert reported what James had said about the incident. Officer McBride had another version of the story and doubted that James had simply been holding his wife down. As Officer Lambert later told me, McBride had heard "people bouncing off the walls" when he arrived. Given what he had seen, Officer McBride thought James should be taken into custody.

Making his way back outside the apartment, Officer Lambert explained to James that he would be arrested. The man offered little resistance, noting simply in a resigned, self-reflective tone, "I ain't never been arrested before.

Forty-five years, and I ain't never been arrested for nothing." James asked if he could go get his shoes and jacket before going outside into the cold night. Officer Lambert told him that he would get them for him. The officer soon returned with the shoes and jacket. The door to the apartment was still open, and I could see some people moving around inside. Suddenly, I also heard his 13-year-old daughter scream, "I don't want my daddy to go away!" James answered back from the hall, seeking to reassure her, "It's OK, honey, Daddy will be all right and will see you again real soon."

Officer Lambert led James down the stairs and placed him in his cruiser. Two other officers had arrived on the scene, one a sergeant and the other an officer with a digital camera to document the injuries. Officer Lambert had the officer with the camera take a picture of the cut on James's ear. Following that, we transported James to the county jail.

Officer Lambert escorted James, in handcuffs, to the small receiving room of the jail, where two correctional officers were working. Lambert removed the handcuffs from James and seated him in a chair in the corner. One of the correctional officers asked James to remove the shoelaces from his sneakers and to place his personal belongings on a table. The officer began entering the items in an inventory bag. The officer then asked James whether he was on medication or had any specific medical requirements. James answered no. The officer then read off a seemingly endless list of diseases and medical conditions, asking James if he suffered from any of them. James again answered no. Finally, he was led to a separate room, where a correctional officer would conduct a strip search and give James his jail clothes. As he left the room, Officer Lambert and I made our way back to his cruiser.

2

On the night of November 8, I accompanied Officer Debnitz as he responded to a domestic disturbance involving a verbal argument between an adult female and male. When we arrived at the address, two cruisers were already at the scene, including a sergeant's car. We caught up with the two officers as they were approaching the residence, a medium-sized house in the poorer section of town. Yelling could be heard from inside the home. One of the officers knocked on the door, using the butt of his flashlight to intensify the sound. The door opened soon afterward, and the officers and I made our way into the home.

Inside, in a small living room, a middle-aged black man stood facing a middle-aged black woman, with some distance between them. Both were visibly agitated. One of the officers asked, "What's the yelling about?" With that, the man burst out, "She's a stupid ho', that's the problem." The woman quickly responded with an insult of her own, "Ho'? You must be talkin' about your mama, then!"

With the argument beginning again, the officers quickly moved themselves deeper into the small room, getting between the two parties. Given the small size of the room, I had to make an effort to remain out of everyone's way. Separating the parties, two of the officers led the man out of the house. I followed. The third officer stayed in the house to interview the woman.

Outside the house on the front sidewalk, the two officers—one of them the sergeant—stood facing the man. I stood behind them. The officer asked the man for identification. Still visibly agitated, the man reached to pull out his wallet and presented his driver's license to the officer. The officer again asked the man what had happened. The man responded loudly with fragments of a story intermixed with insults toward the woman.

"That woman's crazy. She's the type of woman who doesn't know when to stop. I was just sitting there in my chair in the other room, relaxing and having a couple beers, and then she's gotta come up and get on my case. She just wouldn't leave me alone."

While the man was talking, the officer took down his information into a notepad while the sergeant stood watching him. When the man paused with his story, the officer asked whether he had hit her.

"No, man, I didn't hit her. We was just arguing, you know . . ."

"Yeah, but when things get heated like this, people sometimes hit one another. You didn't touch her at all, even brush up against her?"

"No, no, serious. We were just yelling at each other." Giving his answer, the man started on another line, expressing his regret for the incident. "Man, I'm sorry we're arguing and got you out here."

The officer recording his information answered coolly, "Don't worry about it. We all get like that sometimes."

The man started back upon his previous line of argumentation. "She's just such a bitch sometimes. She just won't leave me alone."

"Yeah, I hear you," responded the officer.

The officer, having completed taking down his information, then asked whether the man was employed. He answered yes, explaining that he worked at the local university as a custodian. The officer made note of this. Slowly, the man was gathering his composure. Eventually, the officer talking with him made his way back to the house. There, he spoke with the officer inside the house to compare the stories each party had given. The woman also had reported that no physical contact had occurred during the dispute.

The officer returned to where the man was standing. Addressing him by his name, the officer asked, "Now, Donald, do you have anywhere else you can stay tonight? Given that you guys have been arguing, it would be best if you could go somewhere else for the night."

"Yeah, I'll just go to a hotel and stay there."

The officer continued the conversation. "Good, good. Also, if you need to get some things out of the house, we can go back in now and get them out."

"No, I got everything I need with me," he answered. The man continued to gain his calm as his conversation with the officer continued.

"Alright, but if you want to come back tomorrow to pick some things up, you need to call the police department first, OK? We'll send over an officer to help you pick up your things, OK? We don't want you coming over here tomorrow and having another incident like today."

"Yeah, I got it. So, I'll call you guys then tomorrow to come get my things."

"That's right." The officer handed the man a card with his name on it and the number for the department. The scene was coming to an end. The man began making his way up the sidewalk in the direction of the hotel where he was heading. As he went, the officer inside the house exited, and the woman in the house came out to the porch. The two parties saw each other and immediately began exchanging insults again.

"You fucking asshole," came from the porch.

"You fucking bitch," came from the sidewalk.

The officers spoke up to the man to keep on his way to the hotel.

The man responded, "I'm going to a hotel tonight. And tomorrow, I'm coming here with the cops, and I'm going to get my shit out of here. You hear me?"

One of the officers broke in to reinforce the point to the man, "That's right. Good. You call us tomorrow when you come back. Now let's get going."

With that, the man crossed the street and crossed a deserted lot across from the house. As he made his way up the street and out of the immediate vicinity, the officers started to make small talk about unrelated topics. A short time later, the officers returned to their cruisers and left the scene.

These two scenes capture well the fundamental change in domestic violence policing since the Tracey Thurman case. In the first scene, hearing a physical altercation taking place, officers force entry into the apartment, separate the parties, and conduct an investigation. Upon establishing clear probable cause that a physical assault has taken place and conferring to establish responsibility, the officers take James into custody. In the second scene, the officers note that a verbal argument has occurred, that the parties are still very upset with each other, and that the potential for renewed conflict exists. In response, the officers, despite lacking the legal basis for making an arrest, convince the man to leave the home for the night.

What is also noteworthy in both scenes is how the police move from the "public" to the "private," which owes in large measure to the policing tactics on display. Police scholars (Rubinstein 1973; Sykes & Brent 1983; Bayley & Bittner 1984; Klinger 1995; Alpert & Durnham 1997; Terrill 2003) have classified policing tactics into four basic categories. These are *physical* tactics, where the officer physically engages with other persons and/or materials; *verbal* tactics,[4] through which the officer conveys meaning to other persons without physically engaging them; *spatial* tactics,[5] where officers employ a certain arrangement of people, objects, angles, and space to conduct their work; and *presence*,[6] the act of the police simply being present. Throughout the two scenes, the officers employ each type of tactic and, in the process, cast suspected batterers and suspected victims into different relations of power that facilitate their handling of the violence. In this section, I provide an in-depth description of the operation of these tactics and power relations at five different stages of police–batterer encounters, to explain what happens to abusers in mandatory arrest.

1. Responding to the Scene: The Artful Distribution of Space. The "first minute of response is the most crucial to an officer's safety." So proclaims the instructional video shown police cadets at the domestic violence training seminar I attended, replete with dramatizations of officers being gunned down as they exit their vehicles or advance to residences in response to domestic violence calls. FBI reports on police officers killed on duty bear out this claim (Federal Bureau of Investigations 1975, 1977, 1995, 2002, 2003). In most of the examples described in the reports, the officer is killed with a firearm as he arrives at the scene and is either exiting his vehicle or approaching the residence. The officer is at a distinct disadvantage relative to his assailant at this time. The batterer is barricaded behind the walls of his home, while the officer is in the open. The batterer can use this position to establish sightlines with which to monitor the officer's movements and shoot him. The physical layout of most homes leaves the front door as the primary entryway into the residence. This gives the would-be assailant another clear line of fire for shooting a responding officer. While the door shields the officer's view to the situation inside, his knock on the door gives away his position to the assailant.

A smaller number of deaths occur once officers have entered the residence. The interior of the home also provides advantages to the would-be assailant. The batterer is more familiar with the space than is the officer and knows where he can hide himself and/or weapons. In these scenarios, then, batterers are able to use the material space of their homes to resist the police's response to their violence.

To manage the potential dangers associated with responding to domestic violence calls, officers first rely on dispatchers to provide a detailed description of the scene, including the type of dwelling (apartment or house), the level of conflict, the presence of weapons, and the location of the assailant. More importantly, however, officers are taught to be sensitive to the power of space. For instance, when approaching the residence, officers are instructed to "avoid the use of sirens and emergency lights," which would signal the police's arrival to the batterer as well as "increase the tension of persons emotionally out of control." Officers are also taught to "not park the police unit directly in front of the residence," which would again signal the police's arrival to the batterer as well as offer him a clear line of fire. In advancing to the dwelling, officers once more trained to use the available space to their advantage, by using trees and other elements of the spatial setting to reduce their exposure to sight lines from the home and cloak their presence (International Association of Chiefs of Police 1989).

Once at the entrance, officers are to wait outside long enough to make an assessment of the situation inside. Using a window to peek inside, or simply listening carefully, the officers seek to gauge the number of people inside, the level of conflict, and the presence of weapons, all of which dictate whether they will gain entry by knocking on the door or knocking it down. If the officers knock, they are taught "to stand on the side of the door," in order to deny the would-be assailant another clear line of fire (International Association of Chiefs of Police 1989).

In the second scene provided above, Officer Debnitz is careful to park his car away from the front of the house. Nevertheless, the officers approach the residence rather casually, having been told that the dispute was verbal. On the porch, the officers are able to make a quick assessment of the situation inside. Yelling can clearly be heard. And one of the officers is able to peer into the window and observe that no weapons are involved. In this case, a simple knock on the door is enough to secure entry into the residence.

Responding to domestic violence calls is not always so smooth, of course. In the first scene, Officer Lambert was responding to a domestic call involving a physical altercation at a second-story apartment. Apartment houses are especially troubling spaces for officers, who have to turn a blind corner and walk a staircase to reach the residence. In this case, the lead officer, Officer McBride, approached the front door and heard "people bouncing off the walls." This not only signified that the physical exchange was in progress, but also that the assailant(s) were not sitting on the other side of the door waiting for him to knock or enter. The officer took the initiative and broke down the door to make contact with a man on top of his wife.

In other instances, assailants may try to flee the scene, a common problem affecting the police's response to domestic violence calls (Ferraro & Pope 1993:116). This occurred on another night I was with the police. On the one hand, fleeing suspects lessen the potential threats of approaching a residence. But on the other hand, flight demonstrates that the offender is unlikely to comply with police requests. In this call, the dispatcher had also noted that the dispute involved a knife. Facing a situation of an armed suspect fleeing the scene, the officer directed me to stay in the car and then had the other responding officers, including a canine unit that was on the beat, form a perimeter around the house to prevent the suspect from escaping. As it turned out, the suspect in this case had run out of the house simply to throw away a collection of stolen credit cards, his possession of which had initiated an argument between him and his girlfriend.

On another occasion, the suspect had already fled when the police arrived. The victim explained that her ex-boyfriend had shown up drunk at her house, started an argument, and grabbed her to prevent her from leaving the house. When she called the police, he took off. She provided the officers a description of the vehicle and the direction he was driving. The officers then radioed in to have other officers apprehend the vehicle. Before too long, the suspect reappeared at the scene and explained to the police, "I'm the guy, I'm the one involved here. I came back because I don't want any trouble with the law. I've had problems with this stuff in the past, and I don't want any problems again."

In responding to the scene, officers rely heavily on spatial tactics that, while not acting on batterers directly, diminish their capacity for resisting the police response. The operation of power in this instance is evocative of "the art" of "the distribution of individuals in space" that Foucault (1977) describes as the basis of disciplinary power (141). By placing themselves behind material objects to conceal their advance, the police reduce the lines of force that the would-be assailant could use against them. By enclosing the space around the batterer through the establishment of perimeters, the police limit his paths of escape. At times, and interestingly enough with a batterer who has "had problems with this before," such strategic distributions of space are not required. Instead, the authority of the police and the criminal legal system have already been established in his mind, and the mere presence of the police suffices to draw him back to the scene and acquiesce. Through these tactics and operations of power, the officers bring the "public" sphere of the law through the front door of the "private" sphere of abuse.

2. Establishing Control: Partitioning and Exhausting Abuse. Once inside the home, officers work to "establish control" of the scene. Establishing control is in one sense a matter of manpower. At least two officers are dispatched to each domestic violence call in order to be able to handle each of the parties.

In another sense, establishing control is a matter of skillful practice. While the term "establishing control" evokes images of authoritative strong-arm tactics, officers are taught to shy away from such confrontational "control actions" in policing domestic violence in favor of more courteous, caring "supportive actions,"[7] or what I call "persuasive tactics." The reason for this, beyond the fact that officers are now trained to use nonconfrontational techniques more generally, is again "practical." The assailant or parties are likely to be "heated" and engaged in verbal or physical disputes when the police arrive, presenting the risk that aggressions will either escalate or turn against those intervening against them. This is especially undesirable given that the batterer is more familiar with the material space of his home than are the police officers.

Practically speaking, to establish control when parties are physically or verbally engaged in a dispute, officers are taught to separate the couple as quickly as possible. While this may require confrontational tactics such as pulling one party away from another, actions that run the risk of escalating the violence, the Plainsville officers in the second scene are able to separate the couple with a persuasive spatial technique, simply getting "in between" the parties. To further achieve separation, the officers need to "break the eye contact of the disputants" as quickly as possible (Hendricks & McKean 1995:152). This is accomplished by employing persuasive verbal techniques such as asking questions of the person, which diverts his or her immediate attention from the dispute, and persuasive physical techniques such as mildly "herding" the person away from the other (Hendricks & McKean 1995:153).

Once separating the parties, officers work on "cooling off" "heated" persons. Persuasive techniques are again thought more effective for this end. One persuasive spatial tactic for accomplishing this is to keep the people separated from each other. Officers are taught to position the parties with their backs to each other, with enough distance between them that they cannot easily hear each other. Such a positioning prevents a resumption of conflict that visual or verbal contact could provoke. The perimeter that is formed by this spacing also allows each officer to maintain sight of the separate parties as well as the other officers handling the case.

In place of this spacing, the officers I observed often simply removed the male party from the residence, as occurred in both scenes. This proved necessary given the limited amount of space inside the dwellings with which to achieve an effective positioning. However, this tactic also increases safety by removing the stronger, and often more volatile, person from the domestic setting, with its various weapons and hiding places. Such a tactic evokes Foucault's (1977) notion of "partitioning," placing each person in his or her "own place" in order to exercise control (143). With the tactic, officers literally move the domestic battery suspect from the "private" out into the "public."

"Cooling off" a person also involves verbal tactics and presence. Addressing people by their names works to grab their attention and cool them down. Increasingly in vogue among departments across the country over the last few years is verbal judo. Based on "the principle of judo itself, using the energy of others to master situations," verbal judo is "a set of communication principles and tactics that enable the user to generate cooperation and gain voluntary compliance in others under stressful conditions" (www.verbaljudo.org). As George Thompson, the "founder" of verbal judo, explains it, "you are not counteracting their approach and hammering back at them. Rather, you are moving with them, using their momentum to pull them off-balance . . . it should be redirective rather than confrontational" (Thompson & Jenkins 1993:89). By offering "heated" suspects mild, affirmative statements, officers are able to keep them engaged and exhausting energy, while denying them the stern response that would feed their aggression. The officers "project empathy," a specific type of presence that serves to calm the person and make him easier to talk to (Thompson & Jenkins 1993:30).

In the second scene, the officers employ verbal judo to take Donald down from his irate state. Rather than responding to Donald's aggressive statement, "She's such a bitch sometimes," with a similarly aggressive statement ("Well, you're acting like an asshole"), which could aggravate him, the officers offer a mild, affirmative statement to deflect the abuse of the abuser, "Yeah, I hear you." In doing so, the officers also place the batterer into a different social setting. Similar to the "tea-parties" used by Tuke's asylum to compel the madman to adopt a controlled "social personality" (Foucault 1965:249), the officers' calm, controlled, affirmative talk imposes upon the animated batterer a social setting that functions to bring him to restrain himself. By accepting his verbal aggression, the officers cool him down and exhaust his abuse. By keeping him talking, the officers pull his mind away from the dispute. Through these tactics and operations of power, the police come to bring the order and control of "public" life to bear upon the disorder and conflict they find in the "private" sphere.

3. Investigation: Sorting Batterers from Victims. In the first two stages of domestic violence policing, officers enter the "private" sphere to gain control over it and ensure the safety of the people therein, all of which corresponds to their "order maintenance" function (Wilson 1968). To "enforce the law," officers conduct investigations to determine whether a breach of the law has occurred and make a decision to arrest.

Conducting investigations in domestic violence cases can sometimes be simple, if, for instance, only one party has physical injuries. However, in many cases, domestic violence investigations prove more complicated. First, because two (or more) parties are actively involved in many disputes, determining the primary aggressor, or the person responsible for the violence, often proves complicated. Second, because the disputes involve family members and intimate partners, the disputants and/or witnesses are often unwilling to provide statements about the incident for fear of incriminating a loved one. This is often the case for women who call the officers for protection from their abusive partners, but are unaware of the mandatory arrest policy and opposed to criminal proceedings against them (Hoyle & Sanders 2000).

These obstacles make officers' handling of domestic violence cases considerably harder than researchers have appreciated. That is, researchers in the past have often sought to determine *whether* police make the right decision (to arrest or not) once they respond to the scene (see, for instance, Ferraro & Pope 1993) or *what* personal or situational factors affect their decision-making relative to the evidence in front of them (see, for instance, Hoyle 1998; George 1998; Jones & Belknap 1999; Mastrofski et al. 2000). While important questions in their own right, it is again important to consider *how* the police handle suspected assailants, suspected victims, and witnesses in order to generate the evidence necessary to take an action on the case.

The first step in overcoming the aforementioned obstacles is provided by the spatial isolation of the parties. By splitting up the couple, the officers are able to provide an abused woman the secure and private space she may require to tell her story without fear of retribution from her partner. Separating the partners also ensures that the couple will not be able to collaborate on their stories, should the victim want to protect her abuser. In this way, isolation serves as a tactic that deprives the batterer of his ability to influence and manipulate his partner in their "private" relationship to resist the application of the "public" law.

The separation of the victim from her partner also provides officers the opportunity to shape her subjectivity about violence and her partner. One way the police look to influence victims is through the "Intent to Prosecute" form. When interviewing a suspected victim of violence, the police ask whether she is willing to sign a form indicating her willingness to support criminal prosecution against the partner. The hope of the police and the state's attorney's office is that the act of signing the form will capture the resolve of victims to take legal action against their abusers and deepen and extend it once the police have gone and the case is turned over to the prosecutor's office.

In addition, officers are also required to provide victims and "potential" victims information about intimate partner abuse. Each victim is given a copy of the department's Domestic Violence Act form, which describes the state's laws governing domestic violence and provides contact information for the local shelter and state's attorney's office. The cover of the form announces in bold capital letters, "YOU HAVE THE RIGHT NOT TO BY[8] PHYSICALLY ABUSED. YOU HAVE THE RIGHT NOT TO BE VERBALLY ABUSED. YOU HAVE THE RIGHT TO PROTECT YOURSELF, YOUR CHILDREN, AND YOUR PROPERTY. YOU HAVE THE RIGHT TO SEEK AN ORDER OF PROTECTION BY PETITIONING THE COURTS OF CENTRALIA COUNTY." Officers may also use the opportunity to discuss domestic violence with the victim, to increase her willingness to take action against her abuser.

In interrogating witnesses, officers again rely on persuasive verbal tactics. Officers engage reluctant and/or difficult suspects, victims, and witnesses through different interview techniques. Many of these are described in other studies or training materials (see, for example, Berg 1999:159–65).

For instance, with a difficult suspect, the officers I spoke with would use "persuasion" (Leo 1996:664), telling him that "there are two sides to every story" and that they would have only the victim's side of the story unless he cooperated. In such a case, the silent batterer is encouraged to take advantage of his "right" to speak. The "right to remain silent," meanwhile, one of the most fundamental civil rights, is not mentioned, as the police have no obligation to inform a criminal suspect of his rights unless they are arresting him for questioning. As with the amicable traffic stop, where the officer will lightheartedly ask the driver, "Do you know why I stopped you?" this tactic invites the suspect to incriminate himself by talking about his behavior.

In the training seminar I attended, the instructor emphasized using "theme building" with uncooperative suspects. Taught as part of the Reid technique for conducting interviews, the officer here, as with verbal judo, looks to use the person's aggression productively. As the instructor described it, the officer drops a subtle comment to the suspect ("Boy, a person in your situation would probably want to hit someone," "It must be hard dealing with this") to "hook" him into discussing the event. If the hook takes, the officer then "reels him in."

In the second scene described above, the officers employ a technique akin to theme building when they say to Donald, "Yeah, but when things get heated like this, people sometimes hit one another. You didn't touch her at all, even brush up against her?" The hook to the suspect is that violence is to be expected in such circumstances, especially light violence. Such comments can be effective in eliciting a response, and even an admission of guilt from a person.

The officers I spoke with emphasized that no single interview technique is followed more than others. To the contrary, the selection of interview technique is a matter of personal preference, circumstances, and instinct. For instance, in one case an officer described to me, a woman had called the police to report that her ex-boyfriend, Jesus, against whom she an order of protection, had shown up at her apartment to harass her and a male friend. When the officer arrived at the apartment, he encountered the woman and a man. Asking the pair whether he was Jesus, the officer received no response. He sensed that the woman was afraid to answer. This placed the officer in a predicament. Protocol calls for separating the pair, which would allow the victim to answer freely. However, no other officer had yet responded to the call. The officer later explained, "I don't like turning around on a potential suspect." To overcome this obstacle, the officer changed tactics, asking the woman, "Is Jesus in the apartment? Nod 'yes' or 'no.'" That the woman felt free to nod yes indicated to the officer that the man he was facing was not Jesus, and that Jesus was still somewhere in the apartment. Following this, the officer searched the apartment and arrested her ex-boyfriend.

Other situations call for other interrogation techniques. On another occasion, the police dispatcher had a 911 caller hang up on her. Dispatchers send units to investigate 911 hang-ups to determine whether the call was a mistake or an unsuccessful attempt by a victim to call for help. When the officers arrived at the scene, a Mexican man answered the door and explained that he had accidentally dialed 911 while trying to phone his mother in Mexico. He apologized for the mistake. The lead officer replied calmly that he understood and politely asked the man if he would mind if they just took "a walk around the apartment." Although the man had the legal right to refuse the request, he agreed. As the officers made their way through the apartment, they found a woman crying. The woman later told them that she had been hit and thrown over a chair. The police then arrested the man. Through the strategic use of rapport, the officers were able to construct a "public" encounter with him that helped expose his "private" conduct.

4. Adjudication: The Normalizing Judgment. Once they have conducted their investigations, officers meet to discuss the evidence they have gathered and make a decision on what action to take. Despite the presence of a mandatory arrest policy that curbs officer discretion, the policy still provides police substantial discretionary power on arrest decisions. For one, the Plainsville arrest policy states that for cases not involving an order of protection or felony abuse, officers "should" make an arrest, a wording that recommends rather than mandates an arrest action. Furthermore, even in cases of felony violence, officers must decide whether the evidence indicates a felony or misdemeanor offense.

Police decision making has been a central area of investigation for researchers examining the police's handling of domestic violence cases. A primary concern in this area has been uncovering the extralegal factors, or "personal rules" (George 1998:79), that impact police decision making. Numerous studies have found that arrest decisions vary with the severity of abuse (Hoyle 1998:128; George 1998:84; Coulter et al. 1999:1290). Researchers have also found that officer decision making varies by officer experience, the risk of further violence, the demeanor of both the suspect and the victim, who called the police, and the victim's preference (Finn & Stalans 1995:298–313; George 1998:82–88; Hoyle 1998:128).

To the extent that the demeanor of victims and suspects affects the police's decision making, the performance of persons in and their reaction to the earlier stages of the police encounter figure centrally in the decision making of officers. During my ride-alongs, I witnessed 10 domestic dispute calls, which resulted in three arrests. In the seven nonarrests, five did not involve physical violence of any sort. In the other two, the first perpetrator physically restrained his victim to prevent her from exiting a room, and the second slapped his victim in the back of the head with an open hand. In these cases, the victims did not agree to sign the "intent to prosecute" form. Also, the victims were composed throughout their interactions with the police. The suspects, meanwhile, were also composed. Significant as well, both men lived at separate addresses and agreed not to have further contact with the victim that evening.

In only one case where an arrest was not made did the complainant desire an arrest. In that case, a woman who had called the police requested that her partner, whom she suspected was cheating on her, be taken away. No physical abuse had been reported, however, and the police decided to negotiate a resolution between the partners.

What was interesting in this case was the manner in which officer decision making assumed the quality of a public event. Because the complainant desired an arrest, the police needed to explain their decision not to arrest. Shortly after I arrived on the scene, I watched one of the responding officers explain to the woman, "Ma'am, I can't make him leave for something he said. I don't like the law either, but there's nothing I can do about that. If you want to do something about it, write your legislator." The officer's comment is a form of verbal judo, seeking to deflect the woman's frustration by casting responsibility for the arrest decision to the law. Despite this explanation, the woman persisted in her attempts to have her partner removed, naming for officers the man's girlfriends with whom he could stay. The officer again explained calmly and politely that the officers had no legal basis for taking action. The conversation continued on in this manner for some 10 minutes, with the woman stating that her partner abused drugs and alcohol, and the officer repeating that no legal basis for removal existed.

Finally, sensing that she was losing her appeal, the woman added, "You know what he does? He puts alcohol in the juice of my kids. I have to check their drinks before they drink them." At this, the officer became visibly irritated with the woman. Dropping the verbal judo, the officer responded with what amounted to a threat, "Listen, if you're going to be saying things like that, then I can call DCFS.[9] If you're saying that you don't feel your kids are safe in this house, I can call them and they'll have someone here to start a file in two hours. So, you can't just say that, because then my job becomes to report this to DCFS. Do you want me to do that?" The woman responded that she just didn't want her partner there that night. And the call finally came to an end with the woman stating that she and her kids would go to her mother's house.

The interaction is interesting for a number of reasons, including how officers interact with complainants who do not meet the police's legal definition of violence. But what I want to focus on here is the instructive component to police encounters. Evoking Barbara Yngvesson's (1994) research on how the law comes to have meaning for people through their interactions with legal authorities, this scene demonstrates that police encounters educate complainants and suspects on the law as the officers explain the legal categories informing their work. From the officer, the complainant receives explanations on why her desire to have her partner removed will not be met. In response, she adjusts her complaints, moving allegations of his unfaithfulness to his substance abuse and finally ending with his abuse of their children. The officer clearly finds the woman unconvincing. And finding his verbal judo unable to end their interaction, he moves to a more threatening discourse to silence her.

The instructive component of the police encounter enhances the ability of disputants to manage their interactions with the police in future meetings. In the example where the suspect who had fled brought himself back to the police to be interviewed, his initial explanation for his actions was, "I don't want any trouble with the law. I've had problems with this stuff in the past, and I don't want any problems again." This man gives a clear indication that he has been through the system before on a domestic-related charge. Interestingly, when the police asked him what happened, the man explained that he and his partner simply had an argument and "that's it."

The officer interviewing him, already familiar with the woman's story that he physically restrained her, shifted to theme building to extract more information from him. "But when you were arguing, you might have touched her, no? To prevent her from getting away? That happens a lot in situations like this." The suspect did not fall for the tactic, responding, "No. I didn't touch her at all. Like I said, I've been in trouble in the past, and I didn't want trouble again. It took me a long time to clear my name, so I don't want that again."

The officer persisted, "So, you didn't try to prevent her from leaving or anything?" "No, sir," the man replied, "I'm the one who left. She said she was calling the cops, and I said I would just leave, 'cuz I didn't want trouble. But she called anyways."

If the suspect did grab his girlfriend, it is clear that his past experience with the police and the criminal justice system has taught him how to speak to the police. The man denies any contact, and does not pause in cutting off the officers' attempts at eliciting a confession from him. In addition, he has learned that surrendering himself to the police rather than fleeing is important in convincing the police he is responsible enough to be trusted with a mediated resolution. Interestingly as well, the suspect does not hide his past contact with the system, offering it instead as a learning experience from which he has learned to simply leave the scene rather than continue an argument.

As these examples show, the police encounter during adjudication acquires the air of an "examination" (Foucault 1977:184–94), in which suspects and victims are judged before the "normalizing gaze" of the police authority. In those cases where clear evidence of abuse is not present, the composed, calm performance of victim and suspect persuades the police that they are "normal" people who can be trusted to abide by the informal solution mediated to end the dispute. And while officers' decision making is mostly kept private, the logic of police judgments is sometimes revealed to suspects and complainants. As officers explain the reasons they will not make an arrest, or the reasons they have made an arrest, the "normalizing gaze" of the police and criminal justice system is, in effect, reversed, and citizens come to learn what constitutes the boundaries of criminal behavior. Through such interactions, citizens are able to mold themselves into more knowledgeable legal subjects, at times able to more deftly navigate through legal encounters.

5. Detention: Subordinating the Battering Subject. Taking a suspect "into custody" can be problematic for the police, as the suspect can physically resist the action. In the arrests I observed, however, detention transpired smoothly. This is no doubt due to the efficacy of the power operations the police applied to suspects earlier. Having been removed from their homes, cooled down from their agitated states, interrogated about their behavior, and monitored by at least one officer looking to keep them calm, the suspects readily submitted to their detention by the police.

Nevertheless, detaining domestic battery suspects does bring about further refinements in the officers' policing performance. For instance, during one ride-along, the officers arrested a teenage boy at his home for domestic battery against his girlfriend. The victim, who had a closed cut on her forehead, reported the incident had occurred a few days ago. The teen's sisters and cousins were at home and insisted to the officers that he was innocent and that the girlfriend was just a "baby's momma" jealous because her boyfriend was sleeping around on her. In this case, the family's verbal resistance amounted to a challenge to the police's decision to arrest the teenager. To maintain control of the scene, one of the two officers used verbal judo to deflect the criticism from himself to the state's domestic violence statute, answering, "It's not up to me, the law mandates an arrest."

A similar scene is found in Frederick Wiseman's (2000) documentary *Domestic Violence,* which records the response of a shelter and the police to situations of domestic violence in Tampa, Florida. Toward the beginning of the film, Wiseman follows Tampa police officers placing a batterer under arrest. The man verbally resists the detention, asking, "Why do you always take the woman's word?" The question implies that he sees himself as the victim of an injustice. Rather than responding, "Because guys hit women more often," or "Because you hit her," comments that risk provoking the person, the officers reply, "When it comes to domestic violence, if someone says violence happened, that's what happens." Here, the officers refuse the batterer's game of placing guilt on one of the involved parties and instead deflect it to the law.

Once in custody, the batterer is transported to the county jail. The jail represents "a total institution," in which "all aspects of life are conducted in the same place and under the same single authority" (Goffman 1961:4–6).[10] Parking his vehicle inside a large garage attached to the jail, the officer brings the suspect to an intake room, where he is uncuffed and transferred into the custody of the Centralia County Sheriff's Department, which administers the jail.

In the intake room, the batterer undergoes a series of actions that lead to a "curtailment of the self" (Goffman 1961:18). First, he is made to surrender his personal belongings, "a dispossession of property," in Goffman's (1961) terms, that is "important because persons invest self feelings in their possessions" (18). This includes a suspect's belt and shoelaces, which leaves those favoring baggy clothes to suspend their pants by hand. While inmates are not made to change into jail garb upon intake, a process that the guards refer to as "dressing out," those with beads in their hair, a fashion popular with young African American men during the time of my research, are told they will have to remove them. This represents a "personal defacement" that strips the individual of "his usual appearance" (Goffman 1961:20). The suspect is then made to declare any diseases, medical conditions, and/or other needs that he may have, a verbal tactic that violates "one's informational preserve regarding self" (Goffman 1961:23). Following this, the guard then brings the suspect from the intake room to the holding cell, which holds any other persons who have been arrested in the county that night, to await booking.

Conditions in the holding cell are predictably spartan. Two concrete benches line the walls of the cell. A single exposed toilet sits opposite the heavy metal door. A small window on the door provides guards "surveillance" over the detainees (Foucault 1977:170–77). At some point in the night, the suspect will be brought from the cell out to a long desk manned by two sheriff's deputies to be "booked," which involves taking the suspect's fingerprints and picture and recording his personal information and criminal charges in the county's computer system. Because the Centralia County Court has established bail bond rules dictating that persons arrested on domestic violence charges must spend the night in jail, domestic violence suspects are often booked last over the course of the night.

While conditions in the jail are stark, and life is governed by rules, interpersonal relations between the inmates and guards are somewhat light. Inmates commonly engage in what Goffman (1961) terms "secondary adjustments," "practices that do not directly challenge staff but allow inmates to obtain forbidden satisfactions or to obtain permitted ones by forbidden means" (54). An inmate with beads in his hair, for instance, might not immediately comply with the jail's rules prohibiting them. Or an inmate, though permitted one phone call, will use the phone at the booking desk to make a number of calls and have conversations on the phone while he is being booked.

Guards do not respond aggressively to such transgressions of the rules. Rather, the interactions take on a somewhat sportive form. The guard might repeatedly tell the inmate, "You're going to have to take the beads out. If you don't do it, I'll have to do it," while the inmate sees how long he can defy the rules. As Goffman (1961) notes, "secondary adjustments provide the inmate with important evidence that he is still his own man, with some control over his environment" (55).

However playful, guard–inmate interactions never bring authority into question. At some point, these interactions will be terminated on terms convenient to the guard, who is ultimately able to enforce the rules simply by assuming a firm tone with the inmate: "OK, now, the beads. Let's go." Or, "That's it. You had your one phone call."

Jail administrators view such behavior by guards as a calculated effort to affect the mood of the jail. Upon seeing the surprise on my face at the informality of interactions, the lieutenant at the jail explained to me, "We try to keep it light, because this isn't a good place to be." The comment cuts both ways. While life in jail is clearly harsh on the inmate, the "people-work" conducted by the jail staff takes an emotional toll as well (Goffman 1961:74–83). And interestingly, to help diminish the solemnity of the jail space, guards deviate from the official discourse of the institution (see Goffman 1961:83) to establish a lighter relation to inmates than might otherwise be expected.

Part of the amiability between guards and inmates takes the form of legal talk. These interactions are usually predictable. Finding in the guards a new audience, and one different from the police, the suspects often use the interaction to proclaim their innocence. Guards, on the other hand, respond with the stereotypical "that's what they all say." Commonly, however, legal talk between guards and inmates delves into the details of cases, with suspects asking about the current charges they face, what they are likely to be charged with by the state's attorney, what the judge will set their bond at, and so forth. In such instances, guards assume a lawyerly position, sharing with inmates their knowledge about the criminal legal system. Here, again, individuals' contact with the criminal legal system becomes pedagogical.

Such interactions can become interesting in domestic violence cases. No-contact orders, for instance, are a common topic of conversation. No-contact orders are automatically issued against persons charged with domestic violence offenses and last for 72 hours following an arrest. In addition, the court usually imposes a no-contact order on suspects for the duration of a domestic violence case.

In one case I observed, a man was brought into the intake area after being arrested for making contact with his girlfriend following a domestic battery arrest a week earlier. The man was visibly intoxicated and upset. He began telling his story to the guard, complaining that his girlfriend had actually invited him over to see her. Looking to mollify the suspect by engaging him in conversation, the guard asked where the incident took place. The man responded, incredulously, "At 504 North Pine, I live at that address. That's my house, my place. That's where I have my things. She calls me over to pick up the stuff. And I can't even go over and get my stuff?" The guard answered, "No contact means no contact." The man countered, "But I didn't even touch her. She called me to come over and get my stuff. I didn't have contact with her." The guard, having memorized the text of the no-contact order, replied by quoting the order verbatim, "no contact with person or address." The man, adopting a different tack to convince the guard of his innocence, then replied, "I didn't receive anything saying that." The guard followed with, "Well, I'm just trying to explain it to you so you know." And he continued, repeating a story I heard often from officers, prison guards, and court personnel, "That happens all the time. Girls call a guy over when a no-contact order is in effect. He comes over and she calls the cops." The guard's comments did little to calm the man, and as the guard took him to the holding cell, the suspect continued to brood.

At work in jail are not only the guards and inmates and their verbal interactions, but the "material agency" (Pickering 1995) of the jail space as well. Returning to the case of this suspect, as the night continued, the material conditions of the prison cell, conspiring with an encroaching hangover, began to take their toll on his demeanor. As he was brought out of the cell a couple of hours later to be booked, the man, coughing and speaking much more soberly than earlier, addressed a female prison guard who had since come on duty, "I'm cold in there, can they turn the heat up?" The woman said they would, though they never actually did. Later still, once the man had been returned to the holding cell and the woman was making rounds to check on the inmates, the man could be heard coughing and pleading with the woman, "I'm cold, can I have a blanket or anything?" The woman explained, "No, we don't have blankets."

This last scene is a particularly instructive example of how criminal legal interventions affect gender relations. The man began his interaction with the criminal legal system at his home, which he was legally prohibited to contact, but which he clearly felt entitled to visit given his ownership of the property. In effect, by returning to his home in violation of the no-contact order, the man challenged the provision of the formal "public" law with his own "private" notion of law and justice. His challenge failed, and he was arrested. At the jail, he continued his appeals to justice, seeking in the prison guard a sympathetic audience who might see his side of the story. To an extent, he succeeded, as the guard explained that women commonly manipulate the law to punish their partners. But as the scene continued to develop, the man lost his resistance to the injustice he believed he was suffering and adopted his position as a subordinate in the material space of the public law. The scene ends with the gender roles completely reversed. A woman governs the space in which he now finds himself. And while he previously appealed to the first guard on the basis of rights of ownership, he is left now to appeal to his female superior on the basis of her sympathies, begging her unsuccessfully to provide him a blanket for his comfort.

Discussion

Mandatory arrest policing in Plainsville has changed the police's response to domestic violence. This change manifests itself not only in quantitative terms, but in qualitative terms as well. Forced into action on domestic battery calls by vigorous feminist activism, the police have responded with a repertoire of policing tactics that help them overcome the traditional practical problems associated with domestic violence policing. For advocates looking to protect victims of violence and hold batterers accountable, the performance of mandatory arrest policing described here provides grounds for optimism. Despite the continued use of personalized working rules that account for variability in individual officers' response to domestic violence (Finn & Stalans 1995; Hoyle 1998; George 1998), mandatory arrest policing in Plainsville has altered appreciably the boundaries between "private" and "public" space. The batterer's rule of law (Hobart 2000), constructed in relation to the police's unwillingness to enforce their rule of law upon and into the home, has been disrupted.

The Race and Sex of Domestic Battery Arrests. At the same time, as critics of mandatory arrest measures have noted, such changes, realized through alliances with the state, come at the cost of the problems that the criminal legal system itself engenders. For instance, a number of feminist researchers have expressed reservations about mandatory policing policies for the disproportionate effects they have for African Americans, such as the disproportionate application of criminal sanctions in minority communities (Ruttenberg 1994; Cahn 2000; Coker 2001). The practice of mandatory arrest in Plainsville bears out these concerns. As Table 3 shows, although African Americans comprise 16% of the city's population, they accounted for 60.3% of all domestic battery arrests in 2001, the only year for which I have data on the racial breakdown of domestic battery arrests. This value roughly matches the findings of George (1998), who reports that African Americans comprised 65% of domestic violence arrests in her study of the Plainsville Police Department (131).

The significance of these statistics is not as clear as it may seem at first blush. Without the benefit of previous-year statistics on domestic violence arrests, it is not possible to conclude whether these numbers represent a negative or positive trend. Previous research indicates that while mandatory arrest policies increase the number of all races arrested for domestic violence, the proportion of minority men arrested actually drops (see Stark 2007:58). "If anything," concludes Stark (2005:153), "mandatory arrest policies reduced police bias in arrest."

While my research cannot explain these discrepancies, a couple of points are nevertheless in order. For one, these arrests are not reflections of the overpolicing of African American communities that occurs more generally in this country. Unlike drug arrests, where officers take a proactive approach and look to uncover crime, domestic violence needs to be reported for the police to take an action. And, along this line of thinking, past research has noted that African American women are more likely to report abuse to the police due to the lack of adequate alternative resources with which to manage the violence they endure (Goodman et al. 1999).

In addition, the cases reviewed in this research provide some evidence that the over-representation of African American arrests does not reflect racially discriminatory decision making on the part of the police. Of the ten domestic dispute calls I observed involving intimate partners, eight of the men were black. As noted above, three of these calls resulted in an arrest, and all of the suspects were black. This leaves five cases in which black men were not arrested, including two in which evidence of physical contact existed and the suspects had prior criminal records. Thus, although law enforcement officers may be more likely to arrest black men because they are more likely to have previous criminal records (see Coker 2001), this does not ensure police action in such cases. It is also worth noting that in two of the five cases in which an arrest did not take place, the victims were white women. If the police were to discriminate against black men in domestic violence calls, one would expect to see it in this pairing of the perpetrator's and victim's race. Given these observations, I *suspect* that these arrest numbers reflect a higher level of reporting on the part of African American women rather than racially discriminatory decision making on the part of the police.

While I cannot explain the reasons for the disproportionate number of African Americans arrested for domestic battery in Plainsville, it is important to keep in mind the significance of these numbers for this project. That

TABLE 3—Domestic Battery Arrests in Plainsville by Race and Sex, 2001

Race	Male	Female
Asian	3	1
African American	158	52
Latino	13	0
White	79	41

Source: Plainsville Police Department

is, black men might be expected to understand their domestic violence arrests as being racially motivated. This seems especially likely considering the fact that few of the Plainsville police are minority members.

The arrest numbers in Table 3 also bear out the fears of advocates that women will get caught in the net of mandatory arrest policing. In 2001, 37% of domestic battery arrests in Plainsville were women, a number exceeding those reported in other studies, which range from 10% to 33% (Hirschel & Buzawa 2002; Martin 1997; Lyon 1996; Stark 1996).[11] As with the case of race, I am unable to provide a sound explanation for this high level of female arrests. Researchers have in the past attributed high levels of female domestic battery arrests to officers' reluctance or inability to determine the primary aggressor (Ford et al. 1996). During my field research, I never observed a woman arrested for domestic violence, nor did I observe a dual arrest. Unfortunately, my statistical data from the Plainsville police do not explain whether more than one arrest was made at a given incident. However, the officers I spoke with did mention that they were required to determine the "primary aggressor" in each domestic violence case they encountered, specifically to avoid dual arrests.

More recently, Miller (2001) explains the increased number of women arrested on domestic violence as a combination of men trying to "get to the phone first" during domestic disputes and officers overenforcing the law for fear of litigation should they do nothing. In her study of police understandings of domestic violence in Centralia County, George (1998) notes a similar phenomenon, when one officer tells her that "one way to figure out who is the victim is who made the call to the police" (81). Of course, in two of the three arrests that I observed, it was the man who made the call to the police.

As with race, the importance of these arrest numbers comes in how they shape the understandings and outcomes that follow from an arrest. That is, it will be interesting to consider how women arrested for domestic battery in Plainsville interpret their experiences. To provide a glimpse into this phenomenon, the 30 interviews that follow in this study include 3 from women arrested for domestic violence.

The Gendered Performance of Domestic Violence Policing. The central contribution of this chapter is the identification of the policing tactics that officers use to manage domestic batterers. As noted before, these tactics represent primary points of contact between batterers and the criminal legal system. In the later chapters of this study, I will explain their impact on batterers by describing the effects and meanings they hold for them. Here, however, is an appropriate place to reflect on these tactics in advance and posit some of the lines of investigation that will inform the later analysis.

Poststructuralist studies of discipline (Foucault 1965, 1977) and governmentality (Rose 1996, 1999; Dean 1994, 1999; Dean & Hindess 1998; Burchell et al. 1991) claim that the practices (therapy, punishment, confession, group therapy, consumption) through which authorities govern do not simply suppress individuals, but mold them. In poststructural parlance, these practices subjectify the persons they engage, shaping them into new subjects (the sane person, the healthy patient, the forgiven sinner, the controlled alcoholic, the free citizen). I want to extend this line of thought here to consider how the practices of mandatory arrest policing engage the subjectivities of domestic batterers.

Supporters of aggressive policing measures have hoped that the punitive aspects of policing will disrupt batterers' violence. From the description provided so far, it is clear that mandatory arrest policing, which dislodges batterers from their authority in the home and socializes arrestees into new relations as subordinates to the power of the state, possesses negative consequences for abusers.

However, the tactics of the police encounter do not only punish. What is interesting about the policing encounter is the gender discourse that continually circulates between legal authorities and batterers. For instance, in their interactions with the police and prison guards, batterers will continually resort to the denials, minimizations, and justifications of violence that researchers have noted in the past (Ptacek 1988; Hearn 1998; Eisikovits & Buchbinder 2000; Anderson & Umberson 2001). Donald, in the scene at the beginning of the chapter, blames his wife for the abuse that precipitated the police intervention. He explains, "She's just such a bitch sometimes. She just won't leave me alone." This is a classic justification tactic used by batterers to excuse their abuse. Similarly, the jailed batterer claims, "That's my house, my place," relying on notions of property and ownership deeply entrenched in our culture in order to justify his violation of the no-contact order.

Being placed under arrest modifies some batterers' discourse. If they presented their violence as either justified, minimal, or nonexistent, batterers interpret police action against them as unjustified. As noted in past research with abusive men, a discourse of victimization emerges that presents the batterer as victim of either a criminal justice system biased against men (Anderson & Umberson 2001:369) or a woman acting irrationally (Eisikovits & Buchbinder 2000:135). The man detained in Wiseman's documentary presents the first version of the victimization discourse, when he asks the police, "Why do you always take the woman's word?" The batterer in jail presents the second version of the victimization discourse, when he repeatedly states that "she called me to come over."

For their part, the police, precisely to gain control over batterers, respond by participating in the masculine discourse. To Donald's abusive claim that his wife is "just such a bitch," the officers respond with an affirmation, "Yeah, I hear you," calculated to cool him down. The comment conveys the sense that they understand what Donald is saying, and a connection between them is established. Rather than connecting the abuse to Donald himself, as might happen with a response such as "Well, that's what you think," the masculine justification for violence is affirmed. In this sense, while supportive, affirming statements represent a technique to cool a heated suspect down, verbal judo clearly possesses a gendered, masculine dimension.

The same dynamic occurs when officers use verbal judo to deflect criticism during detention. The criticism lodged against the police decision, the idea that the police are taking an unjust action against the person, supports the victimization discourse. Whatever the batterer has done does not warrant arrest. However, rather than explaining their actions in terms of the batterer's guilt—"we are arresting him because he hit her,"—the police's use of verbal judo permits the discourse of victimization to continue. It simply changes the source of the injustice. The comment, "It's not up to me, the law mandates an arrest," puts the blame for the arrest on the law. The comment "When it comes to domestic violence, if someone says violence happened, that's what happens," places blame on both the law and the victim. Such punishments would not have to occur if people would simply not report their abusers. The batterer himself escapes blame in this discourse.

Theme building involves a gendered discourse as well. The power operation is reversed here, however. Whereas the police remain subdued during verbal judo, in order to restrain the animated person, the police now take an active role, in order to activate the agency of the subdued, silent batterer. To do so, the police use masculine discourses of abuse in an effort to connect to the batterer's own abusive attitudes and beliefs. The question "You didn't even touch her?" minimizes violence. The comment "People sometimes hit each other when they get heated like that" notes the conditions in which some violence would be expected. Again, that the batterer did something wrong or bears any guilt escapes from this discourse.

Theme building for these reasons is an unseemly tactic. It gives the appearance of a male officer approving of or minimizing the man's use of violence against his partner. The police recognize this themselves. At the training seminar, the female instructor teaching cadets this tactic cautioned them about its effects for victims. "If the victim hears, talk about it with her, that it's just a tactic. Tell her, 'He hit you and now he's off to jail.'" That this strategic deployment of abusive masculine discourse might affect batterers was not discussed.

In jail, meanwhile, the guard from the scene above offers somewhat contradictory responses to the batterer's masculine discourse. On the one hand, his explanation of the law, "no contact with person or address," challenges the batterer's justification. On the other hand, his comment, "That happens all the time. Girls call a guy over when a no-contact order is in effect. He comes over and she calls the cops," clearly reinforces the man's discourse of victimization. Here, the batterer is not to blame. Rather, women routinely manipulate the law to punish men.

This consideration of the presence of gender discourse in policing is not to claim that the police and guards always send such signals to batterers. Again, the guard above challenges the batterer's denial. Another case in point was the man who restrained his girlfriend, fled the scene, and returned but was not arrested. When leaving the scene, the man, who could have just as easily been arrested, presented himself as a victim, saying, "She has a brother who is a cop down in Florida, she knows what she's doing. She's putting me through the wringer." The female cop accompanying him to make sure he left the scene offered a quick response that denied his claim of victimization. "No, sir, she's not putting you through the wringer. It's not her decision. It's ours. And you're not getting put through the wringer."

Nevertheless, policing clearly involves performances of gender (Butler 1989). Interestingly, the discursive tactics that batterers use to exercise power over their partners are used as well by the police and prison guards to exercise power over batterers. This reveals a different angle on how the police encounter can reverse the power dynamics of abusive relationships. Just as an arrest transforms the batterer from an authority of the "private" sphere to a subordinate of the "public" criminal legal system, the masculine discourses that are the batterer's currency of control over his partner become a currency of police control over the batterer. How these gendered performances affect men in contrast and in addition to the punitive elements of arrest remains to be seen. To the extent that the policing tactics described here mirror batterers' own tactics, the police encounter could actually reinforce their abusive behavior. What is clear, however, is that the meaning of arrest for batterers remains an open question.

2 | The Practice of No-Drop Prosecution

Following their contact with the police and jail, batterers arrested for domestic violence offenses in Centralia County come to face another primary site of criminal legal power in our society: the criminal court. The Centralia County State's Attorney's Office has followed a no-drop prosecution policy since the mid-nineties.[1] Though not set in writing like the Plainsville police's mandatory arrest policy, the prosecution policy encourages the state to pursue domestic violence cases regardless of the victim's willingness to press charges.

Studies in the field of law and society provide a continually evolving view of the persons, places, and processes through which power operates in the court setting. *Procedural rules*, for instance, protect the civil liberties of criminal defendants (Packer 1968), while the *authority of the prosecutor's office* allows the state to bend these rules to secure convictions (Packer 1968). Defendants in the court setting encounter what has been referred to as the *courtroom workgroup*, the network of relationships between prosecutors, judges, and defense attorneys that prioritizes the efficient processing of cases over doing justice (Eisenstein & Jacob 1977; Blumberg 1967; Casper 1972). In addition to the workgroup, the *pretrial process* informally punishes defendants by making them appear in court on numerous occasions and miss days of work, resulting in an increased willingness to plea bargain (Feeley 1977). Finally, scholars more recently have noted how *discourse* shapes interactions between attorneys, clients, and the courtroom and affects clients' understanding of the law and relation to past events (Sarat & Felstiner 1995; Felstiner 1998; Matoesian 1993).

While these studies provide an authoritative account of the loci of power in the court setting, the adoption of a no-drop prosecution policy in Centralia County has brought about modifications in their operation. These changes take shape as specific tactics used by state's attorneys, defense lawyers, and judges in their interactions with suspected batterers. The tactics operate upon defendants in particular ways, evidencing multiple operations of power at different stages of the criminal justice process. Many of the tactics coalesce into an effort to have suspects plead guilty to domestic violence charges, which most do. However, where there is power, there is resistance (Foucault 1979:95). And in Centralia County, no-drop prosecution plants the seeds of its own resistance, as defense attorneys become more adversarial in the face of what they perceive to be the state's unreasonableness in domestic violence cases, and as domestic violence defendants become less willing to accept plea deals that challenge key aspects of masculine identity. In the section that follows, I describe five dimensions of domestic battery suspects' contact with the court setting, to highlight these power dynamics.

1. Pressing Charges: "Creative Ways of Doing It." Prosecutors have long claimed domestic violence cases are notoriously difficult cases to prosecute because victims, whether for fear of retaliation or emotional attachment to their partners, are uncooperative witnesses (Ferraro & Boychuk 1992:219–20). In encouraging prosecution regardless of victims' cooperation, proponents of no-drop prosecution argue that prosecutors need base their cases on other types of evidence, such as victim statements, medical reports, photographs of injuries, and 911 tapes (Fleury 2002:199; Dawson & Dinovitzer 2001).[2] Nancy, the victims advocate in the State's Attorney's Office in Centralia County, whose job it is to review police reports to ensure enforcement of the no-drop policy as well as meet with victims to encourage their cooperation, echoed this view, noting that an ideal domestic violence case has "pictures," "independent witnesses," officers collecting "physical evidence," "medical reports," and "immediate follow-up with victims."

While possessing a clear vision of what they need in order to prosecute domestic battery cases successfully, the state's attorney's office reported a number of obstacles preventing them from achieving this goal. On the one hand, the necessary organizational support from local police departments was lacking, as only "one police department in the county faithfully gets a taped statement" (Nancy). Possibly, as Davis et al. (2003) observe, with police officers realizing prosecutors no longer demand victims to be present to prosecute a case, they become "less insistent that victims accompany them to the complaint room" (273).

On the other hand, even when the state is able to take what it believes to be a strong case to trial, it sees its ability to win convictions constrained by the local community's definition of what constitutes abuse. Matt, the assistant state's attorney handling misdemeanor domestic battery cases, presented an example to illustrate the point: "I got all the evidence that I wanted to. The 911 tape got in. (The defendant) even said he put his hands on her out of anger, admitted it was out of anger . . . and I'm going up against a defense attorney who's saying things like, 'if this is a crime, then we have to open up new prisons all over the state,' 'when you go home at night, don't you dare touch your wife.' Stuff that is completely inappropriate. And anyways, not guilty within a half an hour. I mean, boom, not guilty in a half hour." Reflecting on why he lost what he felt was a strong case, Matt mentioned a discussion he had with the judge following the case. The judge explained to him, "it was a jury trial, but there weren't any injuries, so you know how these cases go" in Centralia County. Nancy, the victims advocate, repeated the same point when she noted to me that, "in this county, with our juries, you will not get a conviction if a victim is uncooperative."

The Centralia County State's Attorney's Office in this sense views Centralia County as a "discordant locale" (Frohmann 1997). Frohmann (1997) introduces this term to refer to prosecutors' ascription of "stereotypical characteristics of a neighborhood to victims, defendants, and jurors" that they use "to justify case rejection" (533). For Matt and Nancy, the conservative local community in Centralia County, which demands evidence of visible physical injuries and appropriate victims in domestic violence cases, poses a significant obstacle to its evidence-based prosecution policy.

Confronted with this "discordant locale," the state's attorney's office could choose to prosecute only those cases that would fit the community's conservative definition of domestic violence. However, this would violate its no-drop policy. So then, the office does what other prosecutors do when losing seemingly "sure" cases to unpredictable juries—it accommodates itself to plea bargaining convictions (Heumann 1978:111). Matt noted that in the face of these constraints, "we have to find creative ways to prosecute these cases to try to generate pleas of guilty to domestic battery."[3]

Creativity here comes in different forms. One is aggressively charging cases, which raises the stakes for the suspected batterer who wishes to try his case. "If there is the possibility of filing a felony, I will file a felony no matter what, and then I will file a count two, misdemeanor domestic battery. And then I will offer them to plea to the misdemeanor, and I will dismiss the felony. Somebody takes that almost all the time" (Matt, assistant state's attorney).

In addition, the state's attorney's office uses two techniques related to bond conditions. "One is if the defendant is sitting in jail, and he can't bond out, and you offer him a plea to a misdemeanor domestic battery and he gets out of jail tomorrow, he's going to take it" (Matt). Second is "try to find ways to get them in custody if they're out." A key tactic to this end is the no-contact order. "If someone picks up a misdemeanor case, as part of their bond the judge orders them to have no contact with the victim in the case. If we see or get police reports or somehow learn that they're having contact, I can file a new criminal charge, violation of bail bond. And now they're sitting in jail" (Matt).

The use of the no-contact order to generate pleas is an interesting transformation of its intended purpose that reveals much about the state's approach to tackling domestic violence cases. The no-contact order, more commonly known as an order of protection, is a legal measure or spatial technology (Merry 2001) intended to provide women who feel threatened or have been abused by their partners security by mandating that the assailant stay away from her. In contrast to its original incarnation, in which the victim actively seeks the order, a process that various authors have found empowering for women (Ptacek 1999; Buzawa et al. 1999; Buzawa & Buzawa 1996b; Chaudhuri & Daly 1992), the no-contact order here is requested by the state with little to no consideration of questions of victim safety. And in nearly every case, as Matt mentions, the judge consents to the request. In the process, the function of the no-contact order is transformed. As Matt's comments indicate, the state knows and actually hopes that the no-contact order will be violated. And rather than concerning itself with measures to ensure that it would not be broken, which would provide greater victim safety, the state uses the order to lure defendants into violating it, thus allowing for more severe measures to be taken.

These three tactics evidence a specific type of power that the state wields against suspected batterers in its no-drop policy. It is a *"juridical model"* of power (Foucault 1979:82–85) that operates through the prohibition, informing the subject of what he can or cannot do. Faced with a discordant locale that makes trying cases unpromising, the state hopes that the prohibitions of bond conditions and the increased stakes of high charges will weigh upon the suspected batterer and compel him to plead out. And in general, the strategy is successful. While the state's attorney's office could not supply me with its specific disposition statistics, Nancy estimated that roughly 80% of their cases end in pleas, with 15% being dismissed and 5% going to trial, numbers verified in my conversations with defense attorneys.

2. Pretrial Proceedings: Of Warnings, Accusations, and Admonishments. The classic image of the courtroom setting in the law and society literature is that of a workgroup, in which the state's attorney, defense attorney, and judge share common interests and specialized roles in the administration of justice and the disposition of cases (Eisenstein & Jacob 1977; Blumberg 1967). In Centralia County, the operation of this workgroup remains integral in the processing of domestic battery cases under no-drop prosecution. While the state's attorney's office possesses the authority to aggressively charge cases and request no-contact orders, its ability to use this juridical power is bound together with efforts by the other workgroup members to adapt their interactions with domestic battery suspects to accommodate the policy.

The suspected batterer's first contact with the courtroom workgroup on his present case occurs during a prearraignment intake meeting at the county jail, where he meets with a public defender who prepares his case for arraignment. Public defenders handle all prearraignment intake sessions, even if the suspect has a private attorney or plans to retain one in the future. While the public defender typically uses intake meetings to collect personal information for bond arguments and to determine whether the defendant, if facing felony charges, wishes to have a preliminary hearing, the likelihood that the court will impose no-contact orders in domestic battery cases results in her also warning suspected batterers about the orders.

Public defenders have limited time and resources to dedicate to the session. Typically, two attorneys will go to the jail for 45 minutes to meet with what is usually between 10 and 15 defendants, leaving 6 to 9 minutes for each person. The ability of the public defender to complete the intake meetings in prompt fashion is hindered, however, by the defendants' desire to discuss their cases. "Some guys want to talk to you about their cases," one public defender told me after an intake session. "'I don't know why I was arrested, I didn't do it.'" Rather than engage the suspect in a conversation about his case, which takes time and is not necessarily appropriate, since she will probably not represent him in court, the public defender looks to quickly terminate the discussion. "We just tell them to save it and tell their attorneys" or that "this judge is just setting bond, he doesn't want to hear about that today."

The same types of interactions can occur when public defenders warn defendants about no-contact orders. The public defender typically presents the notification in a standardized format, such as, "Now, it says here that the police have charged you with domestic battery. Now, that brings me to another question. In these cases, what usually happens is that the court imposes a no-contact order on you for the duration of the case. Now, do you have some place else you can stay for the duration of the case if that happens? And what is that address?"

The phrasing employed to talk about the no-contact order is significant. For one, the public defender takes care to avoid accusing the person of committing a crime, noting that "the police have charged" him with domestic battery. This helps avoid activating a denial from the suspect, which would erode the rapport between him and the public defender's office. In addition, she not only warns of the likely application of the no-contact order, but she also requests an address. While this information is important for the public defender's office to be able to get in touch with the person during pretrial proceedings, the question also serves to have the domestic battery suspect envision himself living at an address other than his residence, thus imprinting the meaning of the no-contact order upon him.

In most instances, the suspect simply provides the information requested. Some suspects, however, react to the warning by challenging the justice of the no-contact order. For example, I observed one man exclaiming, "But I own the house!" In such instances, the public defender acts to reclaim control of the conversation. In doing so, she must fashion an answer that will not only quickly draw the discussion to a close, and allow her to move on to the next defendant, but also distance her from the prohibition itself. For instance, in this specific case, the public defender responded by explaining, "I know, I don't agree with it either. They're out of control with this stuff down here. But there's probably going to be a no-contact order, and if you don't follow it, you can be arrested again and face another misdemeanor charge for that."

Arguing that "they," which can be taken to mean the court system, are "out of control," the public defender distances herself from the court itself while revealing an insider's knowledge of how the system works, both classic strategies for establishing client control (Blumberg 1967; Sarat & Felstiner 1995) or trust with the client that can later be used to influence their relationship. As such, warning suspected batterers about the no-contact order serves multiple purposes. It forces them to recognize the impending prohibition in order to help them avoid violating it, it allows the public defender to collect information needed to remain in contact with the suspect, and it helps establish influence over him by affecting his view of the public defender.

The actual application of charges and conditions of bond occurs at the county courthouse during arraignment proceedings. Simply appearing at court brings defendants into contact with a separate disciplinary regime, one governed by "transformation rules" (see Emerson 1969:202) dictating appropriate dress and behavior in the courtroom and rituals, such as rising when the judge enters the courtroom, intended to accentuate the authority of the court and person of the judge (Emerson 1969:172–75). Many domestic battery suspects, however, never make it to the courtroom for arraignment. Rather, given that the bond conditions for domestic battery arrests dictate that the person spend at least one night in jail, suspects are often broadcast into the courtroom via a video feed from the county jail, thereby circumventing much of the pomp and circumstance of normal court proceedings.

The suspects' time in front of the judge passes quickly. The judge will call a case number, the suspect rises and approaches the bench or camera, and the judge reads the charges. In doing so, she introduces the suspect's alleged violence to the court for the first time. "You are being charged with domestic battery. It is alleged that on the evening of November 15, 2004, you knowingly and without legal justification made contact of an insulting or provoking nature against Jane Smith of 15 Main Street in that you grabbed the victim by her wrists. This charge is punishable by one year in jail and $2,500 in fines."

After reading the charges, and determining whether the court will appoint counsel for the suspect, the judge then moves to consider bond arguments, which brings up the no-contact order. The judge first asks the state to make an argument for the suspect's bond. In making its argument, the state again brings forward the violence of the suspect, but drops the legalese in reading from the police report. "The victim was in the process of moving to a new residence. According to the police, the suspect became angry, an argument ensued, and the defendant struck the victim in the face. She then called 911. When the police arrived, they noticed bruises on the victim. The victim says there is a history of domestic violence in the relationship and that he has struck her before. The state asks for a no-contact order to be placed on the address where she now resides, as well as a cash bond." The argument, based on detailed descriptions of what the police and victim allege happened, serves as a public accusation made against the domestic battery defendant standing before the court.

Following the state's presentation, the defense is requested to respond. Since the hearing is not intended to determine the veracity of the state's evidence, the defense does not enter counterarguments concerning the facts of the case, although many defendants can be seen shaking their heads as the state reads from the police report. Instead, counsel seeks to paint a sympathetic picture of the domestic battery defendant, drawing the court's attention to his family ties and time spent residing in the community, in an effort to assure the judge that the defendant will appear at future court hearings: "Defendant has a wife with three children to support and has lived in the area his whole life. Given the fact that he has no past 'failures to appear,' counsel asks for recognizance." Significantly, no challenge to the no-contact order is made, leaving the issue of the defendant's violence unaddressed.

As noted before, judges in Centralia County nearly always allow the state's request for a no-contact order. And while explanations are often given for other elements of the bond decision, such as the bond's monetary amount, judges do not provide a rationale for applying a no-contact order in a specific case. Further, in granting the no-contact order, the judge modifies her own interaction with the domestic battery defendant by explaining the no-contact order to him. Here, the three judges I observed handle arraignments each adopted a "firm" judicial manner (Mileski 1974:83; Ptacek 1999:92–111) in addressing the defendant. "As a condition of bond, you are to have absolutely no contact with Ms. Smith. Do not see her, call her, write her, have someone contact her on your behalf. Do not e-mail her. No contact whatsoever. Do you understand?" The explanation serves as an admonishment to the defendant, who is also asked to respond that he does in fact understand. Oftentimes, the admonishment is also accompanied by threats: "If you do make contact with her, you will be arrested and will not be able to get out of jail."

As with the prearraignment intake warnings of the public defenders, the prohibition against returning to one's residence or having contact with the victim usually meets with little resistance. The defendant simply notes that he understands and then exits the courtroom or sits back down at the broadcast room in the county jail. Some defendants, however, whether feeling a "license to speak" from their proximity to the judge (Mileski 1974:67) or an inability to restrain themselves, do react to the admonishment. In one case, the defendant on the television screen protested, "But I own that house, it's mine!"

Judges, like the public defenders, act quickly to reclaim control of the interaction. Here, the judge noted, "Sir, I'm not questioning your ownership of the property. I am, however, exercising my authority to order you not to have contact with that address." While the judge hoped that this response would terminate the exchange, the defendant persisted, "So what am I supposed to do? Go out on the streets? I don't have friends or family here." Again the judge acted to terminate the discussion, ending his reply with what I observed to be judges' ultimate discursive tool for ending conversations, the "thank you." "It is your responsibility to locate accommodations for yourself in the meantime. But you cannot have contact with the address. Thank you, sir." Sensing that the conversation had no further life, the defendant simply offered a sarcastic, "Yeah, thanks," before he grumbled under his breath and sat back down at the jail.

The warnings, accusations, and admonishments that the courtroom workgroup directs at the suspected batterer when assigning the no-contact order and charges are located within an assemblage of force relations whose power is distinct from that operant in the legal measures themselves. It is a classic type of "*disciplinary power*" (Foucault 1977), drawing force from the material setting of the jail and courtroom, the patriarchal figure of the judge, and the rules regulating appearance and comportment in the courtroom. This power functions to render criminal defendants silent, obedient subjects before the officers of the court. The additional verbal tactics of the public defender and the judge, made necessary by the state's strategy of requesting no-contact orders in all domestic battery cases, seek to extend this obedience outside the courtroom. Those suspected batterers resisting their expected roles as obedient spectators are quickly responded to, though public defenders face the added challenge of disciplining the defendant while preserving his trust in their office.

3. Attorney–Client Meetings I: Talking Violence. Following arraignment, defendants eventually meet with their lawyers to discuss their cases. Much of the literature on attorney–client interactions in criminal cases focuses on counsel's role in plea bargaining (Flemming 1986; Mather 1979; Casper 1972; Blumberg 1967). Sarat and Felstiner's (1995) research on divorce lawyers demonstrates, however, that before clients and their attorneys decide how to resolve a case, they must first discuss the facts and construct an understanding of what happened. These discussions are inherently contentious, since lawyers are primarily interested in "what is going to happen" with cases while defendants look to describe "what happened" in their lives (Hosticka 1979:599).

The image of attorneys' and clients' discussion of the past as a contentious process is born out in Centralia County defense attorneys' talk about domestic battery cases. For the suspected batterer, meeting with his defense attorney offers the first chance to tell his side of the story. However, while defendants "really want to talk about the incident, and explain why they didn't do it, and why you should believe them" when they first meet with a lawyer (Sam, private defense attorney), different obstacles await them.

Defendants seeking private counsel, for instance, encounter attorneys whose first priority is money. "We first talk about money. How much they're gonna pay. Because you need to get that out of the way," explained Richard, a private attorney. Bob, another private attorney, added, "I always want someone to know right up front that I am not the cheapest boy on the block. You can always find a cheaper attorney." In addition to ensuring that they will get compensated for their time, private attorneys' talk about finances projects an image of themselves as authoritative or exclusive members of the local bar (Sarat & Felstiner 1995:57), an image that helps them establish client control with the defendant.

Money talk distinguishes defendants' first meetings with private attorneys from those with public defenders. Besides this difference, both public and private attorneys employ similar strategies in collecting facts from defendants that turn their "egocentric" stories into legally viable accounts (Sarat & Felstiner 1995:24). Depending on the individual lawyer, one of two basic strategies is followed.

The first is to have the client tell his story during the first meeting, an approach used by 5 of the 10 attorneys I interviewed (see Table 4). This strategy allows attorneys to begin assessing and preparing their clients' cases from the start. In addition, it wins the attorneys a measure of trust with their clients. Jim, a private attorney, noted, "Well, the first thing is, I don't want the client to think I'm being judgmental of their behavior. So I will listen to their story and let them express their outrage of how this is all blown out of proportion or whatever."

Whatever benefits this approach offers in gaining client trust and allowing an early start to case preparations, it also threatens to saturate the meeting with information irrelevant to the legal matters at hand. "I might have the charge," Diane, a private attorney explained, "and it just says, 'John Smith on October 31, did slap, count 1, did spit on, count 2.' You're starting with chapter 84 in the Life of John Smith, and invariably he takes you back to Chapter 1."

In anticipation of this, attorneys let the clients speak, but with a high degree of control over their stories, to decide "which ones or parts of them to include within the bounds of the case" (Conley & O'Barr 1990:168). This can be done by redirecting the defendant's story when he begins to go off course from the present case: "Now, let's go back to October 31" (Diane). Or it can be done through directed questions that leave the defendant as narrator, but on a topical course dictated by the attorney. Tom, one of the public defenders, noted that he'll "just cut to the chase. Did this happen? That didn't happen? What happened? Did you make a statement to the police? If you didn't, why didn't you? I just want to survey how strong the case is." What emerges from this type of interaction is a story of the defendant's violence that is negotiated between what the defendant himself looks to express and the questions and types of information that his lawyer believes are most important for evaluating the case.

One major drawback with this approach is that clients' stories will often have to be amended, not because they are untruthful, but simply because there are two sides to each story. And in criminal cases, the defendant's story tends to carry less weight than that of the police who made the arrest. Because of this, 4 out of the 10 defense attorneys I interviewed only had defendants narrate their version of events after they had viewed the police report(s).[4] Sam, a private attorney, reported, "Before I want them to go into any great detail, I want to see the police reports, because I don't want to be in the position where somebody's story is completely contradictory to the police report." Richard echoed this point, "I just say, 'I don't want to talk about the details until I've seen the police reports and see what they're saying you did, because I don't know what questions to ask you.' I have a real good idea after I read the police reports about what the case is going to look like." For the domestic battery defendant telling his side of the story, the police reports serve as a primary influence on what he will say he did on the day in question. What's more, while public defenders usually receive the police report prior to their first meetings with clients, private attorneys do not. Thus, defendants retaining private counsel who follow

TABLE 4—Defense Attorneys Interviewed

Name	Race	Practice	Experience	Basis for Fact Collection	Type
Donald	White	Public Defender	8 Years	N/A	Insider
Michael	White	Public Defender	8 Years	Police Report	Insider
Marge	White	Public Defender	4 Years	Police Report	Insider
Tom	White	Public Defender	1 Year	Client Story	Insider
Jim	White	Private	24 Years	Client Story	Insider
Diane	White	Private	9 Years	Client Story	Insider
Sam	White	Private	4 Years	Police Report	Outsider
Bob	White	Private	26 Years	Client Story	Outsider
Richard	White	Private	29 Years	Police Report	Maverick
Gary	White	Private/Public*	20 Years	Client Story	Insider

* Gary has a private practice, but he is under contract with the university's legal services office. Therefore, I classify him as both private and public.

this approach may have to wait some weeks before being able to present their stories to their attorneys.

In addition to the questions of attorneys and the claims of the police, defendants' story-telling is shaped by other evidence. The defense attorneys I interviewed generally agreed on what types of evidence are most meaningful in defining a situation as abusive, though individual attorneys sometimes disagreed on their relative strength. Almost all agreed that pictures and other evidence of injuries, such as medical reports, were the most deleterious evidence for the domestic battery defendant. Tom, the public defender, did however counter that "injuries sometimes don't concern [him] so much, because you can get injuries defending yourself. So, you can explain those away." Similarly, independent witnesses unrelated to the parties of the dispute are seen as damaging to the defense. Marge, one of the public defenders, felt, however, that such witnesses could also sometimes be explained away: "I can poke holes into what they thought they saw. The lighting was poor, do you have the right person?" Finally, while some of the attorneys mentioned not wanting to see a victim testify, other attorneys noted being able to discredit the victim by noting her previous criminal record, if one existed, or simply turning the case into a he said–she said.

In general, the impact of such evidence upon the defendant's story is only as strong as the evidence itself. That is to say, quality matters over quantity. This then places much of the potential for a defendant's story in the hands of the persons gathering and presenting evidence. As Richard noted, "a good policeman can wrap up the case up so tight that there is nothing you can do when you get it. For us, a case that's good is where they haven't really pinned the so-called victim down, they didn't get a taped statement from her, maybe they didn't get good pictures of her injury. There's a lot of wiggle room." And into that wiggle room the defense can construct alternate versions of violent events.

In providing his story, then, the suspected batterer engages with a type of power that is again distinct from those described before. It is a *discursive power,* akin to the confession (Foucault 1979:58–63), that presupposes and harnesses the batterer's desire to end his silence and counter the claims of the state. Inserted in an authoritative relationship opposite his attorney, and positioned against the lawyer's questions, the police reports, outside witnesses, and the material reality of victim injuries, pictures, and medical reports, the suspected batterer constructs his story and, in effect, redefines his relation to his own violent past.

4. Attorney–Client Meetings II: To Plead or Not to Plead. In addition to constructing with clients an understanding of their cases, lawyers work to move the cases towards resolution (Sarat & Felstiner 1995). As noted above, the majority of the literature on criminal lawyers and their clients examines defense counsel approaches to plea bargaining. In general, defense attorneys base their recommendations or advice on the seriousness of the case, the strength of the prosecutor's case, and the expected outcomes (Mather 1979:65–122; Feeley 1979:158–66). In addition to this, and in contrast to earlier research in the field that cast defense attorneys as "con artists" who simply plead out cases (Blumberg 1967; Casper 1972), researchers have noted variance in defense counsel strategy based on defense attorney type. Despite their reputation to plead more often than private attorneys, both Skolnick (1974) and Mather (1979) find that *public defenders* simply comprise part of a larger lawyer category, the *"cooperative" attorney* (Skolnick 1974:97), who are "regulars" (Flemming 1986) or "insiders" (Nardulli 1986) willing to work with the system to dispose of cases. More variety tends to appear at both ends of the spectrum among private attorneys, including *"cop-out" lawyers* who plead everything out (Alschuler 1975); *"gamblers"* (Skolnick 1974:95) or *"mavericks"* (Mather 1979:124) who maintain an adversarial relationship with the prosecutor's office and tend to win or lose big; and *"outsiders"* (Nardulli 1986), who represent fewer criminal cases than do insiders but tend to experience the same outcomes.

The strategies and tactics that lawyers employ in their interactions with clients are also significant. By defining "the legally possible," conjuring up a "parade of horribles" to describe the consequences of not negotiating, citing clients with similar cases who did not negotiate and "suffered disastrous results," casting themselves as the "dean" of the bar, and so forth, attorneys have their clients rethink their present and future (Sarat & Felstiner 1995:57, 26–52). These tactics mediate the intentions of the attorney and client alike and help shape the outcomes and meanings that the client will take away from the courts.

In observing courtroom practice in Centralia County, I noticed each category of defense attorney working domestic battery cases. My interviews, however, included mostly "insiders" (see Table 4). Seven of the ten attorneys I interviewed qualify as insiders in that they represented a steady stream of criminal cases. Of the remaining three, all of whom were private attorneys, two were "outsiders" (Sam, Bob) and one was a "maverick" (Richard). Within the "insiders" group, I did detect a divergence between private and public defenders in their propensity to plea bargain and the tactics employed to move clients to plead.

Both insider and outsider private attorneys mentioned the challenge that arises when they and their clients disagree on how to resolve a case. To move the client toward a negotiating position, the attorneys tend to use two basic strategies. The first is to depersonalize the client's view of the case by having him consider it from another perspective. As Jim explained, "I have to delicately explain to him that this isn't going to look good in front of a jury. I'll say, 'When the jury sees that she's bleeding from the head wound, and when they see that you put your hand through the drywall here, this is not going to be good.'"

The second is to focus on the consequences of losing a trial, a tactic akin to conjuring up the "parade of horribles." "If you have someone come in who's a teacher, and even though they say they didn't commit the domestic battery, are they going to have to ruin a career and never be able to work again at a crapshoot that somebody believes the other side more than them. You might be better off plea-ing" (Sam). Through these tactics, the attorneys attempt to change how the suspected batterer thinks about his case.

For Richard, the maverick, such tactics are not a concern in domestic battery cases, since he doesn't set them for pleas. Part of his reluctance to plead stems from his professed enjoyment of trying cases. In addition, however, he displayed a genuine aversion to the state's handling of domestic battery cases under its no-drop policy, which he described as a "stupid" and "flawed" social policy "dreamed up" by people in "ivory towers."

One reason he disliked the policy was that he believed the penalties associated with domestic battery convictions were too severe. "You lose your right to firearm ownership if you're convicted of domestic battery, even if it didn't involve a gun. If you get convicted of ordinary battery, there's not such a consequence. You're treated like a felon" (Richard). Together with this, he also disliked the state's unwillingness to bargain down to a charge below domestic battery. He explained, "They aren't offering our clients any kind of a deal. There's no incentive to plead guilty."

Although Richard was the lone maverick among the attorneys I interviewed, both private and public defenders alike expressed a similar dislike of the state's no-drop prosecution policy. Even while private attorneys admitted that it generated more business for them, with Jim likening it to a "lawyer's relief act," they had several complaints about it, including that the state was charging "silly" cases that did not really involve domestic violence, that the application of no-contact orders without hearings was unjust, that the policy was politically inspired from the state's attorney's office's receipt of a federal grant, and that the plea offers from the state were formulaic cookie cutters.

Significantly, in the case of private defense attorneys, this animosity toward the state's handling of domestic violence cases was accompanied by an increased propensity to take cases to trial. The two following quotations illustrate this point:

> When the state's attorney's office communicates a proposed plea agreement, there is a form letter. A couple of assistant state's attorneys ago, they added a little checkbox at the bottom of that letter that said, "911 tape has been ordered," and they check that. When I first saw that, I thought, "What a crock of shit this is. What a transparent bluff. 'We've ordered the 911 tape.'" Well, big deal! Bring on the 911 tape. As if I'm supposed to tremble in my boots that they've ordered the 911 tape. Well, the case was dismissed a month ago. (Jim)

> I called the prosecutor, who had such a closed mind, saying, "I think you have it wrong on this one," kind of outlining my investigation. Essentially [her reaction was], "Fuck you." They completely rejected it, "set it for trial then." I called Nancy, the victims advocate, and said, "OK, what's the latest protocol here? I have victims who don't want to go forward, I got a wacky 911 tape, I got a decent guy with his own apartment, he doesn't want to live with them anymore, who do I talk to?" Nancy indicated she agreed with me but couldn't persuade

the prosecutor. So I ended up setting it for trial, and the prosecutor kept backing off. You know, "Will your guy accept supervision?" "I don't know, I'll talk to him." God love him, this guy wasn't going to back down. "I got beat up that day. I didn't do it." And she (the prosecutor) just finally backed off, tail between her legs, and dismissed it. (Diane)

In the first quote, Jim reacts to the state's "evidence-based" prosecution strategy, which he interprets as increasingly adversarial. In the second quote, Diane questions the state's decision to charge her client with domestic battery, and the prosecutor's unwillingness to reduce the charges. Both quotes find the attorneys reacting to central elements of the state's no-drop prosecution strategy and setting their cases for trial. Analogous to the mandatory domestic abuse sentences studied by Carlson and Nidey (1995), the adherence to mandatory prosecution in Centralia County witnesses a certain fracture within the courtroom workgroup and the emergence of a more adversarial form of justice. And, as the two quotes indicate, the state, facing the conservative juries of Centralia County, are forced to either dismiss or risk losing at trial.

Public defenders in Centralia County face a different situation. As past research reveals (Lynch 1999; Heumann 1978:66), public defenders often feel pressure from the courtroom workgroup to plead cases. Tom, the public defender, noted this during our interview: "I don't believe any judge would ever tell you this, but I know, if you get a fair plea, and you don't take it, and you go to trial and lose, the judge thinks you're taking the court's time, and you usually don't get off as good." Added to this pressure is the mistrust and resistance of their clients (Levine 1975:237; Stover & Eckart 1974–75), most of whom are well aware of public defenders' bad reputations. Because of this, public defenders are left to exert themselves more in order to win the confidence of their clients and move them to plead (Flemming 1986:257–61).[5]

Personal style dictates how the public defender goes about gaining client trust. Marge, a middle-aged white woman, looks to gain trust with many clients by employing a personal, affectionate tone with them, sometimes referring to the men as "hun."[6] Tom, on the other hand, said that he forgoes getting to know clients like Marge does. Instead, he tries to be up front and honest with clients, a common tactic employed by public defenders to win clients' trust (Flemming 1986:261).

Of course, what one chooses to be honest about is subjective and can impact how a client views his case. Like private attorneys, two common tactics employed by public defenders are to have the defendant depersonalize his view of the case by considering the strength of the state's case and contemplate the consequences of losing a trial. Interestingly, given the centrality of trust to the attorney–client relation, these tactics sometimes meet with resistance. As Michael, a public defender who was working domestic battery cases when I began my research, described his clients' reaction, "'This is a misdemeanor, isn't it, and they want a 100 hours [of community service]! And two years of probation instead of one year of conditional discharge.'"

In such instances, the lawyer responds to preserve trust and avoid the perception that she is selling out her client. One strategy is to point out that the deal is normal or "conventional" (Sarat & Felstiner 1995:79). Michael notes, "I say, it sounds like a lot to me too. If it makes you feel any better, it's their standard offer, they're not picking on you." Tom employs a similar tack when defendants offer resistance to the plea deal. "What I'll say is, 'Hey, listen, I'm your attorney, don't shoot the messenger. This is typical in every case, they're going to make me an offer.'"

Another strategy is to share the suspected batterer's negative view of the deal. As Marge told me, "It does make them angry. 'This ain't fair. This is ridiculous.' 'I would agree with you that it's ridiculous, but I got to help guide you through this mess, because this is the reality of Centralia County.'" By portraying the deal as "ridiculous," and herself as someone who can guide the person through the "mess," Marge presents herself not only as someone who is on her client's side, but as someone who is needed by her client to successfully cope with the situation.

Perhaps most central for the defense attorney looking to move a case to plea is the appearance that she is doing something for the client. That is, actions speak louder than words. And, in general, the plea bargain operates by having the defendant see his defense attorney move the case from "theoretical exposure," which is the maximum sentence on a charge, to the "standard rate," which is the normal deal on the charge, "making the defendant think he is getting a special 'deal' when in fact he is getting the standard rate" (Feeley 1979:191).

In this process, the cooperation of the state's attorney is crucial, as he sets the sentencing structure in which the defendant and his defense attorney will discuss the deal. Matt, the assistant state's attorney, explained his role in the plea bargaining process as follows:

> For every misdemeanor case, I have as part of the sentence that they have no contact with the victim. . . . (But) that's something I can give to the defense attorney, because the defense attorney needs to tell the client that he did something for him. "Here's what I got for you." I am willing to come down on the public service work hours, which is kind of ridiculous anyways, because I always offer around 70 or 100 public service hours. The partner abuse intervention programs take 70 hours. So, they don't have to do any public service work anyways.

By outward appearances, the space between "theoretical exposure" and the "standard rate" is not that great, as Matt himself indicates. Removing public service work from the agreement is "ridiculous," since the defendant's participation in a partner abuse program, which the state rarely negotiates, covers those hours. In addition, the no-contact order can be removed during pretrial proceedings, though it does require additional court appearances on the part of the defendant. Nevertheless, this plea bargaining framework proves effective. In discussing why people choose to take plea bargains, Michael answered, "One very important thing is the no-contact order. If I can get the no-contact order dropped, that will convince a lot of people to plead guilty."

These tactics employed by both private and public attorneys serve as another form of *discursive power* confronting domestic battery suspects as they pass through the criminal justice system. Like the tactics used by attorneys to shape the suspected batterer's story of violence, these are intended to affect the way he understands his case. Distinctly, however, while those tactics have the client rethink his past, the tactics described here are measured to have him rethink his present and future. And although most operate in the push to have the suspected batterer plead guilty, points of resistance emerge in the increasingly adversarial stance of private attorneys against the no-drop prosecution policy.

The power of suspected batterers to resist the institutional impulsion to plead out their cases emerges from their own personal background as well. Michael, the public defender, explained that domestic battery suspects "are a lot less willing to plead guilty." While he stated that these defendants are "are more convinced of their innocence," 4 of the 10 attorneys I interviewed mentioned that many men refuse to plead guilty because domestic battery convictions prevent them from ever legally owning a firearm again.[7] Experience with the courts matters as well, with prior contact educating the defendant on the workings of the criminal justice system. To this point, Michael noted that "the ones who are less experienced are more willing to listen to their lawyer, and are less likely to have preconceived ideas about what to expect, and I can influence them a lot more."

5. The Plea Bargain: Disposing Justice. Although legal scholars have long given attention to the influences on defendants' decision to plead, relatively little attention has been paid to the operation of power within the plea proceeding itself. This lack of interest surely owes to a belief that it is an insignificant proceeding, a mere formality required to bring a procedural end to a legal process that the defendant himself has already decided to terminate. To some extent, this is true. However, as a final engagement between the domestic battery defendant and the courtroom workgroup before his case moves to the corrections system, the plea hearing contains additional operations of power that are important to a fuller understanding of the domestic batterer's relation to the court.

To begin with, it is important to keep in mind that the plea bargain is one of three ways in which a domestic battery defendant's case might end. Some 15% of domestic battery cases in Centralia County are dismissed, while a small percentage are sent to trial.[8] Because such a small number of cases go to trial, I do not consider them here. Dismissals, meanwhile, only slightly engage the suspected batterer into the operations of the court. The defendant is usually made to appear in court for a pretrial appearance, where he hears his case number read off the docket sheet by the judge, and the state's attorney announces that "it is the state's decision to dismiss the charges in this matter, your honor." But this is the extent of his interaction with the court when his case is dismissed. As such, the dismissal is possibly more meaningful for the defendant in terms of what it does not make him do than of what it does make him do.

Plea hearings, in contrast, are more substantial. At the hearing, the defendant appears with his attorney, may review the contents of the form describing the plea bargain to ensure it is what was agreed upon, and then signs it. Once the session begins, the judge dominates and directs the proceedings. Her tone throughout is "bureaucratic," in contrast to the "firm" tone employed against the defendant when applying the no-contact order (Mileski 1974:83).

A significant number of the judge's comments address the rights of the defendant. For the plea to go forward, the court requires evidence that the defendant understands and willingly waives his right to trial. The challenge for the judge is that few of the citizens appearing before her understand their rights well enough to independently verify that they understand and willingly waive them.

In response, the judge engages defendants in a pair of strategies intended to summon from them subjective performances that meet the procedural requirements for the plea. The first is to address the defendants as a group and apprise them of their rights:

> I'm going to address you as a group, then as individuals. It's my understanding that you are here to accept plea bargains. In making a plea, I am going to ask to ensure that you are entering the plea agreement freely; that you understand that you are waiving your right to jury trial; that you recognize that the state possesses evidence which, if put to trial before a judge or jury, would result in a finding of guilty; and that you understand your right to challenge the plea agreement, if later you wish to do so.

The address informs the group that they will approach the bench as individuals and prepares them for the specific questions they will be asked.

Following the group address, the judge calls individual cases forward. The defendant approaches the bench, often in a tentative fashion that indicates a certain degree of trepidation in facing the judge. After having the state read the conditions of the plea agreement before the court, the judge addresses the person to verify that he is knowingly waiving his right to trial. In doing so, the judge employs the second technique to move plea proceedings forward, which is to pose a repertoire of short statements and questions concerning rights and judicial procedures before the defendant:

> Is this what you're pleading guilty to? Has anyone threatened you to make you plea? Have any other promises been made to you in addition to what is contained in the plea agreement? If you plead guilty, you are agreeing that a factual basis exists in the case against you. Do you understand that, sir? If you plead guilty, you are giving up many rights. Do you understand what a jury trial is? If you plead guilty, you will not have a jury trial. Do you understand that? In fact, you will have no trial at all. Do you understand that, sir? Knowing this, do you still intend to plead guilty?

The questions the judge asks are simple, short, "yes/no" questions. In addition, many of the questions do not themselves directly address the issue of rights and procedures, but only whether the defendant understands a statement made by the judge about these rights and procedures ("You are agreeing that a factual basis exists in the case against you. Do you understand that, sir?"). The judge does not ask, "Is there a factual basis in the case against you?"—a question that could lead the defendant to ask himself what "factual basis" even means or invite resistance from a defendant who does not believe such a basis exists. Rather, the judge asks, "Do you understand?"—a question that invites an affirmative response. It is a commonly used question, similar to "How are you doing?" that induces an almost automatic response ("Good!") in everyday usage. And even if defendants were to consider the question itself, few are likely to want to admit before such an authority figure that they don't understand.

Also, the judge asks the questions in a rapid, businesslike fashion, posing each question immediately following the defendant's answer of "yes (sir/ma'am)" or "no (sir/ma'am)" to the prior question. In addition to allowing the judge to move the case along more quickly, this manner of questioning establishes a swift yet smooth cadence to the exchange that regularly finds the defendant answering with seemingly no reflection at all. Through this technique the judge is able to reduce potentially complicated rights talk to simple yes/no questions, with their own cadence, that the defendant is able to easily respond to. In effect, this technique calls forth before the court and, more importantly, the court record a knowing legal subject who has waived his rights to trial.

Despite these tactics, defendants do not always supply the performance needed by the court. They often respond to the questions in quiet, muted voices or move their heads to communicate their response, behavior that perhaps indicates a continued apprehension before the authority of the judge or a "passive exercise of power" (Sarat & Felstiner 1995:70) in defiance of the plea bargain. To this resistance, the judge simply requests an acceptable level of participation from the participant: "Sir, I need you to answer questions loudly because these proceedings are being audio-recorded." "The tape cannot hear you shaking your head."

During the plea hearing, the violence of the domestic battery defendant, who becomes a legally defined domestic batterer through the process, appears once again. As in the arraignment hearing, it is the state that presents the violence to the court. During his exchange with the defendant, the judge, when coming upon the question of the factual basis of the case, asks the state to present its evidence. Here, the state simply reaffirms the description of violence provided during the arraignment hearing, culled from the police report. The batterer is again left silent, as it is precisely his right to contest the state's claim to his violent behavior that he surrenders through the plea. The story of his violence that he constructs with his defense attorney is never spoken to the court.

The exchange draws to a close with the judge noting for the electronic record that "the suspect has pled guilty to the offense of domestic battery" and directing the batterer to probation services to work out the details of serving his sentence. At this point, the batterer will either leave the courtroom or, as occurred in many instances, use the termination of the proceedings to ask the judge any lingering questions he might have. These questions often concern the return of bond money posted by the defendant, though in one instance a batterer asked the judge, "So, I can have contact with her?", not understanding the conditions of the deal, which allowed him to have contact with his partner, that he had just pled to.

The power operant in the plea hearing is similar to that in the arraignment proceedings. It is again a *disciplinary power* applied by the patriarchal figure of the judge intended to produce a particular type of subject for the purposes of the hearing. During the plea hearing, however, the subject that is desired and brought before the court is not the silenced criminal suspect, obediently receiving his criminal charges and conditions of bond, but the knowing legal subject, verifying in public discussion that he willfully resigns his rights to trial. Nevertheless, elements of that earlier performance remain, as the batterer is made to stand silently as the state again presents before the public the accusation that he committed domestic violence.

Discussion

The implementation of no-drop prosecution in Centralia County has brought about a change in the performance of each actor in the criminal court setting. Faced with a "discordant locale" that does not share the definition of domestic violence encoded into the state's statute and prosecuted by the state's attorney's office, prosecutors shift to an aggressive charging strategy and punitive deployment of the no-contact order in an effort to coerce domestic violence suspects to plead guilty. Public defenders and judges, in response, adjust their performances during prearraignment intake and arraignment proceedings to accommodate the state's charging procedures. Public defenders need alert defendants of the no-contact order, while judges adopt a forceful tone in warning suspects about conditions of the order and the consequences of violating it. In the end, no-drop prosecution deepens the state's infiltration of abusers' authority within the home. Bringing batterers to admit guilt, the prosecutor's office continues the redefinition of "public" and "private" space initiated in the police response.

Gender Politics and the State. While convictions secured by the Centralia County State's Attorney's Office in domestic violence cases evidence the state's capacity to work to advance change in gender relations, this description of the practice of evidence-based prosecution raises deeper questions concerning feminists' alliance with the state. For one, the racial disparities present in arrest statistics persist. The state's attorneys' office did not provide me numbers on the race of defendants or victims, but my observations of pretrial and plea proceedings found a high number of African Americans charged with and convicted of domestic violence charges.

Women of different races remain in the system as well, though not nearly at the 37% level found in the Plainsville arrest numbers. Nancy, the victims advocate in the state's attorney's office, was surprised when I mentioned this percentage of female arrests, which she said sounded very high.[9] Thus, without the benefit of statistics from the state, it is difficult to determine whether the number of women I saw charged with domestic violence reflects the number of women arrested for domestic violence, which is usually much lower than 37%, or an effort by the state's attorney's office to filter these arrests out of the system.

In addition to the persistent racial disparities in the state's processing of domestic violence cases, class also emerges as a concern. Those unable to secure their own counsel are represented by public defenders who need, by nature of their burdensome caseloads, work defendants to plead guilty. This is not to say that private attorneys guarantee a vigorous defense. Many private attorneys in Centralia County are seen to plead defendants out at a higher rate than public defenders. Nevertheless, having the money to hire one's own attorney presents at least the chance to have an attorney who will do more than look to move the case to a plea bargain. Class, of course, intersects with race, leaving poor and working-class African American men at a distinct disadvantage in acquiring adequate legal counsel for their cases.

This description also highlights the importance of community and local culture to advocacy efforts. The "discordant locale" of Centralia County's conservative community represents a firm obstacle dissuading the state's attorney's office from trying cases. This experience highlights a key difference between the potential of feminist activism directed at the police and that directed at the courts. Whereas feminists have witnessed increased domestic violence arrests as a result of their combination of lawsuits, legislation, and pressure on individual departments, their influence on the courts is ultimately limited. Unlike police departments, which are hierarchical organizations whose members can be affected by the efforts of superiors, courts are more egalitarian organizations structured to allow for the participation of the community through the participation of juries. The significance of local community to court outcomes may indicate the need for more broad-based advocacy efforts targeting changes in local attitudes about intimate partner abuse in addition to the organizationally based efforts targeting changes in policing and prosecution practice.

Questions also surround the state's accommodation to the problems of the discordant locale, the plea bargain. While the plea bargain is a conviction that holds the batterer accountable for abusive behavior and forces his enrollment in counseling, it still represents a negotiated settlement to the case. Some have questioned whether such a negotiation does enough to hold batterers accountable. As Friztler and Simon (2000) note, "accepting a 'no contest' plea and other compromises or plea bargains can serve to reinforce distorted thinking by allowing the offender to avoid full responsibility for his behavior. It can also be harmful by causing the victim and the offender to believe that the offender can escape responsibility for present and future acts with some degree of impunity" (31). Others disagree. Hartley (2003), for instance, argues that, "if the defendant pleads or is found guilty, there is a recognition of responsibility" (417). Further, "the prosecution and conviction of batterers can have a therapeutic effect for victims because it can facilitate the reattribution of blame for the abuse of the offender" (Hartley 2003:417). Additional research is needed to identify victims' satisfaction with plea-bargained convictions. I will return to the topic of the effects on batterers in a moment.

Finally, the state's use of no-contact orders also raises questions. The no-contact order represents a central achievement of the battered women's movement that enables women to seek protection from their abusers. In addition, previous studies have shown that many women find the experience of obtaining a restraining order empowering (Chaudhuri & Daly 1992; Ptacek 1999; Fleury 2002), thereby fortifying their ability to manage their situations of abuse. It seems particularly troubling, then, that the function and application of no-contact orders have been changed in criminal cases of domestic violence in Centralia County. In contrast to its original intent, in which the victim actively seeks the order, and the order is given following the court's consideration of the request, the no-contact order in Centralia is requested by the state with little to no consideration to questions of victim safety. In the process, the function of the no-contact order is transformed. The state anticipates the violation of the no-contact order. And rather than finding ways to strengthen the order to prevent batterers from violating it, which would in turn provide greater victim safety, the state waits for defendants to violate it, so that more severe measures can be taken. In addition, the court applies no-contact orders without consulting victims. Given that many victims are uncooperative with the criminal cases,[10] one wonders how this application of no-contact orders affects their ability to manage their situations of abuse. The transformation of the no-contact order under no-drop prosecution thus leaves one to question the compatibility of the state's interest in securing convictions with advocates' interest in protecting and assisting victims of abuse.

The Gendered Performance of No-Drop Prosecution. This chapter highlights three distinct types of power that engage the suspected abuser during court proceedings: a juridical power operant in the no-contact order and aggressive charging policy; a disciplinary power operant in courtroom proceedings; and a discursive power operant in the defendants' interactions with his attorney. These power operations shape the suspected batterer's behavior, decision making, and relation to himself and his partner in different ways that are critical to the state's objective of securing plea bargains. The no-contact order and aggressive charges, for instance, apply leverage intended to have the suspect plead guilty by making the process more punishing.

But these power dynamics, like those in mandatory arrest policing, are also infused with gendered meanings and performances. To begin with, suspected batterers come to the court setting with their masculine discourses of denial, minimization, justification, and victimization. As Sam, one of the private attorneys, noted, the men "really want to talk about the incident, and explain why they didn't do it, and why you should believe them."

Through the processing of their cases in court, men's relation to their violence changes. For one, some men perceive the application of the no-contact order as another injustice forced upon them. Interestingly, for these men, the no-contact order violates a central element of masculine power, private property. Men frequently challenge the justice of the no-contact order on the basis that they "own the house." Thus, an additional version of the victimization discourse emerges.

Men voicing these beliefs challenge the normal operation of the court setting. As noted above, the members of the workgroup look to silence these challenges, to ensure the efficient completion of the tasks before them. But these discursive efforts convey meaning as well. Public defenders respond to these challenges with responses that, similar to verbal judo, quiet the defendant while maintaining control over him: "I know, I don't agree with it either. They're out of control with this stuff down here." Whatever impact such comments afford in terms of client control, they can also be seen to affirm and reinforce the suspected batterer's discourse of victimization.

Unlike public defenders, judges silence batterers' challenges with statements that firmly assert the authority of the court over the man's own: "Sir, I'm not questioning your ownership of the property. I am, however, exercising my authority to order you not to have contact with that address" or "It is your responsibility to locate accommodations for yourself in the meantime. But you cannot have contact with the address. Thank you, sir." These statements follow on the warnings judges give batterers when applying the no-contact order in the first place. Rather than reinforcing the batterers' discourse of victimization, the judges challenge the men's claim to masculine authority. In this sense, one witnesses competing masculinities in the court. The judge, armed with masculinist "prerogative power" (Brown 1995:186–91), asserts the state's monopoly of public authority over the private power and authority that batterers are accustomed to exercising in the home.

Attorney–client meetings represent a central site for the construction of meaning in batterers' contact with the court setting. Rather than simply affirming or denying men's views of the system or stories of violence, defense attorneys reshape them. Like batterers, defense attorneys believe that evidence of abuse can be hidden. As Tom, one of the public defenders, noted, "The injuries sometimes don't concern me so much. Because you can get injuries defending yourself, so you can explain those away." Negotiating between the claims of the police and the other evidence present in a particular case, lawyers work with suspected batterers to construct legally viable denials and minimizations of violence that can stand up in court. In this sense, attorney–client meetings not only reinforce men's views of violence but strengthen them.

Attorney–client meetings also rework how men understand the system attempting to punish them for their behavior. To a person, the defense attorneys I spoke with disliked the state's handling of domestic violence cases, describing it as "stupid," "silly," "flawed," "politically motivated," "sexist," and "a tortured use of the law." From my direct observations of prearraignment interactions, there is little reason to doubt that these views of the state's handling of domestic violence cases penetrate attorney–client meetings. These portrayals of the system actually work to the defense attorney's favor, as they help realize client control. That is, they implant in the defendant's mind the belief that his attorney is indeed on his side, even as she is working to move the case to a quick resolution. What's more, to the extent that defense attorneys sincerely believe the state is acting improperly in domestic violence cases, they may come to empathize with domestic battery suspects. Diane, one of the private attorneys, revealed such a sentiment in talking about one of her clients: "God love him, this guy wasn't going to back down." Such interactions, which have the batterer envision himself as an isolated figure confronting a larger system of forces that simply cannot be beaten (Eisikovits & Buchbinder 2000:136), can reinforce batterers' discourse of victimization by communicating to them that the system prosecuting them is unjust. As Eisikovits and Buchbinder (2000) find in their interviews with abusers whose partners have challenged their power by repeatedly calling the police against them, a batterer comes to believe that "it is not his partner alone that has betrayed and humiliated him but a coalition of which she is but a part" (136).

Defendants' decision making in their cases unfolds in gendered terms as well. As many of the defense attorneys explained, the prospect of losing the right to carry a handgun, one of the core elements of American masculine identity (Connell 2000:214; Sabo 2005:336), makes many men less willing to plead guilty. Interestingly, the men who refuse to cede this element of their masculinity are likely to be rewarded by the conservative juries who do not share feminists' or the state's vision of domestic abuse.

Even if batterers plead guilty, as most do, their stories of denial and victimization do not enter the public arena. The structure of the plea proceeding does not require the batterer to speak of his violence or verbally admit that he has done something wrong. Again, the emphasis of the plea proceeding falls on procedural form, not on batterer accountability. Thus, the court setting, save those rare instances of criminal trials, never formally challenges the batterer's view of himself or his actions. The state contents itself with the belief and hope that counseling will address the defendant's violence.

Of course, before the final verdict on no-drop prosecution can be written, further research is needed on how these practices affect both victims and offenders. In the chapters that follow, I move to do this by reporting the results of my interviews with abusers arrested and prosecuted for intimate abuse. Before that, however, I need first describe the suspects taking part in this research.

3 | Research Participants and Their Violence

This chapter examines the violence and socio-demographic characteristics of the 30 persons arrested and prosecuted for domestic violence in Centralia County who took part in this study.[1] Qualitative research in the past has assumed that intimate abusers constitute a unified category of violent subjects, defined by their efforts to control women (Ptacek 1988; Dobash & Dobash 1998; Hearn 2000; Anderson & Umberson 2001). As noted in the introduction, however, the last decade has seen a growing body of research persuasively argue that intimate partner abuse and intimate abusers consist of multiple types of behaviors and personality types (Stark 2007; Johnson 2006a, 1995; Holtzworth-Munroe & Stuart 1994; Dutton 1998).

Holtzworth-Munroe and Stuart (1994) offer three major types of batterers. *"Family-only batterers"* engage in the least severe violence, limit their violence to family members, and are unlikely to commit sexual and/or psychological abuse; *"dysphoric/borderline batterers"* engage in moderate to severe marital violence, including psychological and sexual abuse, and exhibit deep emotional dependence on their intimate partners; and *"generally violent/antisocial batterers"* commit moderate to severe marital violence, including psychological and sexual abuse, and possess antisocial personality disorders (477–82). Michael Johnson (2006a, 1995) distinguishes among four types of intimate abuse. In *intimate terrorism,* the "individual is violent and controlling, the partner is not"; in *violent resistance,* "the individual is violent but not controlling, the partner is the violent and controlling one"; in *situational couple violence,* "although the individual is violent, neither the individual nor the partner is violent and controlling"; and in *mutual violent control,* "the individual and the partner are violent and controlling" (Johnson 2006a:1). More recently, Evan Stark (2007) has offered a threefold description of domestic violence: *fights,* "in which one or both partners use force to address situationally specific conflicts"; *partner assaults,* "where violence and threats are used to hurt, subjugate, and exert power over a partner"; and *"coercive control,"* in which men use violence, intimidation, isolation, and/or control to "inhibit women's self-direction, compromise their liberty, and cause a range of harms that are not easily subsumed under safety concerns" (234–42, 219).

What is immediately noteworthy in the different classifications is controlling behavior. For years, abuse victims have explained that their partners' efforts to monitor their movements and conversations, dictate personal choices such as going to school or getting a job, denigrate their interests and choices, isolate them from friends and family, and so on, hurt more than the physical violence. Listening to these voices, both Johnson and Stark use controlling behavior to differentiate the most serious types of abusive relationships—intimate terrorism and coercive control—from the least serious—situational couple violence and fights. The lesson to be drawn from this is that if we are to understand intimate partner abuse and to be able to differentiate between different types of offenders, we must account for controlling behavior.

It also is important to highlight how these categories are gendered in practice. Johnson's "situational couple violence" and "mutual violent control" and Stark's "fights" all involve the male and female partner as mutual co-participants in violence. However, Johnson's "intimate terrorism" and Stark's "assaults" and "coercive control" primarily involve men's controlling and violent behavior toward women.[2] Johnson's category of "violent resistance," finally, refers to women's efforts to resist men's intimate terrorism.

Questions exist regarding the place of violence within these categories. Johnson, for instance, believes that physical violence in intimate terrorism is more frequent than in situational couple violence (Johnson 2006b). And while the severity of attacks can be similar, with both types producing serious injuries, intimate terrorism, due to its frequency, causes severe injuries more often than does situational couple violence (Johnson 2006b). Stark (2007), meanwhile, believes that coercive control can be exercised without resort to violence. Through tactics of isolation, intimidation, and control alone, abusers are able to realize their goals of completely dominating the lives of their partners (100). For this reason, legal interventions that require evidence of violence to prove the existence of partner abuse miss a large number of abusive relationships in which victims find themselves.

More research is required to more fully flesh out these categories. Still, these typologies of intimate partner abuse carry the potential to bridge the symmetry debate between family violence researchers (Straus, Gelles, & Steinmetz 1980; Straus & Gelles 1990), who insist that women are as violent as men in intimate relationships, and feminist researchers (Dobash & Dobash 1979; Martin 1976), who contend that intimate abuse is men's violence against women, that has divided domestic violence research since the 1970s. Johnson contends that each group of researchers, due to differences in their sampling techniques, has simply been talking about different types of abuse. While family violence researchers, relying on general population surveys that only asked about and recorded violent incidents, have tended to capture situational couple violence, feminist researchers, listening to victims' stories of abusive and controlling partners gathered from shelter and court samples, have largely captured intimate terrorism (Johnson 1995:288–91).

The need to incorporate such a classification scheme in domestic violence research is intuitive. If not all intimate abuse is the same, then researchers need identify which types they are dealing with. In the remainder of this chapter, I demonstrate the feasibility of doing this, using not only socio-demographic descriptors but also Johnson's categories of situational couple violence (SCV) and intimate terrorism (IT) to describe the persons taking part in this study.

Socio-demographic Characteristics and Criminal History. Aside from sex, the participants in this research were heterogeneous in terms of age, race, employment, marital status, and criminal history (see Tables 5 and 6). Of the 30 persons interviewed, 27 were male. I intentionally recruited male participants, since men are abusive against their intimate partners more frequently than are women, and their violence is more harmful than that of women. Nevertheless, I did include three women arrested for domestic battery in this study, which will help illuminate the experiences of women arrested and prosecuted under mandatory policies.[3]

The average age for participants in the group was 31.1 years. This number falls within the 25-to-34 age group that regularly reports the highest rates of partner violence in surveys (see Brzozowski 2004:8; Stets & Straus 1989:41–42). Respondents' age varied greatly, ranging from 21 years to 58 years. This variance resulted in a standard deviation of 9.19 years.

In terms of race, the group was predominantly split between African Americans (17) and European Americans (11). The two remaining participants were Latinos born and raised in the area. The racial composition of the group over-represented African Americans relative to the general population, but not to the population of persons arrested and prosecuted for domestic violence in Plainsville and Centralia County.

The group was also split evenly in terms of employment status. Seventeen of the interviewees held jobs at the time of their arrest. In Table 5, which provides a summary description of each participant, one can see that these jobs tended to be in the service sector, including gas station attendants, fast-food cooks, and a hotel attendant. Ten of the participants were unemployed at the time of their arrests. Three held disability status. As a whole, this group was comprised primarily of persons with low occupational status.

Only seven of the persons I interviewed were married at the time of their arrest. Moreover, two of these married persons were violent against an intimate partner other than their wife. Of the 23 persons who were not married, 10 were cohabiting with their partners at the time of their arrest, while 13 were living apart from their partners. One man (Doug) I interviewed was married but separated and living with a girlfriend when he was arrested. These numbers help illustrate the point that separation or "leaving," rather than making women safer, increases the likelihood of victimization (see Stark 2007:115–17).

In a study on the efficacy of criminal justice sanctions against intimate abuse, it is clearly important to consider whether respondents have had contact with the criminal justice system in the past. To do this, I provide three descriptive statistics (see Table 6 for a group summary, and Table 7 for participant summaries). The first is the total number of criminal cases brought against the person in Centralia County, including pending cases. Using a cluster analysis, I grouped the respondents into four different groups: 1, 2–3, 4–6, and 7+ cases. For two of the respondents, their domestic violence case was their first criminal case. The rest of the group split relatively evenly, with nine persons having a minor criminal case history (2–3 cases), nine having a moderate criminal case history (4–6 cases), and seven having a major criminal case history (7 or more cases).

To highlight their criminal case histories specific to domestic violence, I report two statistics: total domestic violence cases and total domestic violence convictions. For half of the available sample (14 out of 27 respondents), this was their first domestic violence case. The rest had a prior domestic case, ranging in descending order from five persons with two domestic cases to one person with more than five cases. In terms of convictions, seven of the respondents were not convicted of a domestic violence offense, fifteen had a single domestic violence conviction, and the rest of the group had two or more convictions.

Abuser Type. Differentiating participants according to batterer type proved more challenging than distinguishing them by categories of sex, race, class, marital status, and criminal history. As noted above, the boundaries between batterer types have not yet been settled. Questions remain,

TABLE 5—Pseudonyms, Sociodemographic Characteristics, and Abuser Type

Name	Sex	Age	Race	Employment	Marital Status	Violence Type
1. Ann	F	43	European American	Unemployed	Single	Situational
2. Betty	F	42	African American	Unemployed	Cohabitating	Situational
3. Adam	M	47	Latino	Custodian	Married	Intimate Terrorism
4. Bob	M	35	European American	Disability	Single	Situational
5. Chris	M	46	African American	Unemployed	Cohabitating	Situational
6. Dave	M	38	European American	Disability	Single	Intimate Terrorism
7. Eric	M	21	European American	Painter	Cohabitating	Intimate Terrorism
8. Frank	M	31	European American	Carpenter	Single	Intimate Terrorism
9. Gary	M	22	European American	Gas Station	Cohabitating	Intimate Terrorism
10. Henry	M	53	African American	Unemployed	Single	—
11. Isaac	M	24	African American	Unemployed	Single	Situational
12. John	M	25*	African American	Fast Food	Cohabitating	—
13. Kevin	M	24	African American	Fast Food	Cohabitating	Situational
14. Larry	M	58	European American	Disability	Cohabitating	Intimate Terrorism
15. Mike	M	36	African American	Cook	Cohabitating	Situational
16. Nic	M	29	Latino	Public Works	Married	Intimate Terrorism
17. Oscar	M	43	African American	Construction	Married	Intimate Terrorism

18. Pete	M	45*	European American	Employed	Married	—
19. Quinn	M	32*	European American	Construction	Separated	—
20. Ralph	M	28*	African American	Factory	Single	—
21. Steve	M	43	African American	Hotel	Married	Situational
22. Tom	M	20	African American	Gas Station	Cohabitating	Situational
23. Victor	M	23	African American	Unemployed	Single	Intimate Terrorism
24. Walter	M	32	African American	Employed	Single	Situational
25. Aaron	M	26	African American	Unemployed	Single	Intimate Terrorism
26. Brett	M	38	African American	Factory; Teacher's Aide	Single	Intimate Terrorism
27. Carl	M	42	European American	Cook; Real Estate	Single	Intimate Terrorism
28. Doug	M	41	European American	Mechanic; Real Estate	Separated, Cohabitating	Intimate Terrorism
29. Ed	M	25	African American	Unemployed	Single	Situational
30. Carrie	F	21	European American	Unemployed	Married	Situational

* These numbers reflect an estimate of the person's age.

for instance, as to whether the most severe categories of abuse—intimate terrorism and coercive control—necessarily involve violence. So, it is not clear which categories most accurately depict intimate partner abuse. Also, while the data from which Johnson and Stark created their typologies came from victims, my primary source of data is suspected abusers, who are notoriously unreliable informants on their own behavior. Thus, this study lacks the best type of data—victims' reports—for classifying abusers.

Yet classifying the persons participating in this study remains both possible and instructive. To address the first issue, I chose to employ Johnson's typology of abuse, using the presence or absence of patterns of controlling

TABLE 6—Respondents' Social Background and Criminal Histories

VARIABLE	VALUES
Sociodemographic	
Age	31.1 (mean), 9.19 (s.d.)
Sex	
Male	90.0% (27/30)
Female	10.0% (3/30)
Race	
African American	56.7% (17/30)
Euro-American	36.7% (11/30)
Latino	6.7% (2/30)
Employment	
Unemployed	30.0% (9/30)
Employed	60.0% (18/30)
Disability	10.0% (3/30)
Marital	
Married, Cohabitating	16.7% (5/30)
Divorced/Separated	6.7% (2/30)
Cohabitating	33.3% (10/30)
Single	43.3% (13/30)
*Criminal History**	
Total Criminal Cases	
1	7.4% (2/27)
2–3	33.3% (9/27)
4–6	33.3% (9/27)
7+	25.9% (7/27)
Total DV Cases	
1	51.9% (14/27)
2	18.5% (5/27)
3	14.8% (4/27)
4	11.1% (3/27)
5+	3.7% (1/27)
Total DV Convictions	
0	25.9% (7/27)
1	55.6% (15/27)
2	11.1% (3/27)
3	3.7% (1/27)
4	3.7% (1/27)

* I was unable to gather the criminal records of three of the participants. Therefore, the values presented here are calculated out of 27 respondents.

TABLE 7—Summary of Respondents' Criminal History

Name	Total Cases	Total DV	DV Guilty*
1. Ann	4	4	2
2. Betty	10	3	2
3. Adam	2	1	1
4. Bob	3	1	1
5. Chris	13	6	4
6. Dave	4	4	1
7. Eric	5	2	1
8. Frank	5	3	3
9. Gary	4	3	1
10. Henry	5	1	1
11. Isaac	10	2	2
12. John	1	1	0
13. Kevin	2	1	1
14. Larry	11	2	1
15. Mike	4	1	0
16. Nic	3	1	1
17. Oscar	2	1	0
18. Pete#	—	—	—
19. Quinn#	—	—	—
20. Ralph#	—	—	—
21. Steve	2	2	1
22. Tom	3	1	0
23. Victor	10	4	0
24. Walter	7	1	0
25. Aaron	2	1	1
26. Brett	5	3	1
27. Carl	1	1	1
28. Doug	3	2	0
29. Ed	11	1	1
30. Carrie	4	1	1

* I count plea bargains to lesser battery charges in domestic violence cases as convictions.

I conducted shorter interviews with Pete, Quinn, and Ralph immediately following their appearances in court and did not have the opportunity to record their personal information. These shortened interviews focused primarily on their experiences with the criminal justice system.

behavior to differentiate between situational couple violence (SCV) and intimate terrorism (IT).[4] Again, control tactics are what differentiate the most severe types of abuse from the least severe types. I chose to use these categories, despite harboring some reservations about the terminology itself. Like Stark (2007), I see little resemblance between the tactics of severe abusers and those of terrorists (105). Nevertheless, Johnson's terms are more widely circulated in the research literature. More importantly, his scheme ultimately proved more harmonious with the data than Stark's.[5] I feel more confident, then, distinguishing between the categories of SCV and IT.

To address the second issue, I first turned to the police reports describing the incidents for which the respondents were arrested. Since these reports contain victim statements, they represent a vital source of information beyond participants' narratives. In addition to the police reports, I also looked up participants' criminal history to determine the nature of any prior criminal conduct. By itself, criminal history is a problematic source of information on an individual's behavior, since it registers only those incidents reported to the police and resulting in prosecution. Nevertheless, when used as one measure among others, as is the case here, criminal history can reveal past incidents that help distinguish types of violence. For instance, in one case (Victor), the respondent had prior sexual assault cases as well as multiple prior domestic violence arrests, which evidenced controlling behavior (harassing phone calls to an ex-girlfriend in violation of a no-contact order). Combining this indicator with the participant's own statements that he and his ex-partner had frequent conflicts, I classified this case as intimate terrorism. Finally, I used men's own narratives to help me classify their violence. While these stories possess clear problems in terms of reliability, they did nevertheless turn out to be helpful in uncovering controlling behaviors. That is, many men, not sensing the wrongfulness of control tactics, openly mentioned checking their partner's cell phone call log (Nic) or following around partners they suspected of having affairs (Aaron). Again, when combined with other measures, participants' narratives served as useful sources of information for categorizing their abuse.

I reviewed these three data sources for reports of violence and controlling behaviors, differentiating IT from SCV by patterned use of control tactics. Appendix B contains a summary of the three sources of information (criminal history, victim statement, and participant statement) that I used to categorize the participants. In addition, Appendix B also contains a brief summary of the most recent incident of domestic violence for which the person was arrested.

In Table 8, I list the results of this analysis. As this list shows, I was able to classify 25 cases out of the 30 participants into Johnson's categories. For the five cases I was not able to classify, I did not have police reports or criminal histories for four of the men,[6] while in the other case, the participant was

TABLE 8—Batterer Types among Respondents

Violence Type	Percentage (n=25)
Situational Couple Violence	48.0% (12/25)
Intimate Terrorism	52.0% (13/25)

arrested for domestic violence against his brother, which does not qualify as intimate abuse. From the 25 cases I was able to classify, 13 qualified as intimate terrorism, and 12 qualified as situational couple violence.[7]

Deciding where to place certain respondents proved difficult, especially for conflicts over suspected infidelity, which involve apparent controlling behavior on the abuser's part. For instance, Isaac, suspecting his girlfriend was involved in another relationship, dragged her by her hair from a party, threw her in his car, brought her back to their residence, and continued to batter her there. While this incident certainly demonstrates controlling behavior, Johnson (2006b) explains that "many of the separate violent incidents of SCV may look exactly like those involved in IT or VR.[8] The difference is in the general power and control dynamic of the relationship, not in the nature of any one assault. If it appears that neither partner is generally trying to control the other, that is, it is not the case that the relationship involves the use of a range of control tactics by one or both of the partners, then it is SCV" (562). In Isaac's case, while he viciously attacked his victim, neither he nor his victim, nor past criminal history, indicated that this action comprised a more *general pattern of control*. Therefore, I classified him as situationally violent.

As these points of qualification make clear, this classification is not authoritative. But I offer it still, believing that we cannot in good faith continue to ignore the differences among abusers in domestic violence research. As well, as this review demonstrates, in many if not most cases, it can be fairly simple to differentiate instances where violence arises out of a common dispute and violence in the context of controlling relationships. If tentative, then, this scheme shows that distinctions can be realized, and that stronger ones would be possible in future research with more detailed data.

Severity of Violence. Having some background on who the participants in this research are, it is next important to consider what they are reported to have done that resulted in their arrest. Researchers have differed in how they study or measure domestic violence. Family violence researchers (Straus et al. 1980) examine the severity and frequency of individual violent events, while feminist researchers (Dobash & Dobash 1979; Martin 1976) examine conflict in intimate relationships and the different ways in which men exercise control over their female partners.

Both sets of concerns are useful in further illuminating persons' intimate violence. As such, to provide a fuller description of the violence that led to participants' most recent domestic violence arrest, I reviewed the police reports to determine both the severity of the violence and the nature of the conflict within which the violence occurred. To establish severity, I used the definitions for psychological aggression, physical assault, and injury from Straus et al.'s (1996) Revised Conflict Tactics Scale (CTS2) (see Table 9). To describe the nature of the conflicts, I classified them into categories described in past feminist research (Dobash & Dobash 1998; Ptacek 1988, 1999), which include money, division of household labor, children, jealousy, sex, and drinking. I grouped sex and jealousy together, since both concern men's sexual access to women.

Table 10 reports the results of this analysis. As this table shows, the physical violence reported by victims is predominantly severe, with 17 out of 26 victims reported to have been punched, choked, slammed, beaten up, kicked or having had a knife used against them by their partners (for a summary description of each respondent's violence, see Table 11). Seven victims reported minor violence, such as being slapped, grabbed, or pushed by their partners. Two reported no physical violence. Less psychological aggression is reported, but it should be noted that police look for, and are more likely to record, evidence of physical violence in making an arrest decision. As such, these data most likely under-report the incidence of psychological aggression. In terms of injuries, 14 out of 26 victims reported sustaining injuries of some sort from their partners, with 4 reporting severe injuries.

The conflicts in which violence occurred dealt primarily with sexual access. Thirteen out of 26 cases involved disputes about alleged affairs, having seen a partner with another man, phone calls from persons of the opposite sex, and so forth. After sexual access, the conflicts were somewhat evenly split between those involving money, those involving parenting, and those involving "other" matters, such as arguments over car keys, cigarettes, and loud music. Even though the respondents in this study are disproportionately poor and unemployed, the issues around which they are violent with their intimate partners are issues of sexual access. This is surprising to the extent that one would expect conflicts between lower-income partners to involve financial matters. These numbers thus demonstrate the gendered nature of the conflicts leading to intimate partner violence for these respondents.

In Table 12, I examine the incidence of these abuse items by batterer type. This descriptive table demonstrates a couple of points pertinent to this examination of violence and abusers. First, it reveals a high incidence of severe violence on the part of SCV abusers in this study. Some 58.3% of situationally violent abusers were reported to have committed severe violence, versus 69.2% of intimate terrorists. These percentages are not

TABLE 9— The Revised Conflict Tactics Scale (CTS2)—Physical Assault, Psychological Aggression, and Injury Scale Items

PHYSICAL ASSAULT SCALE ITEMS

Subscale	*Item*
Minor	Threw something at my partner that could hurt
Minor	Twisted my partner's arm or hair
Minor	Pushed or shoved my partner
Minor	Grabbed my partner
Minor	Slapped my partner
Severe	Used a knife or gun on my partner
Severe	Punched or hit my partner with something that could hurt
Severe	Choked my partner
Severe	Slammed my partner against a wall
Severe	Beat up my partner
Severe	Burned or scalded my partner on purpose
Severe	Kicked my partner

PSYCHOLOGICAL AGGRESSION SCALE ITEMS

Subscale	*Item*
Minor	Insulted or swore at my partner
Minor	Shouted or yelled at my partner
Minor	Stomped out of the room or house or yard during a disagreement
Minor	Said something to spite my partner
Severe	Called my partner fat or ugly
Severe	Destroyed something belonging to my partner
Severe	Accused my partner of being a lousy lover
Severe	Threatened to hit or throw something at my partner

INJURY SCALE ITEMS

Subscale	*Item*
Minor	Had a sprain, bruise, or small cut because of a fight with my partner
Minor	Felt physical pain that still hurt the next day because of a fight with my partner
Severe	Passed out from being hit on the head by my partner in a fight
Severe	Went to a doctor because of a fight with my partner
Severe	Needed to see a doctor because of a fight with my partner, but I didn't
Severe	Had a broken bone from a fight with my partner

Source: Straus et al. 1996

TABLE 10—Respondents' Violence: Source of Conflict, Severity, and Injuries in Most Recent Domestic Violence Cases

DOMESTIC VIOLENCE VARIABLE FACT	PERCENTAGES*
Severity	
Physical	
None	7.7% (2/26)
Minor	26.9% (7/26)
Severe	65.4% (17/26)
Psychological	
None	61.5% (16/26)
Minor	7.7% (2/26)
Severe	30.8% (8/26)
Injuries	
None	46.2% (12/26)
Minor	38.5% (10/26)
Severe	15.4% (4/26)
Source of Conflict	
Money/Possessions	19.2% (5/26)
Jealousy/Sex	50.0% (13/26)
Children/Parenting	11.5% (3/26)
Other	19.2% (5/26)

* I was unable to gather the police reports of four of the participants. Therefore, the values presented here are calculated out of 26 respondents

representative of the amount of severe violence committed within each category of abuse. Indeed, it is likely that victims report only incidents of severe violence to authorities. Nevertheless, the numbers echo the point made by Johnson (2006b) that situationally violent batterers can be as severely violent as intimate terrorists in a single incident. Again, the key distinction between these two groups is not lethality, but patterned use of controlling behavior.

With this in mind, the high incidence of severe psychological aggression on the part of intimate terrorists is also worth noting; 46.2% of intimate terrorists are reported to have engaged in severe psychological aggression against their victims, versus 8.3% of situationally violent offenders. Such

TABLE 11—Source of Conflict, Severity of Violence, and Injuries in Respondents' Current Cases

Name	Source of Conflict	Reported Severity of Conflict Tactics	Reported Injuries*
1. Ann	Money	Minor Physical (throws chair at ex-boyfriend)	None
2. Betty	Jealousy/Sex	Severe Physical (strikes partner in head with phone)	None
3. Adam	Children	Severe Psychological (threatens wife with knife)	None
4. Bob	Jealousy/Sex	Severe Physical (chokes ex-girlfriend)	None
5. Chris	Other (loud radio)	Severe Psychological (threatens to hurt girlfriend) / Minor Physical (pushes girlfriend to ground)	Scratch on her neck Bite mark on his chest
6. Dave	Money	Severe Psychological (makes her swear not to call police) / Severe Physical (chokes ex-girlfriend)	Redness on her neck
7. Eric	Jealousy/Sex	Severe Physical (chokes and hits girlfriend in the head)	Bump on her forehead
8. Frank	Jealousy/Sex	Severe Psychological (stalking, property destruction) / Severe Physical (kidnapping)	None
9. Gary	Jealousy/Sex	Minor Psychological (calls partner a "bitch" and a "whore") / Severe Physical (chokes girlfriend)	Victim transported to hospital for neck pain (s)
10. Henry	Money	Severe Psychological (threatens brother with knife) / Severe Physical (hit brother with butt of knife)	None
11. Isaac	Jealousy/Sex	Severe Physical (beats up girlfriend)	Severe bruise on her arm Marks on her cheek
12. John#	Children	N/A	N/A
13. Kevin	Other (cigarette)	Severe Physical (repeatedly punches, then bites partner)	Her lip is bloody Bite on her shoulder
14. Larry	Jealousy/Sex	Severe Psychological (threatens to kill if she calls police) / Severe Physical (repeatedly punches partner in head)	Bruises on her face Her nose is swollen (S)

15. Mike	Other (keys)	Minor Physical (grabs partner by the legs)	None
16. Nic	Children	Severe Physical (throws partner to ground and kicks her)	Red mark on her back
17. Oscar	Money	Severe Physical (drags partner by hair and stomps on her)	Abrasion on her lip
18. Pete+	—	—	—
19. Quinn	—	—	—
20. Ralph	—	—	—
21. Steve	Jealousy/Sex	Minor Psychological (calls partner a "bitch" and "whore") / Minor Physical (tackles partner to the ground)	None
22. Tom	Other (car)	Severe Physical (slams partner against wall, holds to floor)	Bite mark on his hand
23. Victor	Other (flat tire)	Minor Psychological (yells at partner)	None
24. Walter	Jealousy/Sex	Severe Physical (hits partner in head with fists and phone)	None
25. Aaron	Jealousy/Sex	Severe Physical (slams partner against wall)	Swelling on her cheek She goes to hospital (S)
26. Brett	Jealousy/Sex	Severe Physical (chokes partner)	None
27. Carl	Jealousy/Sex	Severe Psychological (insults sexual propriety) / Minor Physical (strikes partner across face)	None
28. Doug	Jealousy/Sex	Severe Psychological (threatens to kill her, disables her car) / Minor Physical (grabs partner by neck)	Her neck is red and sore Scratches on his face
29. Ed	Money	Minor Physical (pushes victim)	Large bruise on her back
30. Carrie	Parenting; Jealousy/Sex	Severe Physical (stabs partner with box cutter)	Severe cut. He goes to hospital (S)

* (S) in the injury column denotes "severe" injuries, as defined by Straus et al. (1996).
# No police report was available for this case.
+ I conducted shorter interviews with these three men immediately following their appearances in court and did not have the opportunity to record their personal information. These shortened interviews focused primarily with their experiences with the criminal justice system.

TABLE 12—Severity of Violence, Injuries, and Source of Conflict by Batterer Type

VIOLENCE DESCRIPTOR	SITUATIONALLY VIOLENT (12)	INTIMATE TERRORISTS (13)
Physical Assault		
None	—	23.1% (2/13)
Minor	41.7% (5/12)	15.4% (2/13)
Severe	58.3% (7/12)	69.2% (9/13)
Psychological Aggression		
None	75.0% (9/12)	38.5% (5/13)
Minor	16.7% (2/12)	15.4% (2/13)
Severe	8.3% (1/12)	46.2% (6/13)
Injuries		
None	50.0% (6/12)	46.2% (6/13)
Minor	33.3% (4/12)	38.5% (5/13)
Severe	16.7% (2/12)	15.4% (2/13)
Source of Conflict		
Sex	41.7% (5/12)	61.2% (8/13)
Money	16.7% (2/12)	15.4% (2/13)
Children	8.3% (1/12)	15.4% (2/13)
Other	33.3% (4/12)	7.7% (1/13)

behavior, for this group of respondents at least, seems to fall almost exclusively within the purview of intimate terrorism. In part, these numbers reflect the use of control tactics on the part of intimate terrorists. To provide an example, in Carl's case, he entered his ex-girlfriend's apartment without her permission while she was asleep, awoke her, began yelling at her about "sleeping around," and then lifted the covers of her bed to inspect her dress. Upon seeing her dressed in a skirt, he lifted the skirt and asked, "Is it still dripping?" What is important to note here is that the impact of control tactics on measures of psychological abuse would be much higher if only the scale measured for the full repertoire of tactics that abusers like Carl deploy. In his case, the Revised Control Tactics Scale would count his demeaning comment under the item "called my partner fat or ugly," a type of "severe psychological abuse." However, it has no items to measure his stalking his ex-partner, which is both a more dangerous form of abuse[9] and more psychologically tormenting for women. Such a consideration only reinforces the need for better assessment tools to measure controlling behavior within intimate relationships.

To conclude, the description of abusers and their violence provided here demonstrates that mandatory arrest and no-drop prosecution policies in Centralia County net different types of batterers and domestic violence. The 30 intimate abusers participating in this study comprised a heterogeneous group, in terms of their social background (age, race, employment, marital status, and criminal history) and the violence they committed. The distinction between batterers and their violence makes clear the point argued by Johnson and others: not all acts of domestic violence are the same. Violence arising from arguments over the volume of a stereo (Chris) and a partner taking the car and leaving her boyfriend without a ride home (Tom) is clearly distinct from stalking and kidnapping a partner terminating a relationship (Frank) and stabbing a partner's favorite stuffed animal with a large knife and then leaving it on display to instill fear in her (Doug). In the chapters that follow, I examine how these differences in the violent subjectivities of intimate abusers impact the operation of mandatory arrest and no-drop prosecution upon them.

4 Abusers' Experiences with Mandatory Arrest and No-Drop Prosecution

The experience of batterers with the criminal justice system is a seldom-considered topic. Two qualitative studies, Eisikovits and Buchbinder (2000) and Anderson and Umberson (2001), have approached it tangentially to broader investigations into the lives of intimate abusers. Both studies find that men arrested for domestic violence possess a sense of victimization. The men interviewed by Anderson and Umberson (2001), for instance, describe themselves as victims of a legal system overtaken by gender politics and media attention following the O.J. Simpson murder trial. Eisikovits and Buchbinder (2000), meanwhile, note the emergence of a "victim identity" in men over time, with multiple encounters with the police and their eventual arrests leading them to perceive the police as allied with their partners against them (135–37). While these are suggestive findings concerning the meanings that batterers draw from their encounters with legal authorities, the role of particular legal practices in producing these meanings remains unclear. In this chapter, I analyze respondents' descriptions of their encounters with the police, county jail, and court setting to understand how intimate abusers interact with mandatory arrest and no-drop prosecution and what meanings these legal encounters have for them.

In examining these questions, I take guidance from ethnographic law and society research that highlights the relational nature of legal power (Silbey & Ewick 2003; Sarat & Felstiner 1995). This scholarship emphasizes power not as "a thing that can be possessed," but as a "probabilistic social relationship whose consequences are contingent upon the contributions of . . . those who turn out to be more powerful (superordinate) and those who turn out to have been less powerful (subordinate)" (Silbey & Ewick 2003:1333). Power, in this sense, is an "unstable and evanescent" phenomenon (Sarat & Felstiner 1995:vii).

Despite the contingent nature of power, patterns of social interaction do become entrenched over time. And those who exercise hegemony do so by "drawing upon the symbols, practices, statuses, and privileges that have become habitual in social structures" (Silbey & Ewick 2003:1334), such as the "rules" through which courts process cases and transform participants' voices (Conley & O'Barr 1990) and the "knowledge of, stature in, and connections to the local community" that court authorities possess (Yngvesson 1994). Still, the substantive outcomes and interpretive meanings of legal encounters are never fixed, and common people possess the capacity to exercise "resistance" in their encounters with legal authorities (Silbey & Ewick 2003; Merry 1995; Sarat 1990).

Extending these insights to the case of domestic violence law, this chapter finds that intimate abusers in Centralia County anchor their experiences of mandatory arrest and no-drop prosecution in police investigations, jail time, and plea bargaining. These events draw batterers into distinct arrangements of power. While police officers work to have domestic violence suspects pronounce their abuse during investigations, court officials press them to give up their right to address allegations of abuse during plea bargain negotiations. In response to these operations of power, suspects deliver legal performances that vary between compliance and defiance and are shaped by their legal consciousness, the tactical force of authorities, and their own abusive subjectivities. In the majority of cases, the police and courts are able to structure the outcomes of these encounters in their favor, leaving them with custodial authority over abusers. Significantly, domestic violence arrests follow abusers' efforts to explain away their violence through stories of diminished responsibility, while plea bargain convictions interrupt their efforts to reestablish control over their victimized partners. Regardless of the substantive outcomes they experience, however, nearly all the respondents in this study understand their punishments as unfair sanctions meted out by an unjust local legal system rather than as the consequences of their own actions. These injustice claims are most commonly formulated on the basis of group identities. In other instances, though, they are the echoes of legal authorities themselves, who use depictions of an unjust legal system as a tactic for realizing the compliance of criminal suspects. In the next two sections, I elaborate these ideas, first reviewing respondents' descriptions of their interactions with legal authorities, and then examining the meanings that these encounters have for them.

Batterers' Engagement with Mandatory Arrest and No-Drop Prosecution

Before looking at respondents' descriptions of their legal encounters, I want to first speak to the "success" of mandatory arrest and no-drop prosecution in the most basic terms available: conviction rates. Of the 30 persons participating in this study, 23 (76.7%) were found guilty on charges relating to their domestic violence offense. Each of these findings of guilt was secured through a plea bargain. This percentage of convictions and plea bargains approaches the percentage of domestic violence cases terminating in plea bargains in Centralia County more generally, which is 80%.

Given that the participants in this study vary in terms of their violent behavior, it is important to consider disposition outcomes by violence type. In Table 13, I do this, summarizing the percentage of guilty verdicts according to the different measures of abusive behavior reviewed last chapter: physical violence, psychological aggression, injuries, and abuser type. As these numbers show, for each of the three measures of abusive behavior, conviction rates increased with severity of abuse. Meanwhile, the conviction rates for intimate terrorists (76.9%) and situationally violent offenders (75.0%) are roughly equivalent.

At the very least, these numbers indicate that the coordinated efforts of the police and county court in Centralia County were most successful in securing convictions against the most severe cases of violence appearing in this sample. This is reassuring on the one hand, since we want to ensure that the most egregious cases of domestic violence are punished. At the same time, these numbers are somewhat disconcerting to the extent that they indicate that intimate terrorists and situationally violent offenders experience similar outcomes from the criminal legal system. As noted in the previous section, while both types of abusers can prove equally dangerous in a single incident, intimate terrorists are more dangerous over time, given the frequency of their physical violence and the range of controlling behaviors they subject their victims to. Without moving too deeply into this topic here, I want to simply state for now that these numbers reflect the disposition of the criminal justice system to determine guilt on the basis of single incidents rather than patterns of behavior.[1] This is ultimately an important point in considering the efficacy of the criminal legal system in fighting domestic violence, and I will return to it in the concluding chapter of the book.

Behind these numbers are the performances of respondents and legal authorities. As the first two chapters of this book revealed, domestic violence arrests and prosecutions expose intimate abusers to a diverse range of power operations. When asked to describe what happens in their

TABLE 13—Percentage of Guilty Dispositions by Descriptor of Violence

VIOLENCE DESCRIPTOR	NUMBER*	PERCENTAGE CONVICTED (n=20)
Physical Violence	26	
None	2	50.0% (1/2)
Minor	7	71.4% (5/7)
Severe	17	82.4% (14/17)
Psychological Aggression	26	
None	16	75.0% (12/16)
Minor	2	50.0% (1/2)
Severe	8	87.5% (7/8)
Injuries	26	
None	12	75.0% (9/12)
Minor	10	70.0% (7/10)
Severe	4	100% (4/4)
Batterer Type	25#	
Situationally Violent	12	75.0% (9/12)
Intimate Terrorist	13	76.9% (10/13)

* I was able to locate police reports for only 26 of the 30 participants.
# The number of persons categorized by batterer type is less because one of the participants, Henry, was violent against his brother rather than an intimate partner. Thus, he does not qualify as a type of intimate abuser.

interactions with the police and county court however, the persons participating in this study neglected to mention many of these operations. The power operations that did register, meanwhile, tended to vary by individual respondent. In their encounters with the police, for instance, Adam and Tom described having officers respond to the scene with guns drawn, while Betty noted the shame of being arrested in front of her mother's house, where the neighbors could see. At court, Carl recounted the challenge of abiding by his attorney's advice to remain silent while listening to what he believed was the state's misrepresentation of the facts of his case, while Walter remembered being admonished by a court peace officer after arriving late to a pretrial hearing.

Amongst this variability, common elements did appear in respondents' stories. When describing the police, for instance, participants gravitated toward discussing officers' investigation of their cases. The challenges of adapting to life behind bars also were present in participants' narratives. And when describing court, they tended to focus on the plea bargain agreements offered by the state.[2] These elements, then—police investigations, jail, and plea bargain agreements—represent the core events of these respondents' legal experiences. In the following three subsections, I review suspects' accounts of these events, focusing on how they describe them unfolding and how they evaluate their experiences.

Police. If clear evidence of intimate abuse is present (serious injuries, violation of an order of protection), the police investigation of domestic violence reports can be a straightforward and somewhat unremarkable process. As noted in the first chapter, however, where such evidence is absent, the police need to question the parties in the dispute as well as any witnesses to establish probable cause. In these instances, police investigations involve domestic violence suspects in a particular type of power relationship in which they are called upon by the state, as represented by law enforcement officers, to provide an account of the events that led to a report of abuse.

In their descriptions, suspects reported responding differently to the police's request for information. For the most part, suspects explained that they simply *complied* with the police by offering accounts of conflicts with their partners. John noted, "They asked, 'Did anybody get hurt?' I basically told them that I all I did was push her off because she was trying to get in my face."

In contrast, some respondents reported different types of actions that *defied* the police's request for information. Bob and Eric, for instance, admitted lying to the police. "They started asking questions and stuff," Eric remembered, "And I was lying. I was trying to lie and say I didn't do nothing to her." Dave, Frank, and Nic, meanwhile, said that they refused to answer the police's questions. Dave said, "Her version of the story was that I grabbed her by the neck. And my version was, well, I didn't say anything to the police." Kevin and Ed finally recounted attempts to contravene the police investigation altogether by fleeing the scene.

These responses of *compliance* and *defiance* resemble what Ewick and Silbey (1998) describe as standing "before," "with," and "up against" the law. Suspects who reported complying with the police investigation can be seen as yielding before the authority of the law, while those who defied the police can be seen as playing with and/or opposing the law. And like Ewick and Silbey's categories, these responses tended to correspond to different legal consciousnesses on the part of suspects. On the one hand, those suspects with little criminal legal experience complied with the police investigation. In addition, some explicitly mentioned trusting the police. Carl, who reported complying with the police, explained that he "was born willing to give them information." On the other hand, nearly all of those defying the police had past experience with the criminal justice system.

Although suspects' responses to the police reflect different experiences with the law, they are not mere extensions of their legal consciousness. From the start, these responses are also shaped by the relations and tactics of power that the police use to conduct investigations. Kevin, for example, fled the police following an argument with his girlfriend. Using Kevin's girl-friend's cell phone, the police called him to discuss the situation:

> I'm constantly telling the officer (over the phone) that I was innocent. I called the police. But he said he just had her side of the story because she's there pres-ent, and I'm just over the phone. So, he kind of lured me back to the house. He said that I wasn't actually going to get locked up. He said it was possible that I could, but that he going to weigh the circumstances. So, that's what got me back at the house. (Kevin)

In this scene, the officer used the same "persuasion" tactic that Leo (1996) found detectives using to have suspects waive their Miranda rights—"there are two sides to every story," and the police will have only the victim's side of the story unless the suspect cooperates (66). As explained in chapter 1, the police possess a repertoire of such tactics that they use in different situations in order to cool down heated suspects, make silent suspects talk, and direct the speech of talkative suspects in particular directions. The tactic used here proved suc-cessful. The officer was able to move Kevin from defiance to compliance and, accomplishing this, was able to interrogate and later detain him.

Suspects are not, of course, powerless in the face of such tactics. They possess their own capacity for legal agency, which they continue to exercise through-out their legal encounters. Ed, the other respondent who fled the scene before the police arrived, experienced many of the same tactics described by Kevin. "Well, they told me that I better come down to the police station so they can talk to me. They were telling me over the phone that they weren't going to lock me up or incarcerate me." Unlike Kevin, however, Ed did not present himself before the law. Interestingly, in explaining why he refused, he cited a past experience observing domestic violence law in action:

> *Why do you think that [you would have been apprehended if you weren't guilty]?* Because I've seen it happen, to a guy at the supermarket. I was sitting in the car, and I've seen it happen. They come out. They were arguing out the store. They got in the car. He was going to start the car up, and she just hits him from the passenger side. She hits him! Like really hitting him a couple of times. She

takes the keys and runs around the parking lot. She kicks him, you know. She busted his cell phone and everything. He calls the cops and they come and get him. (Ed)

This experience convinced Ed that he, as a man, would not be treated fairly in the police investigation of a domestic violence case. As such, rather than turning himself in, he chose to defy the law.

In addition, those who yielded to the authority of the police by complying with their investigations did not simply submit themselves to the law and admit guilt. Instead, in nearly every instance, they provided accounts of violence that diminished their responsibility. Domestic violence researchers in the past have found that abusive men modify their role in situations of abuse by denying their violence, minimizing its severity or harm, excusing its occurrence, justifying its occurrence, and/or describing it as self-defense (Anderson & Umberson 2001; Eisikovits & Buchbinder 2000; Dobash & Dobash 1998; Hearn 1998; Ptacek 1988). Such stories are integral to abusers' efforts to fashion and reinforce definitions of a nonviolent self (Dobash & Dobash 2000:162; Ptacek 1988:145).

In fulfilling the police's request for information, suspects offered similar types of stories that reduced their culpability for violence. Some suspects, like Victor, denied having committed abuse. "They said, 'We got a report [of abuse].' I told them, 'We was fighting, but there was no physical contact. There wasn't nothing.' . . . I told them they had it wrong." Others justified and/or minimized their actions. In his case, Mike admitted having grabbed his partner, but only so that he could get out the door to end their dispute. "I was talking to him, explaining to him everything that had happened, that I pulled her by the legs in order to get out the door, but other than that I didn't put my hands on her." Most commonly, suspects described their actions as acts of self-defense. As John told the police, "all I did was push her off because she was trying to get in my face." These examples reveal how abusers' tactics for preserving their sense of a nonviolent self morph during police investigations into legal arguments affirming their innocence.

It goes without saying that the majority of these performances failed to meet the respondents' primary goal, which was to avoid being arrested. Of the 30 persons participating in the study, only 2, Ed and Walter, were not arrested on the night or day on which the incident was reported to have happened. Ed, who was able to avoid a domestic violence arrest by fleeing, was later apprehended by the police on a drug arrest and charged with domestic battery. Walter, meanwhile, who claimed he could not remember the incident for which he was charged, received a court summons in the mail.

Nevertheless, even if the substantive outcomes of these encounters were one-sided, suspects' narratives demonstrate how the power of law is constructed interactively through the variable performances of both suspects and legal authorities. What's more, these descriptions reinforce Hull's (2003) insight that legal consciousness should be understood as a "layered phenomenon," consisting of "behavioral" and "cognitive" "layers" that operate somewhat separately of another. Batterers' compliance with or defiance of police investigations does not result solely from their legal experience or understandings of the law, but from the tactical force of authorities as well as their own abusive subjectivities.

Finally, it is important to note that the majority of respondents were arrested after they had given the police stories that lessened their responsibility for violence. In this sense, the arrest action not only leaves them in the custody of the state but disrupts their attempts to disown their violence. While I discuss the significance of this later in the chapter when discussing the meanings of arrest and prosecution, it demonstrates how the application of arrest occurs at a seemingly opportune time for challenging batterers' abusive subjectivities.

Jail. The suspect's arrival at jail introduces him to a new range of power operations. As was the case with respondents' descriptions of their police encounters, their narratives about jail touched upon just a few of the elements of power described in the first chapter.

One common element in the descriptions, however, is interaction with guards. Having, in their opinion, been unjustly arrested, many respondents reported explaining their cases to the guards at the jail. Matching what I observed in the county jail, these interactions are depicted as being somewhat playful:

> The guy who did that [booking] was really nice. He was lighthearted and joking around. I felt comfortable with him. You had to hold this thing up to get your picture taken. And I don't know how it came up but I was telling him that they were trying to charge me for lifting the covers up on the bed, and he joked and said, "Well, I'm going to let you take that cover down because . . ." And I said, "Yeah, you don't want me to charge you with domestic battery for taking this cover off me." And he said, "Yeah, I don't want that." We were just joking around. He was a nice guy. (Carl)

For the jail administrator, such interactions can serve to calm heated or disgruntled suspects. At the same time, they can also be seen to generate new meanings through which arrestees understand their experiences. For instance, Carl's playing with the guard about the nature of his case helped reinforce his belief that the charges were dubious and the object of ridicule.

Beyond these interpersonal interactions with guards, respondents' descriptions of jail more commonly gravitated toward elements of power not readily observable to outsiders. This is the harshness of the spatial and material environment of the holding cell and jail routine in general. When initially asked to describe what their experiences in jail were like, participants commonly provided a brief, direct description of the holding cell:

> Once they put you in the cell and you hear that door lock, you know, you're locked up. That's a feeling you don't want to feel anymore, because you don't have no choice to leave or go. You're in there with six, seven other guys and one toilet, you know, no privacy. It's terrible. (Brett)

Others, usually those who were unable to bond out and had to spend more time in jail, also emphasized the quality and amount of food rations:

> They'll starve a man in there. I was always hungry after I ate in there. For breakfast, they're giving you an egg, which can't be a whole egg, some oatmeal, and that's it. For lunch, they'll give you a slice of meat and cheese, some slices of bread. (Adam)

Bound together with these descriptions of the harshness of the spatial and material environment of the jail are the effects of time:

> I couldn't believe they were working so slow. They were talking back and forth to the inmates the way they were, and it just was a bad time. (Mike)

> I'd rather go to prison than sit inside like that. It's probably harder, but the thing that makes the time go so slow is never going nowhere. You're sitting in the same pod. Even if you do nine months, you don't never come outside of that pod at all. You don't never see nothing. There's no movement. If you at prison, you'll be going to work or going to class, go and do this, days go faster there. It's the same way as a juvenile (offender), you always going to school, going to work. You was always doing something. (Eric)

Mike spent just one night in jail before bonding out, and it is unclear whether he understood that domestic violence arrestees are required to spend the night in jail. Nevertheless, the slow pace of booking procedures took its toll on him. Eric, meanwhile, who did not bond out, would have preferred incarceration in a prison to the county jail. With no activities to engage in, and no opportunities to leave his space in the jail, time slowed for him, and the weight of isolation and the deprivations of space and materiality increased.[3]

Suspects failing to make bond engaged in different performances to cope with their time in jail. Frank grew a beard and changed his appearance in order to avoid conflict. "The younger guys don't mess with the older guys . . . if I'd shaved that beard, I'da been in the mix with them guys every day." Bob became a trusty, a work position that allows prisoners with good behavior to receive certain privileges in return for basic custodial work. Isaac, meanwhile, turned inward in order to cope, writing "poems, raps, and stuff like that" to stop himself from having to "think too much."

These are individual strategies for coping with jail. However, the activity mentioned by the most respondents, whether they bonded out or not, is decidedly collective. This is law talk with other detainees in the holding cell. The respondents in this study frequently mentioned discussing their cases with other suspects who either had, had had, or had known someone who had domestic violence cases. Beyond helping pass the time, these conversations are important because they help suspects orient themselves to the criminal proceedings developing against them. This occurs in multiple ways.

First, suspects discuss how their cases look in terms of charges and plea offers. Aaron, for example, described "worrying about the case" in jail. The other inmates, however, after hearing his story, told him, "This ain't nothing but a misdemeanor, a class A misdemeanor." It is of course impossible for a suspect to know the quality of the legal advice he is receiving in these conversations. Consequently, additional anxieties can result. Later on, Aaron noted, "I'm worrying because these jailhouse lawyers don't know nothing. I want to talk to a real attorney and see what's going on." Nevertheless, the interactions allow suspects to begin constructing a matrix against which they can judge the plea bargain deals that the state will later offer them.

In addition to providing a collection of personal experiences from which to understand their cases, law talk in the holding cell deepens suspects' sense that the next stage of the legal game is a team event. And as such, the quality of defense attorney matters. In John's case, he noted that the other guys in jail "usually pleaded out" and that "they all had the same public defender." Determined to fight his case, John decided in jail, "I was just going to go and get whichever one (private attorney) I could afford to get."

Most importantly, these collective conversations identify the key player in the next round of the legal game: the suspect's abused partner.

> I have heard a lot of past experiences that the state's attorney doesn't like to take domestic cases to court, just because there is a lot of instances where the women, they don't want testify against the man, because they want the man out there. *Where would you hear things like that?* You sit down with somebody in the jail, with a similar case, they may or may not have been arrested for the same thing in the past, but they are just talking about it. (Frank)

> In the domestics, there a lot of guys in over there on a domestic. And their fiancées been going up to the state's attorney, man, tell them that she ain't coming to court, she ain't testifying, and she ain't coming to no civil court, nothing. And she telling them that it was a mistake, they was mad and angry at each other. There was a lot of guys' cases there the same as mine. (Isaac)

By sitting down with other suspects who know about domestics, Frank learned that the willingness of the partner to testify affects the state's desire to take a case to court. Isaac, meanwhile, provided a fuller description of the type of performance that an abuse victim can deliver on behalf of her partner in a criminal case, which included confronting the state's attorney and explaining that the abuse she endured was simply a mistake.

In these ways, the holding cell can be seen to function as a depository of local legal culture, in which popular beliefs about the local legal environment circulate and strategies for opposing the state take seed. Thus, while the arrangement of space within the holding cell serves on the one hand as an operation of power that weighs upon suspects' being, it serves on the other as a space that gives birth to resistance. It is, of course, for this reason that the founders of modern incarceration made the partitioning of subjects the first tenet of discipline (Foucault 1977). However, in Centralia County, where the amount of incarceration space is unable to keep pace with the rates of detention, as occurs throughout most of the country, this principle has been either forgotten or ignored. As a result, a unique space is created in the local community where resistance to domestic violence law takes base.

Court. The plea bargain represents a core feature of the modern criminal legal system that enables courts to process heavy caseloads (Alschuler 1976, 1975, 1968). In domestic violence cases, plea bargains can take on added importance. As Mirchandani (2005) explains in her observation of a specialized domestic violence court in Salt Lake City, by routinizing the court's processing of domestic violence cases, plea bargains allow judges the time to confront and challenge offenders' patriarchal beliefs in the court setting (409). As such, the plea bargain serves as a lynchpin in the domestic violence court's union of social control and social change functions. However, as chapter 2 demonstrated, plea bargains have a different significance in Centralia County. Here, the state relies on them not only to process domestic violence cases efficiently, but to secure convictions in the first place.

This framework for prosecuting domestic violence cases involves suspects in a power relation quite distinct from that of police investigations. While suspects are pressed during the police investigation to answer allegations of violence, they are here pressed to give up their right to answer the state's charges that they committed abuse. In this context of power, suspects again respond in one of two ways. They either *comply* with the court's push to have them accept plea bargains, or they *defy* the court by taking their cases to trial.

As in police investigations, defendants' reactions to plea bargains are influenced by both their legal consciousness and the tactical power of the state. With plea bargains, however, the degree to which legal consciousness is bound together with socioeconomic status becomes more pronounced. That is, for suspects who could not afford to bond out of jail, appraisals of plea bargain agreements were as straightforward as Matt, the assistant state's attorney, described before, that "if the defendant is sitting in jail, and he can't bond out, and you offer him a plea to a misdemeanor domestic battery and he gets out of jail tomorrow, he's going to take it." Of the 13 respondents participating in this study who could not bond out of jail, only Ann did not sign a plea deal.

Other study participants, meanwhile, based their responses to plea offers by considering the costs of conviction—whether the potential costs of trying their cases or the certain costs of a domestic violence conviction spelled out in the plea agreement. Ralph, for instance, who had a few friends who ended up in jail on "domestics," said, "I don't want to end up in jail like them, so I'm just going to plea." Quinn, on the other hand, a former police officer arrested for a violation of an order of protection against his wife,[4] reflected on how a domestic violence conviction would affect his life. "Do you realize how bad this [a domestic violence conviction] makes you look?" he asked. "You can never own a firearm. Employers won't hire you. And when the cops pull you over, that V of OP is going to pop up.[5] And that's going to affect how they handle you. I know, we used to do that all the time." With his past experience as a law enforcement officer on his mind, Quinn believed that he had to try his case in order to preserve the benefits that persons without criminal records enjoy in society.

In addition to weighing the costs of conviction, defendants also arrived at decisions on plea bargains by assessing the strength of their cases. In these instances, suspects most often appraised their cases based on the stance of their victimized partners. Suspects who believed that their victims would not cooperate with the state evaluated their cases strongly and rejected plea bargains. In his case, Mike was facing domestic violence charges that were four years old. Describing his thinking on his case, he asserted:

> Oh, I knew it was going to be dismissed, man. Some of that shit in there is three and four years old, you know what I mean? Mine is an old case, OK.

> I knew that Ayanna (ex-girlfriend) ain't living here. How you going to sub-poena her? Her auntie stays in Texas, she's a low-life nobody. These are the people that were there that night. I knew they weren't going to get in touch with them.

Knowing that the state is unlikely to subpoena the main witnesses against him, Mike was confident about his case ("I knew it was going to be dismissed"). As a result, he decided to set it for trial, and, indeed, it was dismissed.

While Mike acted on the basis of given circumstances (he said his ex-girlfriend had moved away), other suspects believed that the prospects of their cases could be swung in their favor if they could have their victims support them. Respondents' ability to control their victimized partners was affected, however, by the web of power relations in which they found them-selves during prosecution proceedings. As noted in chapter 2, the Centralia County State's Attorney's Office regularly has the court issue no-contact or-ders that forbid suspects from contacting their victims. According to partic-ipants' own words, they seldom abided by these court orders. Nevertheless, the orders transformed their intimate relationships, as they worried about getting caught violating them. As a result, many men expressed feeling a loss of power relative to their partners. Mike, for instance, described being concerned that a member of his partner's family might call the police on him to get "crime stopper reward money." Tom, similarly, felt uneasy with his partner when violating the no-contact order:

> We go to sleep, I'm not like going to sleep all the way, just in case she want to get on the phone and dial 911, "he's over here now." I didn't know what she might do. Go to the bathroom and she run to the front room and dial 911 and tell them I'm here or something. She basically got me by the balls right now, and she know it, because she playing it for all it's worth. (Tom)

In these contexts of diminished power, abusers transformed rather than severed their forms of influence over their partners. Their narratives evi-denced different strategies for effecting this end. One way they did this was by trying to be nice. Carl explained that he received this counsel from his attorney, an officer of the court whose formal responsibility it is to uphold the authority of the court. "He said," Carl remembered, "'You're not sup-posed to have contact with her, but remain on good terms with her and, hopefully, I can get her to sign an affidavit saying that she doesn't want any further legal action. It was just all a misunderstanding.'"

Tom whose partner had him "by the balls," also reported presenting a gentler version of his self to maintain influence over her:

> We go to the store and she fussing at me. We just, she was fussing at me, in front of everybody, and all I do is sit there and smile. I don't know what her state of mind is, so I'm just trying to sit down and be nice as possible. She could have came and threw hot grits at me, and I would have just laughed and like, "Ha, ha, ha, you got me." (Tom)

A second tactic suspects used was attempting to generate and/or play upon feelings of regret from their partners about their arrests. Nic, for example, described violating the no-contact order with his wife:

> The last thing I wanted was for the cops to show up while I was at her apartment or she was at mine. I would remind her. I'm like, "Look, remember, you know you don't want to go and deal with these people. You don't want to have an interview with you know and have to deal with that. Part of that is that if the cops come here and I'm anywhere near you, you're not going to jail, I'm going to jail." You know, and she would calm down.

The strategy Nic described for violating the no-contact order clearly builds upon traditional gender roles and expectations. Assuming the role of patriarch, Nic felt it necessary to "remind" his spouse of her supposed uneasiness about legal authorities ("you don't want to go and deal with these people"). He then brought up the fact that he could get arrested for seeing her, which cast him as a potential victim ("you're not going to jail, I'm going to jail"). Implicit here is the expectation that she, rather than he, would have to sacrifice (both her voice and security) for the unity of the family. In doing so, he reported being able to control her during arguments ("she would calm down").

A third way in which the men tried to exercise influence over their partners was through family members. For instance, Nic had his father-in-law, a local cop, write a letter to the state's attorney to explain that his case is a mistake. "He's like, 'Yeah, I understand how arguments can go with Mary, especially when she's all riled up and ready to go.'" This example demonstrates the way in which masculinity can serve as a unifying framework structuring men's assessments of violence and victims. Mary's father, though not especially close with his son-in-law, was still willing to assist Nic because he knew his daughter's combative nature.

More commonly, however, respondents related having sisters and mothers intervene on their behalf with their partners:

> Well, my girlfriend right now, we talk but it's through my mother. They basically put a no-contact on me, so I usually contact my mother to see if she can

basically get a hold of her, because I know guys who have their girlfriends say, maybe it was something then, right there on the day it was happening, that made her call the police. Maybe she was scared or something, but it wasn't really that serious. So I've tried to get her to write letters or to get in touch with the state's attorney to tell him what happened, that it really wasn't as serious as she made it up to be. (John)

So and what sort of communication did you have with your girlfriend [when in jail]? Through my sister, because she [his partner] was wanting me to call, but I didn't be wanting to call because they might be recording it or something, you know, and she just be crying. (Isaac)

I called my mom because they had a phone in there [jail]. So, I called her collect and I tell what happened. She was like, "Well, is she at home now?" And I'm like, "Yeah, she should be." So, my mom tried to call her and everything, and she said, she told my mom that she didn't tell none of them to lock me up and she didn't tell them that I hit her. She told them that I pushed her, but she said I didn't hit her. And my mom, she told her, "Now, you know how those cops are down there. They would love to lock a black man up, especially he don't got no record." (Tom)

These interactions represent a transformation of the gender politics at play in mandatory arrest and no-drop prosecution. While the state is using the police and courts to intervene in abusive intimate relationships to reinscribe gender relations, these sisters and mothers, who embody localized notions of femininity in person, intervene to reconstruct these relationships. John hopes that his mother will be able to have his partner realize that she "made [the violence] up" and contact the state's attorney. Tom's mother adds race to the equation. Against the efforts of the state to make Tom's girlfriend an independent subject by placing a no-contact order against her abusive boyfriend, Tom's mother looks to have her recognize and prioritize not her interests and safety, but those of an underprivileged community—African Americans—and a certain segment of it—black men—who have historically been mistreated in localities like Centralia County.

Suspects' efforts to influence their victimized partners met with varying levels of success. Both Tom and Victor reported having their partners show up at court on their behalf, helping them to defy the state and eventually beat their cases. Other efforts to control partners and ex-partners failed, due to women's own efforts to terminate their relationships. With his attorney out of town on vacation, Carl said he was delegated the task of getting in touch with his ex-girlfriend to make sure that she had contacted the state's attorney's office and notified them of her unwillingness to testify. When meeting her, however, he got into another fight:

> Obviously, when someone throws you in jail, you don't want to be around them anymore. So, she had to schedule a meeting with the victims coordinator. My attorney told me to call her and ask her if she could go and talk to the victims coordinator. He was going to go on vacation, so it kind of fell on me. I said I would call her. So, we got into an argument, and she went and did everything against what she said she was going to do. She was just out to get me. (Carl)

Unable to avoid getting into another argument with his ex-girlfriend, Carl lost what he thought would be her support in his case. As a result, he moved further from trying his case and closer to accepting a plea bargain. And in the process, new meanings were constructed around the experience. His ex-girlfriend's refusal to do what he said and go to the state's attorney's office, a sign of her desire to be independent from him, was interpreted by Carl as a sign that "she was just out to get me."

Apart from the support of their victims, domestic violence suspects also molded their responses to plea bargains in relation to another base of power in the court setting: their defense attorneys. As explained in chapter 2, defense attorneys possess their own propensities for plea bargaining cases. While a minority of defense attorneys are "gamblers" (Skolnick 1974:95) or "mavericks" (Mather 1979:124) who maintain an adversarial stance with the prosecutor's office, most are "cooperative" attorneys (Skolnick 1974:97), willing to cooperate with the state's attorney's office by moving their defendants to plea bargain.

For some respondents, consultations with defense attorneys moved them from defying the court to complying with it. Carl, who thought the state's case against him was ridiculous, noted that he nevertheless pled his case out. Asked why he would admit guilt to charges he thought were spurious, he explained:

> It was happening during the changeover of state's attorney—Nolan, who on his way out—and the new girl was coming in. She was a female and she was going to crack down on domestic violence. My attorney just thought that maybe it was best for me to do this and get it over with. (Carl)

Carl's attorney's depiction of the state's attorney's office is a tactic calculated to establish "client control" (Blumberg 1967). To invoke Sarat and Felstiner's (1995) study of attorney–client relations in divorce cases once again, attorneys rely on a repertoire of such tactics (defining "the legally possible," conjuring up a "parade of horribles," casting themselves as the "dean" of the bar) in order to move clients toward settling their cases (57, 26–52). In the example above, Carl's attorney was able to move him to a plea deal by changing his perception of the fairness of the court process. Carl did not know that the outgoing state's attorney was an enthusiastic supporter of the presumptive prosecution policy. In this vacuum of knowledge about the local legal community, his attorney was able to sketch out a set of "circumstances," an outgoing male state's attorney and an incoming female state's attorney, that could be seen to increase the risk involved with trying the case.

Unlike Carl, other respondents were less susceptible to being influenced by client control tactics because they simply distrusted their defense attorneys. Some, based on past experience, entered the court process skeptical of their attorneys' allegiance to them. Betty, for instance, noted that in her previous interactions with lawyers, "They was on their (the state's) side and they wasn't trying to help me." Others came to distrust their attorneys over the course of their interactions with them, either because the lawyers pushed plea bargains upon them or because they appeared judgmental of their behavior. Steve, who reported grabbing his girlfriend after she spat on him, noted that his public defender was "telling me that she doesn't think I should take it to trial because they going to feel like I should've walked away, even after what she did to me."

For these suspects then, defense attorneys represent another source of uncertainty in the court process. Not knowing whether their attorneys are on their side, many respondents act to mitigate the uncertainty. One way they try to do this is by hiring private representation. As noted above, John intended to hire a private attorney to avoid being represented by a public defender, who he believed would try to force him to plead. With most of the respondents in this study unable to afford a private attorney, however, they resorted to their own control tactics to direct the actions of attorneys whom they did not trust.

Kevin, for example, who was concerned that his public defender would not treat his case with the same care that a private attorney would, attempted to assert control during his first meeting with his lawyer:

> I said, "Listen here. You are an attorney. You're being paid by me, or by the state, or whatever. You are being paid for your services. So, represent me as if I was paying you a hundred thousand dollars, because I am an individual, this is the case, and use your expertise." That's what I'm basically telling him. *What did he say to that?* He smiled at me. He smiled and he said, "Well, hey, you got me." I was like, "Yeah, I know I got because you getting paid. You the lawyer. So, do your job. Defend me to my rights, to the utmost respect of my rights." (Kevin)

Others reported directing the legal performance once negotiations and interactions with the state were already under way. Mike, who did not believe the case against him had merit, directed his attorney to end the case rather than simply continuing it to the next pretrial term. "I told the public defender this needs to be dismissed." Walter was frustrated by the public defender's efforts to seek a plea bargain, even though he had stated he wanted to try his case.

> On one occasion, she actually made it seem like it [the plea offer] was some good news or something. "Good news for who? You or me? It would be good news for you, because you ain't got to deal with this case no more." You know what I'm saying? And I told her, "No. I'm not taking that. Take it to trial. And I mean that." (Walter)

In this example, Walter passed through the client-control techniques of his attorney ("she actually made it seem like it was some good news") to assert control over his legal case.

Suspects' efforts at controlling their attorneys, like those aimed at their victims, met with different results. Tom, interestingly, claimed that he was able to convince the public defender to set his case for trial only upon proving to him that his partner would support him. "He was telling me, 'You don't want to go to trial if she with the attorneys,' . . . I told him, 'No, she out there [in the hallway] with me now. She said she going to tell them [the state] that she told the police that I didn't hit her. . . . So he went out there and he talked to her and he was like, 'OK.'"

Steve, in contrast, who wanted to try his case despite the objections of his defense attorney, recounted arriving late for a pretrial hearing in which the attorney was to announce the case ready for trial. From this error, the lawyer shifted her position on the case and began pushing a plea bargain on him to quash the arrest warrant the judge had just issued for his failure to appear in court.

> She [the public defender] just come over and whisper to me, she tell me, "You already got a warrant out for five thousand dollars," and she says, "you know in the past, he don't take them back." So, I took that plea because I was late for court and she had me thinking that he was going to lock me up. So, that's what happened to me. I made my decision to take that plea because I did not have five hundred dollars there. (Steve)

In a position where he believed he had to plead to avoid arrest, Steve switched from defying to complying with the court's wishes to have him sign a plea bargain.

The substantive outcomes of respondents' court encounters varied more than those of their police encounters. Once again, the state was able to structure outcomes in its favor. Twenty-three of the respondents participating in this study pled guilty to domestic violence charges that required them to undergo counseling. Nonetheless, each of those suspects who refused to comply with the court's plea bargain arrangements experienced a favorable case outcome, either having their cases dismissed (Ann, Mike, Tom, Walter) or winning verdicts in their favor at jury trials (Oscar, Victor, Brett, Doug).

Moving their cases to trial, these defendants profited from a variety of factors weighing in their favor. For one, they benefited from the discordant locale of Centralia County, whose conservative community is unreceptive to domestic violence cases, and their attorneys' ability to speak to this community. By chance, I was able to attend Brett's trial. In his case, Brett's ex-girlfriend had called the police to report that he, having let himself into her apartment and jealous that she had gone out for the night, choked her when she arrived home. In addition, he remained on top of her during the attack until she urinated on herself. During the trial, however, the defense's rendering of the story was that Brett was simply a concerned parent, with a special-needs child, who was worried that his children's mother would not be home with the kids on Mother's Day, which was the following day. During closing arguments, the public defender noted to the jury:

> We have two stories. We have Ms. Jackson [Brett's ex-girlfriend] at the American Legion for three hours, claiming she had one drink. I would have believed her if she had said she had a drink, a soda, and a water. But three hours is a long time for one drink. Plus, she knows the closing hours for the bar. . . . (Marge)

Depicting the victim in the case as an immoral drunk who is more concerned about closing hours at bars than family dinners on Mother's Day, Brett's attorney helped get him a finding of not guilty.

In the cases of Doug and Oscar, the men found that the photos they took of themselves following their arrests proved critical to their victories at trial:

> The guy [police officer] that talked to her, he was a man hater or something. But in court, on the stand, every time anybody asked him what about me, he wouldn't recall. The cuts, abrasions, blood on me, he didn't recall. He exaggerated anything that had to do with the child or this girl. Until the fact that the pictures came out, he would say I don't recall, I don't recall, and my lawyer just threw like 17 pictures down, and that was that. You know, what could he say? He was busted. (Doug)

Through this material evidence, and its positive reception among the members of the jury, Doug was able to overcome the deceit of the "man hater" cop.

Finally, both Victor and Tom were able to get the support of their partners. Victor took his case to trial against the advice of his attorney. At court on the day of the trial, he found out that his partner had agreed to testify for the state, as had the girl's mother, sister, and sister's son, all of whom, Victor explained, "were just really trying to make her think I was a bad person." Upon the stand, however, Victor explained that his girlfriend was ultimately unable to "get up there and testify and say that I hit her and this and that."

Having in place diverse mechanisms and social relationships that help their legal performances, these respondents realized favorable substantive outcomes. Nevertheless, the meanings that they take away from these results very much concern the self. Asked why he thought he was able to win his case, Doug quickly responded, "The fact that I wasn't guilty." Tom, for his part, was nervous before the pretrial hearing that resulted in the dismissal of his case. He had doubts about the case, "I was basically getting ready to be slammed, you know, getting locked up. I was like, 'Man, they going to lock me up.'" In this instance, it fell to his girlfriend, who had first called the police five months earlier to report his violence against her, to reinforce his images of a nonviolent self.

> My girl saying, "Why you keep thinking negative? Quit thinking negative about it. You didn't do nothing. Quit thinking negative." I'm like, "Yeah, you're right." (Tom)

The Meanings of Mandatory Arrest and No-Drop Prosecution

In addition to giving the state custodial authority over intimate abusers, mandatory arrests and no-drop prosecution are intended to teach them that abuse is wrong. In discussing their experiences with the criminal justice system, a few respondents revealed connections between their criminal punishments and increased responsibility for violence. Mike, for example, explained that he realized "after all the shit I've been through" that, even though he just pulled his partner by her legs, "it's just something I shouldn't have did." In his quote, "all the shit" refers specifically to the long court process that he experienced before seeing the charges against him dismissed.

For most of the suspects participating in this study, however, even those who recognized the wrongness of their actions, the lesson of punishment was different. Rather than triggering inward reflections by abusers on the wrongness of their behavior, arrests and prosecutions triggered outward reflections on the wrongness of legal authorities' actions. Overwhelmingly, the respondents in this study believed that they had been mistreated by the police, in jail, and at court.

In the case of the police, for instance, nearly all described some specific aspects of their interactions with the police as unjust. Usually, they claimed that the police did a poor job investigating their cases. To provide a few examples:

> I still think the courthouse, as a matter of fact, the policemen too, they should, when they come on a domestic case, a domestic feud, period, to someone's home, they should look in that more deeper. (Henry)

> We were all sleeping, you know. I said you have my permission to do whatever, but, I mean, it was no asking. They pretty much asked what did happen, but at the same time they were cuffing me. I was already guilty in their eyes. (Ann)

> They don't investigate them like they should. The officers don't. So the state's attorney gets what the officers give him. Like the officer never goes out and does a reinvestigation, you know, to see if her story is going to match up. . . . So, they feel like what they give them at that time is good enough, and they give it to the state's attorney, and the state's attorney goes off of that. You know, it's all lies, it doesn't matter. (Ed)

Interestingly, these respondents are not saying that the police have no right getting involved in their personal affairs. Indeed, with the criminal histories they have, they are accustomed to law as an integrated part of their daily lives. Instead, they would have preferred more, rather than less, police action on their cases. What's more, Ed's comments about the poor quality of evidence that the police provide the state's attorney's office echo what Nancy, the state's attorney's victims advocate, noted in her comments on the quality of the evidence provided to her office by the police departments in the county.

Jail, as has already been touched on, was simply seen by respondents as an inhumane way to treat people. Further, some felt such treatment evidenced that the state had already judged them guilty. As Adam noted, "Innocent until proven guilty? How can they treat someone like that if they're not guilty?"

In terms of the court, most respondents cited elements of its handling of cases that struck them as unjust. For one, the interviewees complained that the court system, and by extension the legal system, is impersonal and insensitive to people's individual situations. In doing so, they identified elements of criminal "process" that Malcolm Feeley (1979) contends represent the true "punishment" for defendants. Walter, for instance, bemoans that in court, "there's no consideration for the other person" and the money and time from work they lose by attending court dates. In addition, many respondents, like socio-legal scholars portraying the "practice of law as a confidence game" (Blumberg 1967), described the court as a close-knit group of professionals who were uninterested in the lives of individual defendants. Frank notes, "I have to come to the conclusion that they all sit around in a bar and have nachos and chips and trade each other lives. 'I give you this guy for that guy, and you let him off, now I will give you this guy.'" Comments such as these were common among respondents and reflected a sense that the system was fixed against them.

In addition to identifying *how* they believed legal authorities mistreated them, respondents also offered rationales for *why* they were treated this way. For instance, male respondents typically believed they were victims of gender bias at the hands of either individual officers or laws and policies designed to protect women. This is not completely unexpected. As Eisikovits and Buchbinder (2000) and Anderson and Umberson (2001) note in their studies of abusive men, abusers who are arrested view themselves as victims of either police officers or domestic violence laws that are biased against men. Participants in this study presented similar views. With regard to the former, men often noted that officers seemed to have "talked to the lady more and tried to get more information from her" (John). With regard to the latter, the participants described the law as "all just women's agenda" (Peter) and "strictly for a woman" (Walter).

While claims of gender bias by men arrested for domestic violence have been noted in past research, what proved surprising in talking to this group of men was that some actually accepted the premise that domestic violence laws favor women:

> Who doesn't protect a woman? You know what I mean? And Mary, she's a very cute girl. At the same time, she's smaller than me. I'm 5' 7", 155; she's 5' 3", 125. She's female; I'm male. So, yeah. So, of course the cops inside are pushing and pushing her, "Tell us." (Nic)

> I believe he handled the situation very fairly. It wasn't . . . it could have been probably handled different, like you know, trying to get both sides of the story. But I guess, that's how life is. I mean, I feel that they look at a woman as very weak, because that call owns you and you ain't got to do nothing. And they assume, they take it from there. (Aaron)

> I think it sucks. I don't think it's no good. I know, I understand. I like to give a female the benefit of the doubt too. I don't agree with jumping on females. I'm totally against that. And I raised my kids—I have a 15-year-old son who's

going to be 16, and I got a 14-year-old, who just turned 14—and I teach them, if they touch anyone—I got two girls—if they touch their sisters, I'm on their ass. I don't care if the girls are right or wrong. You know, I don't like that. But I feel like the law is wrong when they always take the female's side no matter what. (Steve)

These are mixed messages, to be sure. These men feel victimized by the law, but at the same time they believe that society needs to protect women, since they are weaker than men. Nic could understand why the police would want to protect his wife, who, beyond being petite, is also pretty. Aaron too could not fault the police for not listening to both sides of the story, since it is natural to see women as weak. Steve, for his part, feels so strongly against being violent against women that he is violent against his sons when they mistreat their sisters. So, he also could understand the desire to protect women. Of course, that the police "always take the female's side no matter what" was wrong, especially if he was the one apprehended.[6] At the very least, these responses demonstrate the varied meanings that the practice of domestic violence law can take for individual abusers.

Despite the primacy of gender as a framework for claiming injustice, respondents also interpreted their experiences through other, nonprivileged group identities. A wealth of socio-legal research has demonstrated that race plays a key role in how citizens perceive the criminal justice system, with African Americans consistently expressing greater distrust of legal authorities than do whites (Weitzer 2000; Wortley et al. 1997; Hagan & Albonetti 1982). The African Americans participating in this study commonly perceived race as a factor in the police's handling of their cases. These interpretations were touched upon earlier, when Tom's mother explained that his arrest stemmed from the fact that police in the rural county of Centralia liked locking up black men.

Other minority members offered similar views in their stories:

They arrested me. And, I don't know, one of the officers, he was just really smug towards me. He just [had] an air of prejudice about himself. It was like they totally disregarded anything I had said. I mean, it was just the way he was looking at me and just laughing at me the whole time. (Chris)

This black officer was telling me, "Hey, I understand, just go ahead and get your clothes and all and leave." But this white officer came, he said, "No." He said, "Put those handcuffs back on him," just like that. . . . I knew the white officer who told him to put that handcuffs back on me. The only reason I knew him . . . I don't know him, I just knew of him because I'd seen his picture on the TV, and I heard a lot of conflict about what he help did. (Henry)

Chris noted the presence of the officer as prejudicial, while Henry described a specific interaction—favorable treatment by a black officer and unfavorable treatment by a notorious white officer—as evidence that they had been unfairly treated due to their race. In Henry's case, his personal encounter with the local police was woven together with that of his community. The white officer's picture had been on TV, and he was known in the African American community to treat people unfairly. For African American men with prior contact with the police in Centralia County or with ties to community members, family members, and friends with such contact, their arrest for domestic battery represented not a just punishment for being abusive against their partner, but the exercise of unjust power against them by racist police officers.

Other respondents interpreted the criminal justice system's handling of their cases in terms of money. Quinn, the former cop, believed that domestic violence cases simply serve to enrich the state and lawyers. "It's all status and money," he notes, "I mean, there are guys out there who deserve to be arrested. But there's a lot of guys being arrested who don't deserve to be, couples who are trying to work things out. But it's about money. They want their money."

Others echoed these sentiments. Ann and Peter, for example, focused on the costs associated with completing their sentences.

> You're thrown into these classes, you know, a lot of people can't afford them, and they're expensive. . . . I don't think that they [the state] take it seriously because to them it's all a moneymaker. You know, do this class, do that, you know, everything is about money. (Ann)

> And the courts, they just kick you while you're down. Make you pay fines, for evaluation, for classes, but you gotta work to be able to pay them. This deal, my attorney says if I don't take this deal and I lose the trial, it'll be even worse. So, I have to take this. They just take your money. (Peter)

Such comments express a certain class consciousness on the part of suspects, similar to that of people who stand "up against" the law (Ewick & Silbey 1998) and interpret their legal experiences in terms of resources. These respondents, for whom hiring a defense attorney, appearing in court, and abiding by their sentences represented significant financial costs, believed the criminal justice system punished them not to stop their abusive behavior, but to get their money.

Finally, some respondents believed that their past criminal records prejudiced the authorities' handling of their cases. Ann believed her involvement in past domestic violence cases automatically identified her to the police as the aggressor in her current case. She explained, "I had a couple of priors to that with domestics, but once you're pegged in Plainsville, you're pretty well screwed." Dave, for his part, interpreted the state's decision to charge him after his latest domestic violence arrest as motivated by his criminal record: "My record is what hurts me more than the crime that I actually did." Again, these respondents, like the others citing unjust treatment by the police, jail, and courts, believed that they were punished not for what they did, but for who they are.

Respondents' belief that their punishment was unfair arose not simply from their positions in different social hierarchies, but from the practices of power performed by the police and courts as well. That is, in describing aspects of their experiences with domestic violence law that struck them as unjust, respondents frequently echoed the statements that police officers, jail guards, and defense attorneys use to render them compliant with policing and court-setting power. For instance, many respondents reported police officers or jail guards conveying to them the message that current laws are either excessively harsh or simply require them to make an arrest on domestic violence calls:

> So, the police said that when I lifted up the covers on the bed, that was domestic battery. And I asked, "How are you getting that?" They said that anytime you do anything around a person that they don't like, that they can charge you with domestic battery. (Carl)

> The police came up, and for some reason they kept trying to feed me this line that someone has to go to jail on a domestic battery call. You know what I mean? That's what they kept telling me. I'm like, "Well, you know, I moved her by her legs." (Mike)

Each of these ideas is, of course, false. But each is calculated to effect a certain reaction from the suspect. Carl's case is an example of "verbal judo," with the police looking to either calm Carl down or keep him calm by deflecting his criticisms of their actions ("How are you getting that?"). Interestingly, the criticism was redirected to the reporting party ("a person," "they") and an unspecified legal culture that allows minor acts ("anything around a person that they don't like") to be charged as domestic battery. The police's role in the process remains obscure. Mike's case, meanwhile, is an example of aggressive "theme building," with the police looking to compel him to talk by repeatedly explaining that someone has to be arrested on a domestic call. Interestingly, the way in which both comments effect compliance is by sending the message to suspects that nothing they did is necessarily wrong, but that departmental policy or state law is simply strict.

In the process, the suspects come to see themselves as victims of the law.

Other respondents also echoed statements from their defense attorneys that the local legal culture was simply unfair. Following his victory by jury trial, Brett was newly charged for violating the no-contact order that had been issued against him in his case. Left to explain the situation to her client, while moving him to a plea agreement on the new charges, Brett's public defender tells him that he was facing new charges because "the judge, the bailiff, a lot of the people watching felt I should have lost" the trial.

Steve also came to see the injustice of the local legal culture through the comments of his attorney:

> She said that they drop the charges, and most of the time they take the female side . . . she got to the point with, "Well, it's just how it goes. Well, how long you lived in Centralia County?" (Steve)

These comments are directed at effecting "client control," trust with clients that can be used to influence their decision making. Such comments are central to lawyering practice, and, in Brett's case at least, they proved influential in having the suspect accept a plea bargain. Nevertheless, however effective they are in realizing "client control," these comments also come to have a separate meaning for domestic battery suspects. The men come to understand that the deck is stacked against them, and that there is no beating the system. In the process, their sense of injustice and victimization is deepened.

Discussion

Diverse operations of power define domestic abusers' experience of mandatory arrest and no-drop prosecution. In the face of police requests to speak of their violence, the material deprivations of jail, and court pressure to give up their right to address allegations, domestic violence suspects respond through legal performances that fluctuate between compliance and defiance and are interactively shaped by their legal consciousness, legal authorities' tactics of power, and their own abusive behavior. These performances are central to both the substantive outcomes intimate abusers experience and the interpretive meanings these experiences hold. As the case outcomes make clear, the police and courts are able to structure these interactions in their favor, leaving abusers under their administrative authority. Notably, domestic violence arrests and plea bargain convictions disrupt many abusers' attempts to explain away their violence during police investigations and to reestablish control over their victimized partners during plea negotiations. However, while these legal actions give the state a hold over batterers, they do not deliver strong messages about their abusive behavior. Contact with mandatory arrest and no-drop prosecution in Centralia County leaves this group of respondents with a profound sense of injustice, expressed not only in terms of gender, race, and class, but also in the very terms of power that legal authorities use to gain control over them.

Of Punishment and Its Consequences. Sally Engle Merry (2002) describes mandatory arrest and no-drop prosecution as central elements in a new regime of domestic violence governance that seeks to transform male and female subjectivities. Together with batterer interventions groups intended to reform abusers and orders of protection meant to protect women and foster independence, mandatory arrest and no-drop prosecution are meant to function as punishments that will disrupt the intimate abuser's violence against his partner and send both him and society the message that his behavior is wrong. A central goal in this book is to understand the operation of these two elements of domestic violence governmentality upon the violent subjects they seek to subjectify.

Governmentality is an increasingly popular theoretical framework for analyzing the operation of power in society. As mentioned in the introduction, this popularity stems in part from the framework's sensitivity to the intersections of structure and agency, two core concerns of sociology. In this view, society is not simply composed of individuals and groups who either benefit from or are constrained by those who possess and wield power. Rather, individual subjects emerge in society through their participation in different programs of governmentality, or "endeavours to shape, guide, and direct the conduct of others" (Rose 1999:3).

What this description of people's experiences with mandatory arrest and no-drop prosecution contributes to our understanding of governmentality is a clearer sense of the role that individual agents play in the operation of power. As this chapter has shown, the capacities and performances of individual agents are central to the operation of power in programs of governmentality and constituent of the interpretive and substantive outcomes they produce. Individuals enter the criminal justice system on domestic battery cases with vastly different capacities for engaging the operations of power with which authorities seek to engage them. Ed, who had seen domestic violence policing in action in the past, successfully (for a while at least) evaded capture by the police. Doug and Oscar, who had been through the criminal courts before, took pictures of themselves following their incidents that allowed them to secure verdicts of not guilty. Meanwhile, Carl, an unskilled, inexperienced legal novice, seemed at every step of the process to be shuffled along by legal authorities and their operations of power into precisely the performances that they intended for him. But individuals' capacity for engaging power develops in interaction with authorities as well. Carl, after his unsuccessful encounter with the police, later reported in our interview that he would lie to the police if given another opportunity to interact with them. Thus, reflection upon legal performances they either are completing or have completed further informs persons' interactions with authorities.

Another central lesson to take away from this analysis is that the exercise of power, precisely because it is constructed interactively, yields unintended consequences. This chapter has illuminated two unintended outcomes vital for assessing the contribution of mandatory arrest and no-drop prosecution in the fight against domestic violence.

The first concerns suspects' relationships with their victimized intimate partners. One of the goals of mandatory interventions is to disrupt batterers' control and influence over their victims. This chapter demonstrates that arrest and prosecution do disrupt abusers' violence. All but 2 of the 30 respondents participating in the study were arrested on the night of their abuse, disabling their capacity to cause more harm that night. In addition, the majority of them (24 out of 30) were found guilty on charges relating to their attacks, which subsequently subjected them to increased surveillance by the state and, in most cases, their enrollment in treatment groups. What's more, interviews with these abusers reveal that they experience a loss of power in their intimate relationships as a result of the no-contact orders that the state imposes against them.

However, despite these disruptions, this chapter also finds that batterers, faced with the threat of additional legal punishment, resort to different tactics to continue exercising control over their partners during the prosecution of their cases. Abusers play nice as well as play upon their partners' feelings of remorse to influence their relation to the criminal case. In addition, mothers and sisters intervene, to reconstruct the relationships that the state has disrupted.

The interventions of mothers and sisters, especially, underscore the importance of intersectionality in understanding the efficacy of domestic violence law (Coker 2001, 2004). Abusive relationships involve intimate abusers and victims at their core. But these partners and their violence are embedded in a broader social context of family and community relations. Disruptions to the abusive relationship bring disruptions in other relationships as well, which work to reconstitute themselves. In the process, the power of state interventions against intimate violence weakens.

The role of family members and others in supporting domestic violence suspects' resistance to state interventions is a topic to explore further. At the very least, we would want to know what victims think about and experience through these interpersonal interventions. As well, why do these family members get involved? Do they not think violence against women is an important problem? Or do they simply want to insulate sons and brothers from the police and state? If these family members are genuinely concerned about both the seriousness of domestic violence as a social problem and the seriousness of criminal legal interventions in underprivileged communities as a social problem, we might also ask whether their energy and efforts could be harnessed more productively to other types of social interventions.

The second unintended consequence concerns the meaning that punishment has for abusers. A primary goal of mandatory arrest and no-drop prosecution is deterrence—that abusers will tie the pain of their punishments to their exercise of abuse and thus desist from the latter. But rather than seeing their punishments as a consequence of their own behavior, the respondents participating in this study interpreted them as a consequence of the unjust workings of the criminal legal system.

Opposition to the meaning-making power of law emerges from different sources. First are the diverse subject positions that comprise domestic violence suspects. While the intimate abuser, domestic batterer, or wife beater has emerged as a unified subject in the popular imagination, persons who commit intimate abuse occupy a variety of subject positions (African American, laborer, convict) in the social world simultaneously. And through these multiple positions, the respondents in this study defined their legal experiences of injustice. The injustices that African Americans and the working class (Brooks & Jeon-Slaughter 2001; Wortley et al. 1997; Hagan & Albonetti 1982) experience and perceive in the criminal justice system thus check the meaning-making power of domestic violence law.

Of course, the subject position from which most respondents based their injustice claims was gender. The majority of the male respondents believed that the police, courts, or law were biased against men. Rather than reflecting the consciousness of traditionally disadvantaged groups and classes, these claims represent the disquietudes of a historically privileged group as it witnesses the further dismantling of its architecture of advantage. In rearranging the boundaries between "private" and "public" space that have buttressed men's violence against women in intimate relationships, domestic violence law represents another instance of a larger "crisis of masculinity" through which men begin to perceive themselves as "the *real* victims in American society" (Kimmel 1996:305). Regardless of its merit, the sense of victimization expressed by the abusers in this study is again important, as it counters the subjectifying power of the law.

Community also plays a role in refracting the meaning of punishment. In their recent work, Sampson and Bartusch (1998) and Weitzer (2000) highlight how neighborhoods can serve as "cognitive landscapes" shaping individuals' perception of deviance and trust in legal institutions. The legal narratives in this study suggest different ways in which community influences individuals' feelings of criminal injustice. On the one hand, communities carry or are imputed with a reputation that then colors people's legal experiences in those locales. Tom's mother, who lives in a major city, explained to him and his victimized partner "how those cops are down there" in more rural Centralia County: "They would love to lock a black man up, especially he don't got no record." On the other hand, communities also serve as the stages upon which the events shaping people's collective experiences take place. And people tie their personal experiences with the law to these larger experiences in order to define their legal encounters. Henry believes he was the victim of racism because the officer arresting him had been at the center of a local controversy concerning the police's mistreatment of African Americans. Carrie, similarly, explained to me why she felt her probation sentence was "all just about money":

> I know that it was in the paper they wanted to rebuild the clock of the courthouse or whatever. Ever since then the police are doing different stuff, you know, as far as trying to make more money. Like last week they stopped, oh, three hundred and something people on the corner of Roosevelt and Lancaster doing . . . I'm not sure what it's called, public safety search or something. *That's an African American neighborhood?* Yeah. And basically what they were doing was checking to see if you have your seatbelt on, checking to see if you have a driver's license and insurance. And if you don't have it, they ended up arresting 60 people just that day. (Carrie)

In this cognitive landscape, where the courthouse is restoring its iconic clock tower and the police are stepping up a public order campaign specifically in a black neighborhood, Carrie's own experience with the law takes on a new meaning.

Finally, the power of law to serve as a force of social change is inhibited by itself. More specifically, the means by which the law is able to gain power over domestic violence suspects are inimical to subjectifying them in the ways intended. The control tactics that police officers and defense attorneys employ to have suspects cooperate with investigations and accept plea bargains ricochet to alter the meaning of punishment. Similarly, the strong-arm tactics (having suspects sit in jail, overcharging cases) that the state's attorneys' office relies on to secure convictions become the substance of abusers' injustice claims.

Having suspects who are arrested and prosecuted for their violence see themselves as victims is an ominous sign about the efficacy of these criminal legal interventions. As Tom Tyler's (1990) research explains, persons who come into contact with legal authorities and feel they have been unfairly treated are less likely to conform to the law than those who feel they have been justly treated, regardless of the substantive outcomes each receives. As such, the feelings of victimization that the participants in this study express are a bad harbinger. Nevertheless, there is more than one way to judge the effects of mandatory arrest and no-drop prosecution. And in the chapters that follow, I examine how these legal encounters impact intimate abusers' relation to their violent pasts as well as their futures.

5 | Abusers' Relation to Violence

This chapter investigates how batterers come to view their abusive behavior following arrest and prosecution. Abusers' views of their own behavior are important for assessing the impact of mandatory arrest and no-drop prosecution. Feminist researchers have established a link between the stories abusive partners use to describe their behavior and their violent selves (Ptacek 1988; Dobash & Dobash 1998; Hearn 1998; Eisikovits & Buchbinder 2000; Anderson & Umberson 2001). Men describe their violence by denying it, minimizing its severity or harm, excusing its occurrence, and/or justifying its occurrence. In doing so, they insulate themselves from taking responsibility for their actions.

Batterers use these stories to fashion and reinforce particular definitions of the self and the other. For example, in justifying violence, batterers commonly present their partners as intentional provocateurs who "'wind them up,' 'nag,' and generally behave in ways that 'provoke' arguments and violence" (Dobash & Dobash 2000:162; see also Ptacek 1988:145). In addition, Ptacek (1988), in one of the early studies examining batterers' talk about violence, explains that abusive men use denials and justifications to portray themselves as normal, nonviolent persons. This point has been expanded upon more recently by Anderson and Umberson (2001) as well as Stark (2007). Noting how men describe their physical violence as "rational" and "explosive" as opposed to the "hysterical" and "weak" actions of their female partners, Anderson and Umberson (2001) find that "batterers attempt to construct masculine identities through the practice of violence and the discourse about violence" (359). Similarly, Stark (2007) finds, "by contrasting their own propensity for reasoned and rational argument to their partners' 'crazy' views and behaviors, controllers build an elaborate pseudo-logic out of sarcasm, disdain, and insult that they then bring to bear on judgments about women's everyday behavior" (282). Through these gendered depictions of violence and conflict, men construct and naturalize "a binary and hierarchical gender system" (Anderson & Umberson 2001:374).

Arresting and prosecuting domestic batterers is intended to disrupt men's ability, at both the societal and individual levels, to rationalize and normalize violence against women. At the societal level, punishing batterers conveys the message that violence against women is not normal or tolerable (Schneider 2000). At the individual level, the presence of a third party to the violent event, who possesses and exercises the legal authority to punish the guilty party, complicates the batterer's ability to simply explain away his violence by denying its existence or displacing responsibility for it to the victim. Optimally, it is hoped that punishment "thwarts denial and evasion of responsibility" (Waits 1985:267).

To evaluate the efficacy of mandatory arrest and no-drop prosecution, it is important, then, to consider how batterers relate to their violence following contact with the police and courts. Do they continue to deny, minimize, excuse, and/or justify their abuse? And how do they depict themselves and their victims? Do arrest and prosecution affect these representations? If so, how?

This chapter pursues these questions by examining different dimensions of abusive men's narratives of violence.[1] The first section of the chapter reports how respondents described the events that led to their arrest, highlighting how they depicted themselves, their victims, and the interactions between them. The second section assesses change by comparing the descriptions of violence that respondents provided me with those they provided the police, focusing on any breaks or differences between the two descriptions.

Taken as a whole, the analysis of respondents' narratives finds that most offenders continue to evade responsibility for abuse following their arrest and prosecution. In contrast to past research, however, abusers disown their violence not only by denying, minimizing, excusing, and justifying it, but also by offering stories of self-defense. The differences among these stories are critical in men's construction of gendered subjectivities. While men justifying and excusing their violence tend to construct and affirm traditional masculine identities, those who offer denials or self-defense stories tend not to affirm any masculine identity, depicting the violence instead as originating from aggressive, crazed female partners. Men reassert their masculinity when describing their intimate relationships beyond the violent event itself. However, in doing so, many respondents offer nontraditional descriptions of the masculine self as caring and accommodating. Through such portrayals, men further distance their selves from violence and deepen the image of their selves as victims of controlling, promiscuous, crazed, and manipulative women.

Batterers' Narratives of Abuse

Relating Violence. Past research with batterers has found that these men generally offer four types of stories to describe their violence, each of which modifies their role and responsibility in the violent act (Ptacek 1988; Dobash & Dobash 1998; Eisikovits & Buchbinder 2000; Anderson & Umberson 2001). In *denials,* batterers simply deny that any abuse or violence took place ("I didn't touch her"). In *minimizations,* they admit that violence took place, but minimize either its seriousness ("I just pushed her") or the harm resulting from it ("No one got hurt"). In *excuses,* they admit that violence took place, and do not question its seriousness, but reduce their culpability by blaming the episode on being under the influence of alcohol, drugs, or strong, uncontrollable emotions ("I was drunk and I hit her"). In *justifications,* they admit their violence, do not question its seriousness, but rationalize it as a justified response to provocations from their partners ("She was pushing my buttons").

The respondents in this study offered the same types of stories to describe their violence. They denied it (in 11 out of 27 cases), minimized it (in 7 out of 27 cases), excused it (in 4 out of 27 cases), and justified it (in 7 out of 27 cases).[2] However, despite the prevalence of these descriptions, respondents frequently offered two additional types of stories to depict their violence: *self-defense stories* and *responsibility stories.*

In the self-defense story, the narrator admits to having engaged in violence. But he describes his actions as a response to physical aggression initiated by the partner. To the extent that violence is characterized as a response to the actions of the intimate partner, the self-defense story resembles a justification, where the abuser explains that he is violent in answer to provocations from his partner. But the self-defense story is distinct in that the partner is not only verbally provoking, or "pushing buttons," but actually engaging in physical violence that the man perceives and portrays as threatening.[3]

Some examples help demonstrate the difference. In his interview, Steve explained that he got into an argument with his girlfriend after she brought up the topic of his wife and the possibility of him leaving her. Eventually, he said, the argument became physical, after she spat in his face.

> I've been messing with my girlfriend for about three to four years. OK. And she start to talk about, you know, I wasn't ever going to leave my wife, and I'm not never going to be with her, and that's what started the argument. . . . So we're

sitting there and we're talking, we're arguing. So, all of a sudden she slaps me. I asked her not to, you know, don't put her hands on me. So, I sit there twenty minutes after we started arguing, and she spits on me. OK. So, when she spit on me, that's when I grab her by the hair. (Steve)

This is a typical justification story. The offender explains that the partner does something to him—in this case bringing up an uncomfortable topic and spitting on him—that he interprets as antagonizing and meriting a physical response. Tellingly, his partner does become physically aggressive with him ("all of a sudden she slaps me"), but this action does not prompt a physical response from him. Rather, he explains, it is being spat upon that made him violent.

In contrast to this justification story is that of Carl, who went to his exgirlfriend's apartment, upset that she had gone out by herself and had not been returning his phone calls.

I went over to my girlfriend's house. She was in bed, and we were discussing some things. I walked to the foot of the bed, and I noticed that she didn't have any underwear on. I bent over the bed, and I said, "Look, you don't even have any underwear on." I don't remember exactly what was said, but that's why I was bending over the bed. At that time, she turned and put her hands down on the bed, gritted her teeth and just came up and kicked me right across the face. She then leaned up and started toward me. When she did that, I swung at her to get her away from me . . . all I did was stop her from coming at me. (Carl)

In this description, the respondent presents his violence as a response to a physical assault by his partner. Overlooking his psychological abuse in the scene, wherein he insulted his partner by implying that she was indecent because of the way she was dressed in bed, he centered his description on her actions and the threats they posed. All he did "was stop her from coming at" him.

Surprisingly, *self-defense* stories were the second-most common description of violence offered by the respondents in this research, appearing in 9 out of 27 cases. In these descriptions, the same basic pattern is repeated. An argument arises, the partner attacks, and the respondent is left to defend himself.

I was lying in bed, listening to music. My friend came in and she turned the music off. I got up and turned it back on and asked her what was her problem. When I turned around to face her, she pushed me on the bed. And when I went to stand up, she just grabbed me by my neck and started scratching me. And I grabbed her and held her real close to me to stop her from hurting me any further, and she bit me extremely hard. So, I pushed her away from me, and I'm not sure if she fell over a box or whatever in the room, but she got up and she ran into the front room and called 911. (Chris)

She came home ready to argue, because she's like, "I couldn't get out of work. My boss said if I don't show up tomorrow, then I'm going to get in trouble." And I was like, "Well, what do you want me to do?" So we throw down then. We argued. It escalated. There was a lot of things getting thrown around with her throwing my bag around. So, you know, our neighbors hear all the banging and everything. She's throwing my bag and I would push her off me. I was trying to get out the door. They heard the back door slamming. She was slamming the door like, "No, we're going to argue about this," and I'd move out of the way. I never really hit her. . . . I mean one time, I had to, she was all over me. She was ripping at my coat and stuff, and I picked her up and I pushed her over to the couch. (Nic)

What happened was we were driving. I stopped and picked her up. She had a beer. I quit drinking over six years ago. I wasn't going to give away my transportation license, so I quit drinking. Her four-year-old was between us, and I'm like, "OK, whatever." So I take her there and let her have a beer in the truck. We weren't going very far. We were going out to the park to have a picnic. She snagged my phone, and I went to reach for my phone, and she went ballistic in the truck. She had boots on, kicking everything. So, I held her over against the door and pulled over the truck. She got out and kicked the hell out of my truck. I went to the police. (Doug)

Although distinct from the other types of descriptions presented by batterers, the self-defense story mirrors denials, minimizations, excuses, and justifications in that it allows the batterer to separate himself from the violence he participated in. He was violent, but only in reaction to an outside threat to his well-being. Blame, as in the justification story, lies squarely on the partner, who in these cases has become violent against him. At first glance, then, this review of batterers' descriptions of their violent behavior provides strong evidence that they do not come to accept responsibility for their abuse following their contact with the criminal justice system. In 23 out of 27 cases, the respondents in this study evaded responsibility for the violence that resulted in their arrest.

However, not all the respondents disowned their violence. In four cases (Larry, Mike, Aaron, Ed), the respondents offered stories of *responsibility*. In these descriptions, the men admit not only that they were violent, but that they are the ones to blame for the violence. Aaron, for instance, who was violent against his girlfriend after discovering she was involved in another relationship, noted, "I can't blame nobody but myself, you know. I look now, I suppose to have self-control over that situation." Similarly, Mike, who grabbed his girlfriend during an argument, explained:

> I was going to leave. She was pissed off and didn't let me leave. First, she took the keys, then I found the keys. Then, you know, by me pulling her away from the door by her legs, which I shouldn't have did, now I see that after all the shit I've been through, her grandmother came around the corner with a little .25 pistol. . . . It's just something I shouldn't have did. (Mike)

In these examples, both Aaron and Mike provide clear statements that they did something wrong. What's more, Mike's comments suggest that the criminal justice system, which he referred to as "all the shit I've been through," played a role in having him recognize his culpability.

But if these men admitted guilt, their stories in each instance were accompanied by other descriptions of violence that served to diminish their responsibility. Later in his interview, for instance, Aaron wove his admission of guilt together with both a denial of violence *and* a justification: "fingers point at me like I was the bad guy. You know I never hit a woman a day in my life. I can say it provoked from her. I mean, it's so much you can take. Man. Really. Especially when you know you love the person." Mike, in the same manner, dressed his admission with a series of excuses and justifications, which dominated his narrative more generally: "Like I said, the alcohol was in me, her Aunt Tina was getting on my nerves, and she [the girlfriend] was getting on my nerves, drunk and shit."

By mixing responsibility with other types of accounts, these stories end up functioning much the same as excuses. The man admits that what he did was wrong. But the admission goes together with a number of mitigating factors that lessen his culpability. In the process, the admission of guilt loses much of its meaning. These stories, like the other descriptions of violence reviewed above, indicate that the men in this study have not taken responsibility for their violence following arrest and prosecution.

It is also interesting to consider these descriptions of violence by abuser type. In Tables 14 and 15, I do this. Table 14 lists each participant by abuser and story type, while Table 15 summarizes the group results. As Table 15 shows, both intimate terrorists and situationally violent abusers used each type of story to evade responsibility for violence. And roughly speaking, both groups use each story to similar degrees. The one exception is "minimization" stories, which 38.7% of intimate terrorists used versus 11.1% of situationally violent offenders.

It is difficult to conclude too much from these correlations, given the low number of respondents. They are nevertheless worth reflecting upon. That

TABLE 14—Pseudonyms, Abuser Types, and Stories of Violence for Male Respondents

Name	Abuser Type	Story Type
1. Adam	Intimate Terrorism	Denial
2. Bob	Situational	Excuse, Justification
3. Chris	Situational	Self-Defense
4. Dave	Intimate Terrorism	Minimization
5. Eric	Intimate Terrorism	Justification
6. Frank	Intimate Terrorism	Denial
7. Gary	Intimate Terrorism	Justification, Minimization
8. Henry	—	Denial
9. Isaac	Situational	Denial
10. John	—	Self-Defense
11. Kevin	Situational	Denial, Self-Defense
12. Larry	Intimate Terrorism	Excuse, Responsibility
13. Mike	Situational	Excuse, Responsibility
14. Nic	Intimate Terrorism	Minimization, Self-Defense
15. Oscar	Intimate Terrorism	Self-Defense
16. Pete	—	Denial
17. Quinn	—	Denial
18. Ralph	—	Minimization
19. Steve	Situational	Justification, Minimization
20. Tom	Situational	Justification, Self-Defense
21. Victor	Intimate Terrorism	Denial (first arrest); Minimization (second arrest)
22. Walter	Situational	Denial
23. Aaron	Intimate Terrorism	Denial, Justification, Minimization, Responsibility
24. Brett	Intimate Terrorism	Excuse, Justification, Self-Defense
25. Carl	Intimate Terrorism	Self-Defense
26. Doug	Intimate Terrorism	Self-Defense
27. Ed	Situational	Denial, Responsibility

TABLE 15—Male Respondents' Descriptions of Violence by Abuser Type*

Description of Violence	Situationally Violent (9)	Intimate Terrorists (13)
Denial	44.4% (4/9)	30.8% (4/13)
Minimization	11.1% (1/9)	38.7% (5/13)
Excuse	22.2% (2/9)	38.7% (5/13)
Justification	33.3% (3/9)	30.8% (4/13)
Self-Defense	33.3% (3/9)	38.7% (5/13)
Responsibility	22.1% (2/9)	15.4% (2/13)

* The numbers of stories by type reported here do not match the total number of stories reported in the text, since 5 of the 27 male respondents could not be classified by batterer type. Also, the female respondents have not been included here.

minimizations represent the most frequent type of story from intimate terrorists and the least frequent story from situationally violent abusers might owe to the two groups' dissimilar experiences with abuse. Intimate terrorists engage in a wider range of abusive behaviors than do situationally violent abusers. As a consequence, they might actually perceive the abuse in question as minor compared to other incidents they subjected their partners to and which may not have resulted in an arrest. Situational abusers, meanwhile, may simply lack the extended personal histories of abuse to assess a particular incident as minor.

Aaron, an intimate terrorist, recounted the police's investigation of his case and remembered, "They were trying to run a little trick talk on me. They were like, 'She said this and that.' But I'm still saying, 'I didn't hit her.' Grabbing your arm is not hitting, to me it's not. [begins to laugh]." His account leaves out the fact that he also slammed his girlfriend's head against the wall, resulting in a visit to the hospital. And one is left to wonder what "hitting," versus merely "grabbing," would entail. Similarly, Victor described the events that led to the second of his two domestic violence arrests. At his girlfriend's house to pick up court papers relating to the first case, his girlfriend became upset with him for violating the no-contact order and refused to help him locate the paperwork. In response, Victor reported:

I told them, "I'm not leaving until I get those papers. I need them court papers to fax down there to my public defender so that they can squash the warrant that'd been issued." So I told them I wasn't leaving. She started walking around the house, and I grabbed her. It wasn't no like physical contact, like beat your brow. It was just like, "Stop playing, baby. Can you just go and grab the papers."

Like Aaron, Victor in this scene distinguishes between grabbing a partner when she chooses to walk away after refusing to do what she's told and real "physical contact" that involves blows to the "brow." More familiar with the range of controlling and violent behaviors that they can and have used against their partners, intimate terrorists then might be more inclined to view the behavior for which they were arrested as "minimal."

Another interesting difference between the story-telling of intimate terrorists and situationally violent offenders is the number of stories they use to describe their violence. As Table 16 shows, a greater percentage of intimate terrorists presented only one explanation of the events leading to their arrests as compared to situationally violent offenders. While 61.5% of intimate terrorists offered just one story to characterize their violence, only 33.3% of situationally violent offenders did the same. Conversely, 66.6% of situationally violent abusers used multiple stories to convey violent events, while 38.5% of intimate terrorists did so.

One example of situationally violent abusers' combining story types was Mike, who as noted above claimed responsibility for grabbing his girlfriend but also excused it because "the alcohol was in me" and justified it because "she was getting on my nerves." Bob similarly excused responsibility for grabbing his girlfriend by the neck because he and a friend had finished a "twelve-pack" and "a fifth of tequila" that day. At the same time, he justified the attack, clarifying that "the only trick about this girl is she just gets this thing where she goes finds another little boy. She thinks it's cool to bring him over to the house and says, 'I'm going to go out drinking with this guy.' That don't sit right." Steve, who justified pulling his girlfriend's hair because she spat on him, also minimized the violence. Pulling her hair hard enough to remove two pieces of a braided weave, he simply explained, "You know, the braids is very easy to fall out when they weaved in."

This apparent propensity of intimate terrorits to "stay on message," and situationally violent abusers to mix story types, might best be explained by the controlling nature of the former. Continually managing how others treat and perceive them, intimate terrorists may possess either a greater faculty for or concern with publicly describing their behavior. Indeed, it would make sense that these men, being more frequently violent and controlling of their partners than situationally violent abusers, have had more opportunities to hone their skills at describing their abusive conduct in a consistent

TABLE 16—Number of Stories Used to Describe Violence by Abuser Type

Abuser Type	Single Story	Multiple Stories
Situationally Violent	33.3% (3/9)	66.6% (6/9)
Intimate Terrorist	61.5% (8/13)	38.5% (5/13)

manner, resulting in fewer fluctuations between story types. Again, these are necessarily tentative suppositions, but they help in thinking about how batterer types matter in legal interventions against domestic abuse.

Gendered Subjectivities in Violence. In addition to providing insight into their relation to violence, respondents' narratives also illuminate how these men construct the self and other through violence. Previous studies have found that men construct and affirm masculine and feminine subjectivities *through* their descriptions of violence (Dobash & Dobash 1998; Hearn 1998; Anderson & Umberson 2001). Anderson and Umberson (2001), for instance, note that abusive men "depict their violence as rational, effective, and explosive," all positive traits associated with masculinity, while they describe their partners' violence as "hysterical, trivial, and ineffectual," which tap into and reinforce negative stereotypes of women (363). Further, in absolving themselves of responsibility for violence, batterers often present their partners as "controlling," "demanding," or "dominating" women (Anderson & Umberson 2001:367) who "wind them up" or "provoke" them to be violent (Dobash & Dobash 1998:162).

Respondents' narratives bore these ideas out. Men frequently described themselves as "angry," "pissed-off" tough guys during their violent episodes, while portraying their partners as "controlling" or "demanding" women who initiated the conflict that led to violence.

Nevertheless, batterers' descriptions of violence also paint a more complex picture of the relation between violence and gendered subjectivity than that described in past research. First, the types of masculine and feminine subjects appearing in batterers' accounts of violence are more numerous than previous research has indicated. Men affirm themselves not only as strong, lethal, no-bullshit guys in enacting violence, but as other masculine subjects as well. For instance, in describing his violation of an order of protection against his ex-girlfriend, which fell within a pattern of highly abusive behavior, including the eventual kidnapping of the woman, Frank affirmed his identity as a caring father. He notes:

So I went to the drugstore and—lo and behold!—right across the street there is my son with his mom, waiting at the bus stop. So I stopped the truck . . . yeah, I wasn't expecting them . . . it might have run through my mind that they might be there. Well, I got to stop at the drugstore. I don't know what I was thinking. So, I stopped the truck there, and I stayed on my side of the street, and I just waved because I haven't seen him. You know, I manage to see my kid every day. I pick him up from school every day. I am part of his life. I am part of his social environment and everything. I am his dad.

In this account, Frank lets slip out that his "chance" encounter with his ex-girlfriend ("lo and behold!") might actually have been planned on his part ("it might have run through my mind that they might be there"). Regardless, his stalking and violation of the court order intended to protect her is justified on the basis of being a father ("I pick him up from school every day. . . . I am his dad").

In other stories, men affirm themselves as breadwinners, another positive masculine subject, through their violence. Eric, for example, punched his girlfriend and looked to initiate sex with her after she did not come home after a night out with friends. In narrating the scene, however, he explained that he was upset because she had spent the money he gave her to pay for bills.

I was paying all the bills and everything on my own. I was giving her everything. Really she didn't have to do nothing. Just be there for me. And what happened that morning, I wouldn't never put my hands on her, but that was, I was screwed, you know what I'm saying, all my bills wasn't paid, how I'm gonna explain this? (Eric)

Eric's attempt to reframe the conflict as one primarily concerning finances falters to the extent that he lets out that he had expected his girlfriend to fulfill a traditional feminine gender role for him, to stay at home and "be there" for him, which he believes involves doing "nothing." This notwithstanding, he presents himself through his violence as a responsible, hardworking breadwinner who is concerned about the household's finances.

Not all presentations of the masculine self in violence are positive. Some men affirmed themselves as drunks and alcoholics in their stories. Larry, who elsewhere in his interview reported harassing his girlfriend for fun, described the conflict that led to his violence as follows:

She didn't really want to put this [calling the cops] on me. But at the time, when you're mad and you're fighting, you know, you blow up. And I don't blame her. I mean, we were both drinking that night, and I wish I'd never drunk. I shouldn't even be drinking, because I'm an alcoholic and two alcoholics don't get along with alcohol and stuff. (Larry)

It is worth noting that Larry's violence in this episode left his partner with severe injuries, including a large bruise under her left eye and a severely swollen nose. Larry does not blame her, however. Nor does he blame himself. Rather, he is simply a drunk who never should have drunk that night.

What is important to note in these descriptions is not merely the multiplicity of masculine subjects men affirm through violence. Rather, it is that in each case the men affirm masculine subjectivities that possess a certain license for violence. The father has historically possessed the authority to be violent against his family for the sake of discipline and order. While this license for violence has diminished, thanks in large part to the activism of battered women's and child welfare advocates, Frank still presents his abuse toward his ex-girlfriend as a justified demonstration of his love for his child. Likewise, the breadwinner, having provided for his household, has earned the right to be violent if his partner loses the money and leaves him "screwed." Even the drunk, though certainly not an appealing masculine subject, provides a cover for violence, as he is understood to not have the ability to control himself. For these men, then, the concern is not just, or even primarily, to present themselves as tough, strong men, but to subjectify themselves into gender identities with the authority to be violent. In this sense, the construction and presentation of masculine subjectivity allow men to further justify their violence, in the case of the abusive father or angry breadwinner, or to further excuse their violence, in the case of the violent drunk.

This multiplicity of violent masculine subjectivities in men's stories is mirrored by a multiplicity of feminine subjectivities against whom violence is justified. As noted in past research, the "controlling" partner who pushes buttons and provokes violence is one such feminine subject. Another appearing frequently in men's narratives is the promiscuous, cheating partner:

It's a terrible feeling, you know? Because, number one, when you think a person really love you and right just betrays you with another human. It hurts. It really do. (Aaron)

If you have a girlfriend and she's going out with other guys and taking your money while she's doing it, and she's waking you up while you're trying to sleep . . . I work nights, and she called me during the day that day to go and buy her a tire and go put it on her car in the middle of my night so that she could go out that night with another guy. Are you just going to ignore that? (Carl)

Like the controlling partner, the promiscuous partner incites men to violence. However, what the partners are guilty of is not annoying men, but hurting them ("It hurts") and their masculine pride. Such immoral betrayals provide these men justification for violence ("Are you just going to ignore that?").

As these points demonstrate, if men's descriptions of violence reinforce a binary, patriarchal gender system (Anderson & Umberson 2001:359), there is greater multiplicity within the gendered subjectivities occupying this system than previously recognized. This is the first way in which men's narratives of violence paint a more complex picture of the relation between violence and gendered subjectivity than described in the past. The second concerns the manner in which, in most respondents' descriptions of violence, masculine subjects are difficult to discern at all. That is, the respondents provided scarce detail about what they are doing or thinking at the time in which violence occurs.

This is especially the case in self-defense and denial stories. In these stories, men simply drop out of the picture and become shadows of themselves. The self-defense stories listed above provide a sense of this. Chris was just listening to music when his partner comes in and starts a fight. Nic was simply "trying to get out the door" during his argument with his wife. Doug was just reaching for his phone while driving his girlfriend to the park for a pleasant picnic with her daughter. Details of the masculine self in these stories, who these men are at the moment of violence, what they are thinking, and how they see themselves, are virtually absent.

Significantly, the disappearance of the masculine self is accompanied by the introduction of a new feminine other: the crazed female. Distinct from the controlling partner and the provocative partner, the crazed partner does not provoke violence from the man. Rather, she suddenly, with seemingly no reason or explanation aside from her own pathology, enacts violence.

> She snagged my phone and I went to reach for my phone and she went ballistic in the truck . . . she was just nuts, man. (Doug)

> I was running from her and her rage. . . . She busted her own lip in her own rage. I don't know how she did it. But she busted her own lip. (Kevin)

> I kept asking if she could get the court papers, she started yelling and getting all crazy and stuff. So she called her sister out the back, and her sister come out the back and she really talking crazy and stuff, yelling. (Victor)

> I called her and I told her to come and pick up her clothes, and she came. When she came, I go in the bedroom and sit on the bed, watching her pick

her clothes up, because I didn't want her to start tearing up my stuff, because that's what she started doing. And I told her quit slamming, you know, them drawers when she get her clothes out and stuff, and then when I told her that, she started knocking stuff off the dresser. I said you going to do that, you got to go. Then she really got mad and started going over to the dining room, trying to knock off something, and something sound like it broke, and I went to raise up and see what it was, and that's when she came at me with her arms. I couldn't honestly see what she had in her arms, because it happened so fast. I just looked up and I had no time to describe it before she hit me with whatever it was that she had. (Oscar)

The violence of the crazed partner is not the "weak," "ineffectual" violence noted by men in past studies of intimate abuse (Anderson & Umberson 2001:363). Rather, it is a quick ("it happened so fast"), powerful ("ballistic"), out of control ("She busted her own lip in her own rage") violence that threatens the respondent ("she hit me with whatever it was that she had") as well as the perpetrator herself ("she busted her own lip").

The appearance of the aggressive, crazed partner thus possesses a critical function in men's evasions of responsibility. As is the case with the controlling partner or cheating partner in justification stories, the crazed partner in men's self-defense and denial stories serves to absolve batterers of blame for their violence. It is the feminine rather than the masculine subject who takes up the violent performance here. However, introducing the crazed woman deprives these men of a corresponding masculine identity to affirm through violence. If a husband can hit his wife for cheating on him, if the no-bullshit man can hit his partner for being controlling, these men offer no masculine identities to assert in relation to a physically abusive woman. Indeed, rather than an affirmation of masculinity, one witnesses in these stories the loss of masculinity, both symbolically (what man would be afraid of a woman?) and literally (the men simply do not appear in these stories). These stories demonstrate that many men do not affirm masculine identities through violence. In neglecting to justify violence or own up to it in any way, these men simply censor their masculine selves from the script. Appearing nonviolent comes before appearing manly for them.

Gendered Subjectivities in Intimacy. In describing the violence that led to their arrests, the men participating in this study invariably embedded the incident within the broader context of their relationships with their intimate partners. And if many respondents neglected to affirm masculine identities when describing the violence that led to their arrest, all the men I interviewed did so in discussing their intimate relationships. In unfolding their descriptions of abuse out into descriptions of intimacy, respondents offered depictions of the self and the partner that deepened the image of a nonviolent self and a negative, suspect feminine other. In doing so, they further distanced themselves from violence while planting it more firmly in their partners.

The wider context of their intimate relationships provided men the opportunity to anchor their narratives in events, actions, and details that cast their masculine self in sharper contrast. Some men, for example, gravitated toward descriptions that highlighted their strength, seriousness, and ability to meet responsibilities, all of which are traditional traits of positive masculine subjects, and all of which have been noted in past research (Eisikovits & Buchbinder 2000:43–47; Anderson & Umberson 2001:363, 372).

More commonly, however, men eschewed such traditional, stereotypical depictions of masculinity and instead invoked traits that could be thought to comprise new forms of masculinity. For instance, many men emphasized their ability to be accommodating in their intimate relationships and to practice restraint when arguments arise:

> She will bring it up every day, about our daughter going somewhere, or me going out, until I tell her who I was with. . . . And she always bring it up until I have to tell her, "No, I won't do it anymore," and I asks her before I do it. So, it's a constant argument, every day, until I give in and say, "OK, then, I won't do it." (John)

> I was like that [temperamental], you know. Me and her used to talk about that because my temper be gone, you know, but I learned to stop myself, I try to stop myself. That's why I stopped playing cards. (Isaac)

> Oh, we have arguments, but like I said, I just don't . . . just like I do all the time. If she wants to argue, she going to argue by herself. (Oscar)

> Sometimes I get real angry and stuff, and I do really want to fight and stuff. You know, I do really just want to push her off and tell her to get out of my face and stuff like that. And some people might not have the type of patience and endurance I have. . . . Some people might be having, like, real bad tempers because I have a little temper. But my temper, I know how to control it. I know how to calm down, to sit here and say, "No, this is wrong. I went too far. I'm sorry." Some people might not have that catch and just, really, snap out. (Victor)

These men, unlike strong, lethal masculine subjects, recognize their power and the possibility for violence. And rather than succumbing to their anger, they take various steps to avoid violence and be different. They give in, walk away, and stop engaging in those activities, such as card playing, that activate their tempers. In depicting themselves as accommodating and under control of their emotions, these men define themselves against the backdrop of truly violent men, who do not possess "that catch" that allows them to avoid violence.

Other men continued this discursive movement away from traditional strong masculinity. Beyond being accommodating and self-controlled, these men described themselves as caring and compassionate, toward both their partners and other family members:

> I wanted, actually, to have counseling, see if I was wrong by asking her to do these things . . . you know, I wanted to be fair. Sometimes two people that love each other and been together for so long, it's hard for you to talk and communicate with each other. So, I said we'll ask a second person, and if I'm wrong, then this person will tell me. *So, the counseling was more your idea?* Yeah. It was my idea. She's not a real . . . I don't know, you can say loving person, like, she's not a hugger, and I am, you know. She's don't like telling people personal things about anything. (Brett)

> Her mother likes me and I never even met her. Jennifer is from Chicago, but her mother liked me and she kind of told me to look after Jennifer, because she knows how she is. She said Jennifer is kind of off a little bit, just try to look after her. (Kevin)

> They had found some marijuana in the house also that was there. My friend, she's on parole. So they asked whose it was, and I told them it was mine. I don't really smoke marijuana. I have in the past. But I bought it for her, because that what she likes. She doesn't never go anywhere, really, because of her seizures and stuff. I'm pretty attentive to what her needs and stuff are. (Chris)

> I've treated her girl just like she was my own. I looked out for that little girl, and this girl [his girlfriend] twisted everything around and makes it looks like I'm the bad guy when the father knows how I've treated his kid. (Doug)

These men claim to have made various sacrifices of themselves for the good of their partners and their families. Brett, a self-described "hugger," wants to seek counseling in order to be "fair" and see whether he is being too demanding in the relationship. Kevin sacrifices himself to watch over Jennifer, who even her mother admits is "off a little bit." The fact that her mother immediately liked him, despite never having met him, further speaks to his good nature. Chris, meanwhile, sacrifices himself by taking the fall on a charge of marijuana possession, which he originally acquired to help his sick, homebound girlfriend, to save her from a parole violation. Doug makes a sacrifice by looking after a child that is not even his own. Like Kevin, he invokes a family member outside the intimate relationship, the child's father, as testament to what a good and generous caregiver he is.

Accompanying these descriptions of accommodating and caring masculinities performed in the intimate relationship are depictions of partners that reinforce the feminine subjectivities introduced earlier. As men extended their narratives of violence and anchored their stories in events and actions that allowed them to present a positive self, they tied their descriptions of their partners to events, actions, and details that deepened the image of the partners as controlling, promiscuous, and crazed.

> *The Crazed Partner.* She ran away from home; she was arrested for running away from home. She spent time in a juvenile deal. The girl is 20 years younger than me, but she carries so much baggage, and I became affected by it. . . . I thought that she was young, and she had grown up and that she was better than that now. (Carl)

> *The Controlling Partner.* We started dating and everything and getting along, and about two months into our relationship, she gets mad because I quit my job to go into another job, and she's like, "Well, you got to come up with the rent money." (Gary)

> *The Promiscuous Partner.* One time she was out with a friend . . . they was pretty much in a place where this friend knew everybody that was there and [she] was just tagging along. . . . So, this friend end up leaving and getting arrested and [she] still sitting in some people's house that [she] don't know, don't have a clue who these people is. . . . After we established that the friend got arrested or whatever, I was like, you know, "Where you at, so I can come pick you up?" "Well, I don't want you to come get me, I don't want you to come get me." Well, the only way you're not gonna want me to come get you is if you're out there doing something that you don't have any business doing. (Walter)

In addition to reinforcing the negative feminine subjects introduced earlier in the descriptions of violence, men also used the context of the intimate relationship to introduce another feminine subject. This is the manipulative partner who uses a particular situation for her own personal gain. While the manipulative partner shares characteristics with the crazed partner (both display "abnormal" behavior) and the controlling partner (both want to exercise power over men), this feminine subject is distinct in her willingness to use the criminal justice system as a tool for gaining power over men.

> That's the only person I do know [in town], and that's why I believe she was doing that [calling the police], trying to show me she was in control and she had the power. Because she knows I'm down here now, and she know people here, and I'm basically the stranger. I'm here alone. She got a little cocky or something about it. I don't know. Maybe she getting a rush off of it. (Tom)

> She's got three kids, and only one lives with her. . . . It happens to be my best friend's, ex-best friend's, brother's kid. He said to me, "Look man, Doug, it doesn't matter if it's you there or another guy, the same thing's going to happen." . . . I mean, she had him kicked out of his own house. And she didn't live there! That's how twisted she is. She's a lawyer's secretary for 20 years. She knows the law, or at least she thinks she does. (Doug)

> I'm tired of playing her little runaround game, "If you don't do this for me, I'm gonna call the cops on you and put you away," and all this stuff. So, I'm not going to be running in circles around you and just let you get by with me paying for you. In terms of that, basically, I was helping her. I was supporting, on my behalf, providing. And she's getting mad at me 'cause I wasn't putting enough effort to it. (Gary)

> So, my wife calls me after she gets the order of protection on me and wants to get together. So, we have sex all night long, and then she disappears for two days. She comes back, has a black eye, and I get arrested for domestic battery. (Quinn)

Manipulative women use the law to kick men out of their houses (Doug), keep them in line (Tom), take their money (Gary), and punish them (Quinn). In using the law for themselves, these women are seen, like the crazed partner, as "twisted." However, unlike the crazed partner, the manipulative partner has a clear—however warped—goal in mind: control over men.

By inserting these subjects into their descriptions of their intimate relationships, the men in this study further negotiate their relation to violence. They again distance their selves from violence while having it gravitate toward their partners. If violence might be expected from strong, aggressive men, it is difficult to imagine from these controlled, caring men. Conversely, with women that are crazed and manipulative, it becomes easier to imagine violence emanating from them. Indeed, what emerges in these men's narratives of violence and intimacy is a reversal of the victim and abuser roles that feminist research on domestic violence has established so clearly. For those men who censor themselves from their descriptions of violence, who paint themselves as caring and compassionate, and who depict crazed and manipulative partners, it is they who are the victims of abuse, while their partners are abusers.

Some men are explicit about the role reversal:

> We were just two different people. She was violent, man. (Kevin)

> She used to hit me a lot. I used to ball up. She used to hit me a lot back home. She used to hit me a lot. So much so, I'd ask myself how much can a person take? (Aaron)

> I'd try to go and walk, you know, walk away from it and go cool myself down. I'll leave her sit there, let her cool herself down. . . . But she, you know, she just don't want to learn. And so, I'll walk away and she'll come running behind me, start punching, kicking, and whatever. (Gary)

> When I first met her, she said something about being a tough girl. She said she was going to kick somebody's ass, and I said, "Oh, you're a tough girl!" And she said, "Yeah, just look at all of my records—they're all for domestic violence." My jaw dropped, and I had this feeling in my stomach. (Carl)

But the message need not be stated so explicitly. Rather than portraying themselves as strong, lethal, powerful tough guys, these men describe themselves as hurt, damaged, victimized subjects. They have been accommodating in an effort to make their relationships work, but their partners have decided to leave them regardless (Frank, Brett). He is a lonely stranger in town, and she has manipulated that fact to control him (Tom). He paid the bills and tried to be a good guy, but she continued going out with other people (Nic, Eric). In the end, then, not only do these men not take ownership over their violence following their contact with the criminal justice system, but they lay claim to a new identity, that of victim, which functions to further distance their selves from the violence for which they were punished.

Punishment and Change? Batterers' Narratives of Abuse across Time

That respondents continued to evade responsibility for violence and presented themselves as nonviolent men victimized by aggressive female partners bodes poorly for the hope that abusers will take responsibility for their behavior following contact with the criminal justice system. However, even if the majority of respondents evaded responsibility for violence in their narratives, it is still important to consider whether changes have occurred in their stories following contact with the police and courts.

To determine this, I compared the descriptions of violence respondents told me with the stories they told the police. In the 24 cases I was able to compare,[4] I found that only 6 respondents (25.0% of the sample) changed their relation to violence. In 18 out of 24 cases (75.0%), respondents demonstrated no change in their relation to violence. That is, if the respondents offered a minimization, self-defense, or other version of their violence at the time of their arrest, they in most cases maintained this relation to violence in their interviews with me. For most of the batterers participating in this study, then, their relation to violence endured through their processing in the criminal justice system.

In the six narratives demonstrating change, four did not demonstrate what could be thought of as positive change. In these cases, respondents' descriptions of violence to me exhibited a lateral movement from one type of evasive account to another. Such lateral movement does not indicate an increase in the respondent's responsibility for violence. Bob moved from *minimizing* his violence to the police, noting that "he and Angie had an altercation" but "everything is okay," to *justifying* his violence to me: "She just gets this thing where she goes and finds another boy." Dave moved from *denying* his violence to the police—"Dave denied having any physical contact with Colleen,"—to *minimizing* it in his account to me: "I grabbed her by the collar, and as soon as I did that, I let go." Kevin changed from a *self-defense* story—"Kevin said that Jennifer tried to push him out of the apartment and started to, 'swing on him'"—to a full *denial:* "She busted her own lip in her own rage. I don't know how she did it, but she busted her own lip." Finally, Nic shifted from a *denial*—"Nic said at one point the talking became yelling, but then it went back to talking. I asked Nic if anything physical had taken place. Nic said no there was no physical contact made at anytime,"—to a *self-defense* and *minimization* mix: "I never really like hit her. . . . I mean one time, I had to, she was all over me. She was ripping at my coat and stuff, and I picked her up and I pushed her over to the couch."

In contrast, two cases did demonstrate some positive change. Both Mike and Aaron reported more responsibility for violence in our interview than when speaking with the police. In his case, Mike moved from a *self-defense* story—"Lori hit Mike approximately 5–6 times,"—to a story of *responsibility:* "It's just something I shouldn't have did." Aaron, meanwhile, changed from a *denial*—"Aaron stated flatly that he never touched Zoe during any altercation. He went on to say that he was the one that was threatened with a knife,"—to a story of *responsibility:* "that morning of the physical contact, I can say truly was because I grabbed her by her arm. She may have pushed me, and I grabbed her by her arm and slammed her to the wall."

However, as noted before, these stories of responsibility were interlaced with other descriptions of violence that diminished the respondents' ownership of the violence. In addition to admitting responsibility, Mike also *excused* his violence, explaining that "if drinking hadn't been involved, and her Aunt Tina running her mouth a little bit . . . all that shit probably could have been avoided." Aaron, for his part, *minimized, denied,* and *justified* his violence, explaining both that "it was not physical, or like punches, but I grabbed her by her arm," and "I never hit a woman a day in my life. I can say it provoked from her. I mean, it's so much you can take. Man. Really. Especially when you know you love the person."

Nevertheless, even if they were not full admissions of guilt, these stories are worth considering for what they reveal in terms of the effects of criminal justice interventions. As touched upon earlier in the chapter, there are clear indications in these cases that contact with the criminal justice system played a role in the changes these men experienced in relation to their violence. Mike, who was not convicted of domestic battery but had his case open for a long period of time, which necessitated multiple trips to court, noted that he now understood he should not have grabbed his girlfriend "after all the shit I've been through." The notion that the "process is the punishment" (Feeley 1979) springs to mind here. Apparently, the informal punishment associated with frequent court appearances made him see that grabbing his girlfriend was wrong.

Aaron, meanwhile, later reported in his interview that he had already attended some of the partner abuse classes that he was required to complete following his guilty plea to domestic battery charges. Further, he explained that the counseling was premised on open discussions of violent behavior, "I got to take family life skill classes. It helps you, just like me and you one-on-one talking. And I'm laying it down to you and seeing where the problem is at, that's what type of counseling it is. Yeah. They trying to help me, so I appreciate that." In this case, Aaron's partial admission of responsibility could be an effect of his participation in the counseling group, which encourages participants to discuss their behavior openly.

For these two respondents, then, the operation of power in the criminal justice system affected their relation to violence. Interestingly, operations of power within the criminal justice setting seem to play a role in the other stories of change as well. In these cases, though, contact with the police and courts seemed to result in men distancing themselves from violence. Bob made this point explicitly in his discussion of the police's response to the scene.

So, I go out there and he's asking questions. He says, "Hey, you tried grabbing her?" You know, me, I've got to deny this, you know, because if I even admit to grabbing her, I'm going to jail. I said, "I don't know what the hell you talking about." This, that, and the other. All of a sudden, I'm denying it and saying, "I didn't rough her up or nothing." (Bob)

Believing that he would be arrested for any admission of physical contact, Bob chose to deny making any sort of contact with the victim at all.

Though less explicitly, Nic and Dave offered similar explanations of their interactions with the police. Nic explained, "So the cops outside are like, 'What have you got to say for yourself?' I'm like, 'Nothing.' I'm thinking, I don't want to get arrested. I don't want her to get arrested. You know, that leaves the kids end up going, getting her grandfather called, or who knows." Dave, likewise, noted, "Her version of the story is that I grabbed her by the neck. And my version was, well, I didn't say anything to the police."

These men reveal how interactions with the police brought them to change their description of violence. Bob chose to deny everything. Nic and Dave opted to say as little as possible. Each of these men had had prior contact with the criminal justice system, as did the majority of the respondents participating in the research. And these quotes would seem to indicate that this past experience taught them not to be forthcoming in their interactions with the police. As such, the changes these men displayed in their descriptions of violence could be thought to speak not so much to a change in their relation to violence, but to a change in their relation to the social interaction in which these narratives were constructed. In other words, they approached talking to me differently than they approached talking to the police.

All the same, in these four cases, the narratives that they switched to in relating their violence to me still represent evasions of responsibility. Furthermore, excluding Bob, these men were unable to provide much detail about themselves in their descriptions of violence. They represent three cases where the masculine self falls out of the description of violence. Therefore, these narrative shifts by the men do not represent efforts to "come clean" and confess the truth, but rather efforts to establish a new relation to their violent past that can be presented in different social encounters.

Discussion

Following contact with mandatory arrest and no-drop prosecution, abusers continue to evade responsibility for violence. In addition to denying, minimizing, excusing, and justifying their violence, they also avoid responsibility through self-defense stories. In the few cases where men do admit responsibility for their abuse, they combine their admissions with evasions, thereby diminishing their claim to violence. While abusers construct and affirm masculine identities as strong, powerful men when describing their violence, many neglect to do so. Instead, they describe strong feminine subjects who are said to bear responsibility for the violence. Descriptions of intimate relationships deepen these gender constructions, with men noting their capacity for accommodation and caring while emphasizing their partners' controlling, promiscuous, crazed, and manipulative nature. Through such depictions, men distance themselves from their violence while laying claim to a victim identity. Notably, these discursive constructs appear durable, with most participants not changing their relation to violence through time. Those who do change more often demonstrate negative, lateral movements between stories of evasion rather than positive, progressive assumptions of responsibility.

On Defending the Masculine Self. The most intriguing finding in this chapter probably involves men's sense of victimization both within violence, which they express through self-defense stories, and intimacy, which they express through depictions of the self as caring and compassionate and the partner as manipulative, cheating, and crazy. This constellation of narrative elements is interesting because it runs against much of what we have learned about abusive men, violence, and gender in the past. That is, based on prior research with batterers, we would expect men to present and affirm themselves as tough, strong subjects through their violence. Having them portray themselves as victims of their partners' abuse to other men, whether dressed in police uniforms and not, contradicts much of what we have learned about them. Given this, one wonders from where these constructions of violence and the self emerge.

On the one hand, I believe the stories of victimization and self-defense identified here have something to do with the changing nature of gender relations in society. If we take the men's narratives, look beyond their normative assessments of women, and consider for a moment who these women described as crazed, controlling, cheating, and manipulative are and what they are doing, one gets a sense of this change. These are women who often own or rent the apartments the men are living in; have lives outside of their intimate relationships and are unwilling to settle down with these men; are willing to contact the police when their partners become abusive; and are also apparently willing to fight back when their partners become abusive. These are not the nagging wives and partners described so often by men in other studies of batterers (Ptacek 1988:144; Dobash & Dobash 1998:162; Anderson & Umberson 2001:367). Rather, these are strong, independent, empowered women willing to use different resources to negotiate their situations of abuse and to pursue their self-interest. In this regard, these women resemble the low-income single mothers highlighted by Kathryn Edin and Laura Lein (Edin & Lein 1997; Edin 2000) who are unwilling to accept intimate relationships with men who are abusive and controlling, have erratic employment, and cannot be trusted to be faithful, mature, and financially responsible. To the extent that these women do not match the traditional, stereotypical depictions of self-sacrificing women, they strike the men as crazy and manipulative. And men, in turn, feel threatened and/or hurt.

Conversely, for men, their inability to easily affirm masculine identities through the performance of violence also points to wider changes in gender relations in society. At the very least, this speaks to the efficacy of the battered women's movement and feminism more generally in changing social attitudes about violence against women. It is not too grandiose a claim to say that feminism has removed domestic violence from popular culture's collection of positive masculine behaviors. Hitting a woman in contemporary America is commonly accepted as wrong. Rhett Butler today does not slap Scarlett O'Hara. Indeed, hitting a woman in the movies and on television immediately casts the male character as a villain. And it is not necessarily other men who will come along to mete out justice. Rather, it could just as easily be Jennifer Lopez, who portrays a battered woman who fights back to exact revenge on her former abusive partner in *Enough*. The cultural scripts that men can use to relate themselves to their violent behavior have changed (Kimmel 1996).

Yet the new forms of masculinity that will replace the old are not entirely apparent or appealing to men. This dilemma could already be sketched out in the 1970s. The television comedy *All in the Family* vividly contrasts an older type of "autocratic" masculinity in the character of Archie, who is antagonistic toward the countercultural movement of the period, and a newer type of masculinity in the character of his son-in-law, who if tolerant toward racial minorities and women is also sluggish and weak (Stark 2007:46–47). "The show," as Stark (2007) explains, "suggests that the choice men face is to change with the times or become trapped in a loser's personality like . . . Archie" (47). Today still, in a "metrosexual" world where even sexual preference becomes "immaterial," because the male "has clearly taken himself as his own love object and pleasure as his sexual preference" (Simpson 2002), what a real man can instead be is not clear. Thus, absent strong masculine subjectivities to fit their abusive behavior into, many of the men in this study simply censor themselves out of the story altogether.

On the other hand, men's stories of victimization are not simply products of macro-level changes in society. Rather, these narratives arise in conjunction with the mandatory arrest and no-drop prosecution policies intended to disrupt abusers' violent subjectivities. Men's contact with the police and courts clearly impacts their construction of and adherence to victim identities.

This is so in at least three ways. First, at the most basic level, self-interest matters. And as this chapter has shown, the police investigation places men, at least those with prior contact with the criminal justice system, in a position where they attempt to evade responsibility for violence by denying its occurrence or claiming that they were the ones victimized to avoid arrest. One observes a similar dynamic in divorce and custody proceedings, where men will "insist they are the 'real' abused persons," to benefit from the law (Stark 2007:97).

Second, as the last chapter demonstrated, domestic violence suspects' interactions with legal authorities leave them with a sense of injustice. Men believe that they were punished not because they were violent, but because the police and domestic violence laws are biased against them. Importantly, men read these experiences not simply from their own positions of masculine privilege that are threatened through the arrest and prosecution action, but through the very operations of power that the police and courts use against them to exercise influence upon them. As such, abusive men's encounters with the law add a layer of experience in their lives through which they see themselves as victims.

Third, men's narratives of their contact with legal authorities evidence that at least some men embrace victim subjectivities as a way to reaffirm masculinity. Anderson and Umberson (2001) note this dynamic with men claiming that they "took the fall" to "protect" their partners from being arrested by the police (Anderson & Umberson 2001:369). "Taking the fall" allows abusers to use their interactions with the police as opportunities to present themselves as honorable men who "protect" their women. Men in this study too depicted their arrest or conviction as a case of taking the fall to protect their partners or families from state sanctions. As Isaac stated, "It [the criminal charge] should be thrown out. But they [the state] won't let me beat it, because they threatened my girl to take my baby away if she don't testify. So that's why I ain't going to trial."[5] In such accounts, the respondents affirm themselves in their interactions with legal authorities as masculine martyrs willing to shoulder the pain of criminal punishment to save their partners. Of course, as their descriptions of their intimate relationships during criminal proceedings indicate, men use this notion of having suffered to control their partners through feelings of remorse.

Through these dynamics, we begin to see the ways in which mandatory arrest and no-drop prosecution fail to have men assume responsibility for violence. Men's contact with the police and courts does not result in their recognition of themselves as perpetrators of violence, but in a continued evasion of violence, and the emergence of a masculine victim identity. But these are not all the outcomes resulting from respondents' encounters with the criminal justice system. In the last chapter, I move to examine the broader range of changes in subjectivity that abusers experience after being arrested and prosecuted.

6 Change in the Lives of Abusers

Past studies examining the impact of arrest and prosecution in changing batterers have focused on the question of recidivism, whether those punished for domestic violence are found to repeat their criminal behavior. The arrest experiments sponsored by the National Institute of Justice (NIJ) established that arrest deters men with a particular type of "stake in conformity," possessing a job (Maxwell et al. 2002).[1] More recent studies examining no-drop prosecution have consistently found that aggressive prosecution fails to deter subsequent abuse (Davis et al. 2003; Ford & Regoli 1993; Buzawa et al. 1999).

This chapter also considers the changes that abusers experience following their exposure to mandatory arrest and no-drop prosecution. Unlike the studies mentioned above, however, it does not seek to determine rates of recidivism. And perhaps it need not, since the gaps in this area of research do not concern *whether* offenders abuse again as much as *why* or *how* they abuse again. That is, while the sophisticated experimental designs and quantitative analyses of the arrest and prosecution studies confidently establish the outcomes resulting from these policies, they provide little insight into the context into which those outcomes are realized.

This chapter provides a look into this context by relating how research participants talked about the changes in their lives following contact with the police and courts. Specifically, it does this by examining two distinct temporal dimensions of abusers' experiences. The first is oriented to the past and includes the changes that the respondents reported having already experienced as a result of their legal encounters. The second is oriented to the future and includes the changes that respondents reported they are making or will make in their lives as a result of their encounters with the law.

This analysis finds that mandatory arrest and no-drop prosecution produce disparate effects in intimate abusers, including a greater religiosity following extended terms in jail as well as feelings of loss in different aspects of their lives. The detrimental consequences of these legal encounters for suspects are broader than previously noted. Beyond the actual and potential loss of jobs and intimate relationships, they also publicly expose the "private" violence of batterers, leaving them with stigmatized identities as criminals and "wife beaters" that affect various aspects of their daily lives. Abusers engage in different strategies to mitigate the deleterious impact of their stigmas, including defining themselves as distinct from "real" domestic batterers. In describing their futures, respondents express a will to avoid repeat contact with the criminal justice system. Additionally, they describe what I refer to as "self-governance projects" to realize this goal. Displaying different configurations of relations between the self, intimate and familial partner(s), and other social forces, these self-governance projects carry different implications for batterers' careers in intimate violence. While some evidence deterred violent subjectivities, others display reconstituted violent subjectivities calculated to better avoid detection from legal authorities.

Intimate Abusers and Change Experienced

Before examining the changes that respondents reported experiencing following arrest and prosecution, I want to first look at an element of change in their lives that did not necessarily figure centrally in their narratives but is nevertheless critical for considering the efficacy of mandatory arrest and no-drop prosecution. This is disruption of abusive intimate relationships. Historically, women victimized in violent relationships have faced the question, "Why does she stay?" But the fact that women who leave abusive relationships are actually at increased risk of severe assault demonstrates that "there is no greater challenge in the abuse field than getting *men* to exit from abusive relationships" [emphasis added] (Stark 2007:130). And indeed, disrupting violent relationships stands as one of the central goals of the current regime of domestic violence governance (Merry 1995).

In chapter 4, I noted that arrest disrupted the abusive relationships of this group of research participants in the short term, with 28 out of the 30 participants having been arrested on the night they were violent. Respondents' accounts of their lives following arrest and prosecution reveal that this disruption often comes to be permanent. At the time of their arrest, 21 out of the 29 respondents were violent against intimate partners with whom they were in active relationships, according to victim statements in the police reports (see Table 17).[2] Five were no longer in intimate relationships with their victims, while another three were in relationships whose status was uncertain. According to respondents' narratives, 12 out of the 21 active relationships (57.1%) had terminated by the time of their interviews. Additionally, the three relationships of uncertain status had ended.

Without victim reports, it is difficult to corroborate that these relationships did indeed end. Respondents, who evade responsibility for the violence they commit, may just as easily misrepresent the nature of their current contact with ex-intimate partners to conceal ongoing abuse. Nevertheless, accepting that this is an imperfect measure, the rate of relationship termination following contact with the criminal legal system reported here is higher than that reported in past research. In their Milwaukee arrest experiment, for instance, Sherman et al. (1992a) found a 45% separation rate for persons incarcerated overnight. Similarly, Campbell et al. (1994), in a longitudinal study comparing the categories of battered and not battered women, found that 43% of the battered women had left their abusers at the time of their follow-up interviews (105). Based on this group of abusers, then, mandatory arrest and no-drop prosecution achieve a high rate of long-term relationship disruption.

While termination of intimate relationships is a vital measure of the efficacy of criminal legal interventions against domestic violence, for abusers themselves it is but one meaningful outcome. In their narratives of change, a host of other results also proved significant. Here, I group these into three general categories: religiosity, loss, and stigma.

Religiosity. One change noted by six of the men participating in this study was becoming closer to their faith as a result of their contact with the criminal justice system. In each case, this change was connected to spending extended amounts of time incarcerated. Unable to bond out following their arrests, and exposed to prolonged periods of material and spatial deprivation, these respondents established a new relationship to religion. As Isaac noted, reflecting on his time in the Centralia County Jail, "I'll just say I pray more now. I just pray more."

The connection between jail and religiosity represents a more general element of incarceration culture (Ballesteros 1979:111–12). "They call it Christianity in jail," Aaron explained in his interview. "Christianity in jail, that's the only time you pick up a Bible." Despite the dismissive tone, respondents' increased religiosity in jail played a central role in their definition of self and the reasons for their detention. Aaron said later of his time in jail, "I did a lot of reading. It [reading the Bible] basically helps me. It help me. It help me sit down and realize who I am. What's my reason for being here, you know."

TABLE 17—Pseudonyms and Relationship Status of Respondents

Name	Relation Before Arrest	Relation After Arrest
1. Ann	Ended	Ended
2. Betty	Active	Ended
3. Adam	Active	Active
4. Bob	Active	Ended
5. Chris	Active	Ended
6. Dave	Ended	Ended
7. Eric	Active	Active
8. Frank	Ended	Ended
9. Gary	Active	Ended
10. Henry	—	—
11. Isaac	Active	Active
12. John	Active	Ended
13. Kevin	Active	Ended
14. Larry	Active	Active
15. Mike	Active	Ended
16. Nic	Uncertain	Ended
17. Oscar	Active	Active
18. Pete	Active	Active
19. Quinn	Uncertain	Ended
20. Ralph	Active	Ended
21. Steve	Active	Ended
22. Tom	Active	Active
23. Victor	Active	Active
24. Walter	Active	Ended
25. Aaron	Uncertain	Ended
26. Brett	Active	Ended
27. Carl	Ended	Ended
28. Doug	Active	Ended
29. Ed	Ended	Ended
30. Carrie	Active	Active

Reflection on oneself and one's actions in the solitude of jail is of course an intended effect of the penitentiary system (Newbold 2003:150–51). Through such effort, the offender will come to repent his crime. However, such reflection does not necessarily lead to a critical self-appraisal of one's criminal conduct. Instead, through the embrace of religion, it recasts the reasons for detention into spiritual, rather than criminal, terms. Chris noted in his interview:

> I've come to the conclusion that I had turned my back against God. And so now God turned his back against me. I feel like I'm being punished for living in the sinful ways that I have, living with women without being married to them. I had drank with some of them. And I had tried smoking marijuana with some of them.

Rather than viewing his detention as a punishment for unlawful abusive behavior *against* his intimate partner, Chris came while in jail to understand it as a punishment sanctioned by God for sinful behavior *with* intimate partners out of wedlock. In the process, the meaning of punishment for him was (re)defined.

For these men who believed that they were innocent of any statutory crime and were victims of an unjust legal system, religion offered a moral template for interpreting their actions that supersedes the laws dictated and exercised by state authorities. The notion that they had been punished for some higher purpose became a defining characteristic of their legal encounter. Like Chris, Aaron noted that his punishment was a sign from God. And like Chris, the crime committed was not abusive behavior against a woman, but immoral living against God with a woman. "My God," he said, "want me to sit down and acknowledge him more. Get a closer relationship instead of using this materialistic money and women." Kevin too explained that "what [he] did in the past," in terms of sinful living, "came back on [him]." As such, "This domestic dispute is just a piece of the puzzle. I think I was locked up for another reason, just to read through what's really going on around me."

In addition to helping infuse alternative meanings into the reasons for their punishment, religion also offers batterers a resource by which they can reorder the morality of the space and society in which they are participating. Rather than viewing themselves as bad, they see those who would incarcerate fellow human beings in such inhumane conditions as bad:

> I think these people are slaves to the devil. They come here and get paid for locking people up. And the politicians, they change the laws, and repeal them, and change them. I see the devil working at these people's backs. (Adam)

By embracing God, Adam located a moral resource for resisting the power of the jail and the inculcation of a negative moral identity.

The shift to a deeper religiosity on the part of intimate abusers provides further evidence that mandatory arrest and no-drop prosecution fail to increase responsibility for violence. Although few in number, these respondents found in the heart of the state's punitive criminal legal apparatus the cultural resources to redefine their criminal behavior in new ways that distanced them from violence. As such, the experiences of these men underscore the unpredictable outcomes resulting from the state's exercise of power against situations of intimate abuse.

Loss. A more common change reported by respondents was loss. Interviewees described experiencing loss in different aspects of their lives following their encounters with the police and courts. For some, the loss was financial. Tom, for instance, lost the job he had just begun after he failed to appear to work following his night in jail. "I didn't go back to work on that next day or anything because I was kind messed up," he explained, "So I called up and told them that I wasn't going to be able come in. And they said they needed me to come in that day, and if I wouldn't come in, then don't come back at all." Doug similarly emphasized the financial costs involved in taking his case to trial. "Financially, it's been devastating," he said, "Financially, it sucks, man. There's several thousand dollars that I had put up in the state's hands for no reason." In citing that there was "no reason" to have needed to spend money on his case, Doug reaffirmed his belief that the case against him was a sham.

Others noted loss in terms of family and intimate relationships. Brett focused on his partner's decision to leave him, depicting it as a hurtful void in his life:

> It [the criminal case] nearly destroyed my family. We no longer live together. She's living with another guy now. She threw it away. Those few months apart, we couldn't talk, we couldn't communicate. It destroyed my whole life. I'm hurt. I'm mad. It's just hard for me, man, and there's no way to fix it.

Brett blamed both the no-contact order imposed during his case ("we couldn't talk, we couldn't communicate") as well as his ex-girlfriend's own lack of commitment to their relationship ("She threw it away") for the loss he feels. Seeing his "life" destroyed, Brett assumed a fatalistic stance, claiming there's "no way to fix" the pain he suffers.

Carl described loss in terms of his intimate relationship as well as the surrogate family that her children provided him. "It all happened at the same time," he described, "breaking up with the girlfriend, the girlfriend going out with other guys, losing two kids that I love, I can never get past the kids." John too focused on the loss of contact with children. Thinking back to his time in jail, he recalled, "I was basically out of work and hadn't seen my daughter, basically on the verge of losing a lot of things."

In addition to the loss of persons in their lives, respondents reported the loss of trust in personal relationships. In some cases, this loss of trust involved relationships that remained active after the resolution of respondents' criminal cases. Steve, for instance, who was violent against a girlfriend he was seeing outside of his marriage, lost the trust of his wife. "My wife still don't trust me," he revealed, "When she see my cell phone ring . . . normally, I mean, I had this phone for about 10 years, and my phone ring, she would never touch it. Now, when it rings, she grabs it like I got an answering service. She just don't trust me."

More commonly, loss of trust was described by respondents whose partners had reported their abuse to the police. Having trusted their partners to endure their abusive behavior, these men interpreted their partners' calls for help as acts of betrayal. As a result, their trust in their partners was affected. Victor related that his experience with the criminal justice system was "affecting [him] a lot with the trust" he had for his partner, who appeared on the day of his trial to testify against him. His girlfriend did not ultimately testify against him. However, rather than interpreting her refusal to cooperate with the state as a show of faith in him and the relationship, he understood it as a betrayal.

For Doug and Chris, the loss of trust extended to personal relationships in general:

> I don't have any trust anymore for anybody. That's what it's done to me. I lost all that. I lost my balls. She was the one person, I mean, I could have murdered somebody or something like that, and if I told her, she would never say a word. (Doug)

> My faith and trust in women are really down now. I mean, I'm the type of person, if you treat me nice, then I'm going to think you're a nice person. I see now that it takes time to really get to know a person. I just can't take your word for it. (Chris)

For Doug, the fact that a trusted partner, whom he thought could be trusted with knowledge of his abusive self ("I could have murdered somebody . . . she would never say a word"), refused to endure his abuse any longer meant that he could no longer trust anyone. The loss of trust involved a loss of masculinity as well ("I lost my balls"), a response conveying how Doug interpreted trusting a partner with his abusive self as a particularly masculine characteristic. Chris, in the same way, interpreted his partner's contacting the police as a betrayal. As a result, his trust in women has been lost, and he noted that he will take more time in the future to evaluate partners before putting his faith in them.

These findings add greater insight into the variable costs of arrest and prosecution for abusers with different "stakes in conformity" (Sherman 1992). Those with jobs (Tom) and financial resources (Doug) risk losing them as a result of time missed from work and the expenses required to retain an attorney. However, even those unemployed and unmarried abusers with "nothing to lose," such as Victor and Chris, in fact lose much in losing trust in their partners. Importantly, they lose the assurance that their abuse can simply be hidden away from public view. And while this revelation generates feelings of betrayal in abusers, so too does it, as we will see next, increase the costs of their violence by generating a stigmatized identity through which others come to see them.

Stigma. In addition to these "losses," many respondents expressed concern with what they had gained through their experiences with the criminal justice system: a stigmatized identity as a criminal and "wife beater." In his collection of essays on the topic, Erving Goffman (1965) defines stigma as a "deeply discrediting" attribute (3). The attribute is relational rather than essential, meaning that what "stigmatizes one type of possessor can confirm the usualness of another, and therefore is neither credible nor discreditable as a thing in itself" (Goffman 1965:3). As a relational quality, a stigma comes to be identified by its possessor only through her or his interactions with other persons. "Those who have dealings with him fail to accord him the respect and regard which the uncontaminated aspects of his social identity have led them to anticipate extending, and have led him to anticipate receiving" (Goffman 1965:8–9).

Respondents' narratives revealed that that their legal encounters had left them with stigmatized identities that contaminated different everyday social interactions. For one, encounters in the formal economy forced respondents to identify themselves as convicted criminals, which hindered their ability to secure employment and other financial services. Carrie, for example, was working at a large retail store when she was arrested for abusing her boyfriend. Promised a promotion before the arrest, she found that the promotion never materialized. She explained, "They treated me differently after I called them and let them know I was arrested. [They were] treating me, you know, as if, 'Okay, well, if she sticks with this overnight position, then maybe she'll just quit and we won't have to fire her.'" Identifying for herself the stigmatized identity, Carrie understood it to harm her ability to locate subsequent employment. "They [potential employers] treat you differently," she reported, "They pretty much treat you like you're a criminal even though it could be for something small. So, it's really hard to find employment right now."

Other respondents related similar problems following their encounters with the law. Chris wanted to get life insurance, to save his family "the burden of burying me and all that," but the insurance company told him, "because I have felonies with violence, I can't get life insurance." John noted that people "look at me differently" at work since his arrest. Carl mentioned his conviction affecting job applications. "I've had to fill out a job application since then and had to put 'yes' where it says, 'Have you ever been convicted of a misdemeanor or felony?'" Doug "was doing specialty work, 160 bucks an hour, specialty welding at the [local] car plant," a side job he would often get through a friend of a friend. After his arrest, he stated, "I don't get that no more."

While the stigma affecting respondents in these interactions was that of being a criminal, the stigma impacting them in other interactions was that of being a domestic batterer. Carl explained, "I feel like I'm marked as a wife beater or a hothead and I go out and get into bar fights and stuff like that." Steve, for his part, described the shift in the way his friends perceived him.

> My friends, a couple of them call me Mr. Goodbar. Mr. Goodbar, don't do shit wrong. I would crack on their asses when they have a fucking domestic, you know. I'd be the main one calling them a dumb fuck. My friends tell you about me, he's a good guy, no problems, no violence, and when he hears about it, he's the first one to try to make the motherfucker feel bad. So then, after all these years, now I have a domestic. It's a big change. They look at you like, "You ain't shit."

Here, Steve related undergoing a fundamental transformation in his social identity at work. At one time viewing himself as the primary person who would stigmatize men arrested for domestic violence ("I would crack on their asses when they have a fucking domestic"), he now reported being the one stigmatized ("They look at you like, 'You ain't shit.'"). In the process, he had lost his identity as a good person ("Mr. Goodbar") in the eyes of his peers.

The stigma of being a batterer affects intimate relationships as well. Aaron described a date with a woman who knew he had been convicted of domestic violence. When he tried to get close to her, the woman became apprehensive. "I was trying to hug her, and she like, 'Aaron!' I'm like, 'What's wrong!?! I ain't going to hit you! I wouldn't do that.'" Through the public exposure of his intimate abuse, Aaron's future relationships with intimate partners have been affected.

Learning that others now see them and will relate to them differently as a result of their domestic violence arrests, respondents reported making efforts to conceal their stigmatized identities in order "to pass" (Goffman 1965:80) as "normal" citizens, friends, and intimate partners. In effect, having had their intimate abuse revealed, batterers worked to reprivatize the violence through various acts of deception. Trying to find employment after his encounter with the law, Mike did not mention his criminal history to potential employers. He explained, "I've just gotten lucky [that] a couple jobs have not [done background checks]. A friend of a friend that I knew at the farm supply shop hooked me up with a guy at a flooring surfaces job. So they really didn't really do a background check. They just went off the word of this guy I knew for a long time, and I got a job."

Aaron and Carl hid their batterer stigmas from potential intimate partners. Aaron, who above described one woman being afraid of him after learning of his domestic violence conviction, noted, "I don't tell them, because I think they'll look at me different." Carl echoed this response. "I'm certainly not going to tell a new girlfriend that I've been arrested for hitting on my other girlfriend. I suppose that's not something that I'm happy with. I wouldn't feel right in a relationship not telling her, but I don't think I would . . . she'll look at me in a different light." Fearful that their stigmas will endanger the possibilities of future intimacy, these men have simply chosen to keep these elements of their identities hidden. In addition, Carl anticipated feeling guilty about his foreseen attempts "to pass," fulfilling Goffman's (1965) claim that passing in "intimate relationships," which are "ratified in our society by mutual confession of invisible failings," will cause a possessor of stigma "to admit his situation" or "feel guilty for not doing so" (74).

Beyond these efforts to manage stigmatized identities in different social interactions, respondents' narratives also evidenced attempts to manage stigmatized identities in relation to the self. Like the men mentioned in the last chapter who described themselves as caring and accommodating, these men looked to define their selves in contrast to persons who they claimed were truly violent:

> This could be your 13th or your 12th interview. A lot of those guys that you interviewed previously could have had this stuff that went on in their lives with that abuse in a domestic relationship. I'm not that kind of person. I'm not a violent person. (Kevin)

> Some of these cases are domestics. These guys are really hardcore. Some of these guys are in on domestics, and they're catching these domestic cases. They are really domestics. They will beat their girlfriend up. I've seen guys beat their girlfriend up at the clubs. (Ed)

Similar to the abusers Bancroft (2002:296) works with, who have "a mental image of what a 'real abuser' is like, and it isn't 'him,'" these men looked to differentiate themselves from those "hardcore" cases that "really" are "domestics." In doing so, they worked to insulate their self-identity from the contamination of the stigmatized identity they perceived in the gaze of others.

Respondents frequently offered statements that similarly attempted to distinguish themselves from truly violent persons. "I don't hit women. I've never hit a woman," Ralph claimed, presenting as evidence of his innocence the incriminating fact that "this is my first domestic." Such contradictions are inherent to these efforts as respondents, who were contacted for the research project precisely because they had committed abuse, attempted to describe themselves as something other than batterers. Doug adds, "I've restrained her. I never hit her. I can't hit a woman. If I did, she'd still have scars or something." Like Ed, he saw the difference between real domestic violence and his own behaviors in the severity. If he were really violent, and not just physically restraining, his violence would leave marks.

These attempts to define the self as nonviolent are important to consider in assessing the efficacy of mandatory arrest and no-drop prosecution. On the one hand, like the increased religiosity reported by respondents, they provide further indications that the abusers participating in this study did not come to claim responsibility for their abuse. This surely counts as a shortcoming of these policies. On the other hand, they, like the findings on loss, evidence punitive aftereffects accruing from arrest and prosecution that increase the costs of committing intimate abuse. Having had their private intimate violence publicly exposed to friends and other relations, these respondents faced the burden of stigmatization in their private and public lives. Again, batterers who were employed either lost or risked losing their jobs and experience difficulty in locating new ones. And those with seemingly "nothing to lose" in fact can be seen to be losing or at risk of losing much. This includes not only the possibility of locating employment or securing vital financial services such as life insurance, but also the possibility of future intimate relationships as well as social acceptance as good people. In response, abusers seek to reprivatize their violence and (re)define their selves to resist contamination from stigmatized batterer identities and "pass" as normal, nonviolent citizens and intimate partners.

Intimate Abusers and Change Imagined

The review of outcomes discussed thus far in this work has established that domestic violence offenders do not assume responsibility for their actions following their arrest and prosecution. Nor do they perceive their punishments as just. However, in discussing the changes they foresee in their lives, respondents expressed a clear will to avoid future contact with the criminal justice system, a subjective orientation important in efforts to change criminal offenders.

This sentiment was common among the participants, though it was often expressed in different terms. Adam, who had previously spent time in a federal penitentiary before spending time at the Centralia County Jail on his domestic violence charge, simply noted being tired of incarceration, "Man, I don't want to go back there [jail]. I'm tired of being tired, I got sick of being sick." Ann, on the other hand, had defiance on her mind. Having once failed to comply with the terms of her probation, which landed her back in jail, she was determined this time around to complete her sentence, to avoid jail and defy those who believed she was incapable of doing it. "If I have to do everything twice, I will just [do it] to show them, 'You know what? Screw you. I am going do it.' I have to do it. I can see what happens if you don't. Bam, you go to jail." Mike viewed avoiding the law as part of being a mature, masculine subject. "I'm a grown-ass man," he said, "I shouldn't have nothing like that [criminal case] over my head." Part of this mature masculinity was having the ability to freely move through different social interactions without the stigma of criminality revealing itself. He continued, "I should be a citizen, a law-abiding citizen, so I can go over to anybody and put my name in the computer and, 'Oh no, there ain't nothing against me.'"

Having felt the punitive costs associated with being arrested and prosecuted for domestic violence, these respondents had no desire to feel them again. In addition, and more significant to the efforts to change batterers' behaviors, 26 out of the 30 persons (see Table 18) participating in the study described different courses of action that they were pursuing or would pursue to realize this will, including trying to quit abusing alcohol, working on anger management, and ending intimate relationships. To conclude this final section of findings, I review four types of strategies described by respondents: *submitting the self, controlling the self, freeing the self,* and *fitting the self.* As this review demonstrates, each type involves a different strategy for working the self in relation to intimate and familial others, as well as larger social forces, to avoid renewed contact with the law. In essence, these serve as amateur projects of "self-governance" (Valverde 1998),[3] personally defined programs of action calculated to manage the self away from situations that would result in further punishment. Involving dissimilar configurations of relations between the self, the other, and social forces, these four self-governance projects hold different implications for batterers' careers in intimate violence.

Submitting the Self. The first of the four strategies involves religion once again. This is *submitting the self* before God to avoid problems. To provide an example, Betty, after her arrest, found herself angry at her cousins, who

TABLE 18—Strategies of Self-Governance, Abuser Type, and Deterred Violent Subjectivities

Name	Self-Governance Strategy	Abuser Type	Deterred
1. Ann	Free Self	Situational	Y
2. Betty	Submit Self; Free Self	Situational	Y
3. Adam	—	Intimate Terrorism	N
4. Bob	Control Self	Situational	Y
5. Chris	Submit Self; Free Self; Fit Self	Situational	N
6. Dave	Control Self; Free Self	Intimate Terrorism	Y
7. Eric	Free Self	Intimate Terrorism	N
8. Frank	Free Self	Intimate Terrorism	N
9. Gary	Free Self; Fit Self	Intimate Terrorism	N
10. Henry	Submit Self; Free Self	—	Y
11. Isaac	Submit Self; Control Self	Situational	Y
12. John	Control Self; Free Self	—	N
13. Kevin	Submit Self; Free Self; Fit Self	Situational	N
14. Larry	Submit Self; Control Self	Intimate Terrorism	Y
15. Mike	Control Self; Free Self	Situational	Y
16. Nic	Free Self	Intimate Terrorism	N
17. Oscar	Submit Self; Control Self	Intimate Terrorism	Y
18. Pete	—	—	N
19. Quinn	Free Self	—	Y
20. Ralph	Free Self	—	Y
21. Steve	Free Self	Situational	Y
22. Tom	Control Self	Situational	Y
23. Victor	Control Self	Intimate Terrorism	Y
24. Walter	Free Self; Fit Self	Situational	N
25. Aaron	Control Self; Free Self	Intimate Terrorism	Y
26. Brett	—	Intimate Terrorism	N
27. Carl	Control Self	Intimate Terrorism	Y
28. Doug	—	Intimate Terrorism	N
29. Ed	Free Self; Fit Self	Situational	N
30. Carrie	Control Self	Situational	Y

had corroborated her partner's story to the police that she had battered him. Feeling betrayed by her own family, she looked for divine intervention to deal with the anger:

> I prayed to God, asked him to help me take that anger away from me, and he did because I was really hating. I wanted to go and really retaliate. That's what I felt at that time, but I didn't want to feel like that. And I just want to go on with my life, and I'm not going to be bothered with them [her cousins]. I'm not even going to be near that side of town.

As Betty's example demonstrates, in submitting the self to God, the individual perceives her own self to be an incapable force for handling the problem before her. Betty was "really hating" and wanting "to go and really retaliate." The emphasis "really" signals that this is an unusually strong emotion she was experiencing. The resolution to this problem, which if not solved promised more violence and potentially another encounter with the law, was found not through the self alone, but by through a correspondence with God, which provided the self divine intervention ("I . . . asked him to help me take that anger away from me, and he did").

Six respondents cited this strategy of submitting the self before God. And in these other projects, the relation of forces was similar to that described by Betty. The person yielded the self to the power and authority of God in the hopes of realizing change.

> She's [partner] a real religion girl, and she's real honest. I got a good woman, and I don't want to lose her. She stood by me on my operations, dropped me off at school, you know, I appreciate all that. The more I think about it, when I get done, I'm going to church and changing my life. I'm tired of going over in that court. (Larry)

> Whether it be Christian, Muslim, or whatever it is, we always have some kind of relationship with God. So she [my mother] just telling me to just put God first and talk to God about it [a problem]. I'm like, "Sure, cool." (Kevin)

> I'm a God-fearing man and marriage is very important. I'm going to hang in there until death do us part. That's what the Bible says. Whatever she [wife] got on her mind . . . she got a hidden agenda. But you got to be careful, just don't get me caught up in nothing again. (Oscar)

For Larry, going to church was the vehicle through which he could change his life. Kevin's mother had him promise to prioritize God to deal with his problems. Oscar believed following the dictates of the Bible was central in his effort to not get "caught up in nothing again."

These examples also demonstrate that what respondents perceived the self receiving from God and religion differed in each case. Betty received divine intervention to remove the anger from herself. Larry, on the other hand, saw religion as a means for maintaining a supportive social network around his self. He described the various ways in which his religious intimate partner had taken care of him. Afraid that his alcoholism and violence would result in his losing her, leaving him alone and unable to care for his self, he thought to change his life and become more religious. Oscar, for his part, found a set of moral guidelines by which to manage his self. His partner might be scheming, and trying to involve him in trouble, but adherence to the word of the Bible will allow him to avoid it.

Given the variability in how these respondents relate the self to God and religion, submitting the self as a program of self-governance carries different implications for respondents' intimate and family violence. In Betty's case, this strategy possesses a preventive component, promising to help her avoid conflicts with her family that could lead to violence. Larry, an alcoholic, similarly believed that the support of his partner, as well as the church community, will better help him manage his alcohol problem, which would prevent future violence against her. In Oscar's case, religion played a more ominous role, dictating that he should "hang in there" with his marriage to a partner, whom he described as having a hidden agenda, "until death do us part." Considering his history of controlling and violent behavior against his partner, Oscar's project for change does not promise to positively affect his abusive behavior in the future.

Controlling the Self. The second strategy of self-governance is *controlling the self* during conflicts. This strategy was noted by 11 respondents. Most often, they described it simply in terms of "walking away" from conflicts:

> I'm more focused on making sure that I walk away from trouble. In other words, if you reached across the table and slapped me right now, in the past I might have done something about it. Now, I would probably just walk away, because I don't feel like the police would believe me if they got here and I said that you slapped me across the face. (Carl)

> I promise you, I won't make that mistake again, of putting my hands on somebody and having to be carted off, arrested. Before that happens, I know I'm going the other way. (Mike)

Every time we get into an argument, it's in the back of my head that she probably call the police and they going to say, "Oh yeah, we did pick him up before for a domestic." So, basically I just let her win the argument now. You can have the conversation. And I walk out. I'm gone. I got my own car now. I'm riding out. (Tom)

Now, when we argue, if we get into an argument, we'll just walk off, or one of us will stop the argument, agree to it much faster, like, "Okay, you're right. Right." Just play the dumb role and go in the other room. (Victor)

In these examples, a much different notion of self is at work than that present in submitting the self. Here, the self is viewed as a sufficient force of individual change, capable of controlling situations and preventing violence. Rather than calling upon God for help, the self can simply "walk off" or "go the other way."

As the quotes of Tom and Victor demonstrate, those espousing this strategy of self-governance viewed domestic violence as a dynamic interaction that escalates from arguments to physical violence. In their experience, a certain borderline divided the performance of arguing with the performance of violence. And again, it is the self that will manage this boundary, stopping the individual and having him walk off before the interaction reaches the level of violence.

The lingering effects of criminal legal punishments are also on clear display in these examples. The injustice Carl believed he experienced during his encounter with the police figured centrally in his adoption of this strategy of self-governance. Not believing that police would believe him, even if he were a clear victim of abuse, he decided that walking away is the best way to "avoid trouble." Mike too had being "carted off" on his mind in deciding that it is better to "go the other way" than put your hands on someone. These comments reveal how the expressions of agency embedded in these self-defined projects are shaped in relation to the exercise of power by legal authorities.

In terms of implications for future intimate violence, controlling the self is the most promising of the four projects, despite the fact that these respondents view conflict as an inevitable part of intimate relationships. Indeed, they cannot imagine relationships without it. And Tom reported having been in several arguments with his girlfriend since his arrest. Nevertheless, the fact that these persons viewed their selves as the force capable of stopping conflicts with intimate partners before they escalate into violence offers the hope that they will not repeat their violent behavior in the future.

Freeing the Self. The third strategy of change respondents described was *freeing the self* from personal relationships, whether from the particular intimate and/or familial partner(s) they abused in the past or intimate partners in general. This was the most often mentioned strategy, noted by 15 respondents. Like those *controlling the self,* the respondents adhering to this strategy believed conflict is an inevitable part of personal relationships. Distinctly, however, these respondents will avoid rather than manage these conflicts by forgoing personal relationships:

> She's [sister] a vindictive bitch and I can't trust her and be around her. Of course, she wants to be best friends. But I can't trust her, because the second I let my guard down, and, you know, "I love you, sister. Let's please forget about the past," that's about the time she'll pick up the phone and call 911. (Ann)

> I don't plan to have any further relationships with her, because we two different people. (Kevin)

> Man, one thing this teaches you, don't ever get married. I can't tell you how much this has screwed up my life. (Quinn)

Believing that her sister would call the police again if they got into one of their frequent sibling fights, Ann promised herself to simply not have a relationship with her. Kevin too saw himself and his girlfriend as an incompatible pair, leading to his decision to terminate the relationship. Quinn's experiences with the law following his conflicts with his wife led him to give up on the institution of marriage altogether.

Freeing the self can be a more complicated project than controlling the self, since it requires material resources. Henry, wanting to move away from his brother who called the police on him, noted, "My life is going to be a lot different. I'm getting away from my brother. I'm getting my own place. He's just going to have to do it on his own from now on." Of course, for this group of participants, who are predominantly low-income, gathering the resources necessary to be free is a challenge. For this reason, Chris combined a program of freeing his self from intimate relationships with submitting himself to his church, a community center offering the promise of employment. He noted, "I am going back to my church and just, you know, trying to get a job, getting my own place. I guess I'll stay in a shelter until I can get back on my feet."

Freeing the self as a mode of self-governance also possesses a darker character in terms of its meaning for the partners of abusers. For one, the narratives of some respondents illustrate that freeing the self also served as a strategy for retaliating against partners who either called the police or are cooperating with the state:

This relationship, it's been going on for a while. But I've been thinking, I don't think I'm going to continue with it after this particular incident that happened, especially if she's not willing to go in there and tell what really happened, what went on, and try to make things at least easier for me. (John)

I'm not with her anymore. We were off and on. But after this, I haven't seen her or spoken with her since. *Why's that?* 'Cuz she lied and got me involved with all this now. (Ralph)

The sense of betrayal that abusers described after their partners reported their violence is evident in these examples. John was upset that his partner might not "try to make things at least easier" for him, while Ralph felt betrayed, claiming that his ex-partner had "lied" to authorities and got him involved with the law. In response, they both planned to punish their partners by terminating the relationships. The fact that they planned to retaliate by terminating the relationship rather than physically assaulting their partners is encouraging, and it gives further evidence of the efficacy of punitive criminal legal interventions in altering the violent subjectivities of abusers. However, the actions of these men, both of whom were employed at the time of their arrest, also cut their partners off from vital sources of income and increased the punitive costs they endure for having asked the state for help with their violent relationships (Davies et al. 1998:51).

Conversely, freeing the self can also serve as a masculine defense mechanism to manage feelings of rejection and mask their "emotional dependency" on their partners (Dutton 1998:45). Independence and autonomy are core characteristics of the "self-made man" idealized throughout American history (Kimmel 1996:13–43). And indeed, plans to free the self from intimate relationships are expressions of this masculine ideal. Feeling betrayed by intimate partners, these abusive men have decided to go it alone. However, for some batterers, the decision to go it alone had been made for them. Their partners had called the police on them, had taken orders of protection out against them, and were cooperating with the state to terminate the relationship. Rather than admit to themselves that their partners had rejected them, these men reported that they decided to live on their own.

Frank's ex-girlfriend, for example, took various measures to terminate their relationship, including calling the police and obtaining a restraining order. In response, Frank stalked her, even kidnapping her on one occasion. Eventually, he was arrested for violating the order of protection. In discussing his future, Frank noted that he was going to "go on and live [his] life":

I've got to live my life. [If] she wants to live her life without me in it, that's fine. You know, I'll spend my money and drive up here when I can from Peacock and pick up my kids. . . . I've made the changes I need to make. Someone else needs to make the changes. I'm going to go on, and live my life, and do what I can, and just accept things the way they are instead of trying to change [them] my-self. If it's something that's meant to be, if we're meant to be together again, who knows? But I've got to go on and live my life. I can't just fold up and curl up in a little ball and hide from the world.

In this sequence, Frank presented his relationship with his ex-girlfriend in ambiguous terms, using the word "if" to depict the situation as uncertain. Thus, he hid the fact that his ex-partner had repeatedly voiced her desire and acted to end the relationship. Further, he also presented his self as the engine of change that will resolve the uncertainty. Rather than waiting for his partner to make up her mind (which she of course already had), he was going to take charge because he could not "just fold up and curl up in a little ball." Through this plan, then, Frank denied the rejection of his partner.

Of course, one hopes that Frank, and other batterers who announced plans of freeing the self as defense mechanisms, will still pursue their plans of independence. Given his history of stalking, as well as the num-ber of distortions present in his thinking, it is hard to be confident that he will. Still, the fact that he has imagined himself living in a town, Peacock, that is located 90 miles from Plainsville, provides some hope that the punitive impact of his legal encounters has terminated his abusive and controlling behavior.

Finally, in addition to serving as a defense mechanism, freeing the self can also function as an offense mechanism through which men conspire to get partners back or meet new ones. For these men, freeing the self is not a permanent course of action. It is a temporary strategy designed to give them the time to empower their selves to financial and emotional indepen-dence, which they believe will make them more attractive to others:

> Hopefully, I'll be able to get back with Leisha. I just I hope I don't always have to be looking at her that same way I did before she thought I wasn't shit. She said, "Hey, you do this, you do that, you know, get everything together," be-cause I wasn't really working for the last two or three months in Texas. So that right there set the tone that it's time to do something different. . . . I need to come to the table with something. If I want to get with Leisha, get back with her, I need to let her know that, "Hey, I can do all the stuff that we were doing on my own. Got a car, got a house, and I'm working." (Mike)

> We're not kids no more, but I think we both know what we need to do. Once I get these [batterer intervention] classes done and I'm off probation, I'm gonna go to Job Corps. So, that will give us some time apart and let us know what we

really want. If she wants to be with me when I get back, then we'll be able to live life the right way financially. (Eric)

And have you been in any other relationships since then [divorce from wife]? A couple here and there. *And how are those?* I don't really care. I usually tell them exactly that. I just don't really care. . . . A lot of girls call me and I say, "No, I don't want to go." *What do you think that's about?* Oh they're just horny. . . . I just really don't care. They don't sense that I'm going to be with them. So, it's sort of a neat little psychological deal. (Nic)

Both Mike and Eric wanted to get back together with intimate partners they were no longer with. To do so, they believed they needed to demonstrate their ability to be independent breadwinners. Mike stated explicitly that employment status affected his ex-girlfriend's perception of him ("she thought I wasn't shit . . . because I wasn't really working"). To change that perception and renew the relationship, he will show her that he can support both of them by himself ("I can do all the stuff that we were doing on my own").

Nic, meanwhile, found himself becoming more sexually appealing to women as he cared less about them. While he professed that he "really" did not care about establishing future relationships with women following his divorce, it was not clear what he did not care about, the possibility of new intimate relationships or the women contacting him. In either case, the fact that he viewed his expressions of indifference toward these women as "a neat little psychological deal" evidences that he did indeed value the relationship to potential partners that he interpreted his independence giving him.

These men are clearly tapping into the idealized notions of American masculinity noted above. In pursuing and performing prized gender identities as independent men and capable "breadwinners" (Morgan 2005:169), they look to achieve new masculine subjectivities that will translate into greater power in their intimate relationships. Mike and Eric were confident they could attract their partners back, so long as they could secure the resources necessary to make them good providers. Nic played the part of the tough, emotionally detached man who could not be bothered to care about women. Performing this role, he realized a new authority relative to the women who contacted him.

The implications of projects of freeing the self clearly vary with regard to careers in intimate violence. Abusers who sincerely have exited or plan to exit intimate relationships possess a plain strategy for avoiding domestic violence in the future. Conversely, those abusers who used independence either as a defense mechanism for denying their partners' rejection or as an offense mechanism to increase their power in intimate relationships do not hold the same promise for avoiding future abuse. In the case of the latter, increased financial and emotional strength in the relationship would provide these men additional mechanisms through which they could exercise new forms of control over their partners.

Fitting the Self. The final strategy of self-governance reported by respondents to avoid renewed contact with the criminal justice system was *fitting the self* to the "right woman." Respondents pursuing this approach, all five of whom were men, had experienced intimate relationships that did not work out in the past. Rather than giving up on relationships altogether, however, these men related that they would seek out new partners who would be more compatible with them.

In discussing his future and the possibility of new intimate relationships, Gary noted

> I'm just gonna keep the opportunity open and look for somebody that actually has the intentions that I like, that could manage stuff on their own, that is right for my tastes basically.

Implying that his last relationship was hampered by his and his partner's dissimilar interests, Gary hoped a new partner might better fit his self.

If "finding the right partner" echoes themes of individual choice and compatibility, elements of relationships that are highly valued in contemporary society (Cate & Lloyd 1992:33), as an approach to the self-governance of domestic violence, it has grave implications. Having had previous partners report their abuse to the police, these men sought companions who could be trusted to endure their abusive selves without contacting authorities.

> If you're gonna call the police on me, then it's not gonna stop. It's not gonna stop, and I choose not to deal with them type of women. In every relationship, you're supposed to trust, you're supposed to have faith in people, and you're supposed to be able to count on them. So, if you do that, I'm gonna do this, and that's walk away from you. There's too many other women out there that's gonna treat me a lot better. (Walter)

> It's [a relationship] like a team, you know. We got the coach, the father, the little children, like the teammates or whatever. We got to work together. We all in this together. This is a household, so we got to portray that it's a household. We all have to put forth an effort to hold it together. If it's not held together, it'll fall apart. We got to respect each other; it's all about respect. (Kevin)

Walter explicitly stated that he expected his partner to not call the police on him, which he considered a show of "trust" and "faith." If his partner could not be trusted to accept his abuse, he, like the partners who free the self, would retaliate by terminating the relationship. In addition, he would seek out a new partner who would treat him "a lot better" by not calling the police. Kevin's comments were seemingly more egalitarian ("we got to work together"). Of course, his concept of the family "team" is highly patriarchal. The "father" is coach. The "children" are teammates. Tellingly, he failed to mention a role for the "partner" or "wife." For Kevin, the woman who would be willing to take on this type of partnership is the right woman for him.

In contrast with the previous programs of self-governance, this one involves no strategy for working on the self, whether through God, self-control, or independence. Indeed, these men, who evaded responsibility for violence, found nothing wrong with their selves. Having been punished for being abusive, what needed to change was not the self, but the partners with whom the self interacts. By finding a partner willing to endure this self, these men foresaw themselves being able to live their lives without renewed contact with the criminal justice system.

Gloomily, these men looking to fit the self were confident about their chances of finding the "right woman." Walter believed there were "many women out there that's gonna treat [him] better" by not calling the police. Unfortunately, he is probably correct. Set against the backdrop of a conservative community that does not convict domestic batterers, and a society that equates intimate abuse almost solely with severe violence against helpless victims (Stark 2007),[4] the efforts of these abusers to find partners willing to accept their controlling behavior will be buoyed by larger cultural forces. In this sense, batterers' individual strategies for avoiding detection conspire with larger gender structures, threatening to reprivatize these men's intimate abuse.

The four programs of self-governance that intimate abusers construct carry different implications for careers in violence. In three of these programs —submitting the self, controlling the self, and freeing the self—some signs of a deterred violent subjectivity can be detected. These abusers want to avoid repeated contact with the punishments they were exposed to, and they express intentions to avoid those behaviors of domestic violence that led to their arrest. Betty calls upon God to remove the anger from her to avoid renewed violence. Others will rely on the self to walk away from conflict when arguments arise. Others will free the self from relationships that they perceive to be inherently conflictual.

Conversely, those fitting the self to the "right woman," submitting the self to the moral dictates of God rather than the state, and freeing the self to deny rejection and to strengthen themselves in future intimate relationships demonstrate little concern with avoiding the behaviors that led to their arrests. Rather, they reconstitute their violent selves to avoid detection. These strategies then evidence subjects who have not been deterred from violence.

It is important to keep in mind, however, that these projects are not mutually exclusive. Some participants expressed the intent to pursue different strategies for change within the same narrative. Indeed, 13 out of the 30 respondents mixed plans of self-governance in their interviews (see Table 18). And like the individual projects themselves, these combinations can be evaluated in terms of their prospects for future intimate abuse.

On the one hand, some combinations rendered negative projects, such as submitting the self, into more promising ones. For instance, Oscar, who vowed to stay in his marriage until "death do us part," also noted, "I'm more susceptible [during arguments] to just give in quicker . . . she wins because there's no way I can win, because if something happens, I'm the one that's going to go to jail no matter what happens to her." As such, Oscar both submitted his self to God and controlled his self. This mixing of subjective orientations provides greater promise that he will avoid violence in the future. Eight out of thirteen of the combined responses involved categories of submitting, controlling, or freeing the self. These combinations exhibited deterred violent subjectivities.

On the other hand, combinations involving fitting the self gave otherwise promising projects a more ominous tone. Five out of thirteen respondents offered such combinations. One example was Ed, who said that he was looking for the "right woman" and also expressed an ability to free the self from relationships. "When she shows me signs of that [calling the police], I'll know how to break away from that earlier. I'll start seeing similar traits . . . then it's time to leave before it even escalates." While it is positive that he would break away from the relationship or conflict before it escalated to violence, the concern, of course, is that he would move from relationship to relationship until he found a partner who would be willing to endure him without contacting authorities. These combinations of stories evidenced nondeterred violent subjectivities.

To the extent that the threats posed by intimate terrorists and situationally violent abusers differ, it is important to consider these projects and their evidence of deterred violent subjectivities by batterer type. In Table 19, I do this, summarizing deterred violent subjectivities by batterer type (also see Table 18 for individual listings). This table shows that the projects described by situationally violent offenders demonstrated a higher percentage of deterred violent subjectivities (66.6%) than did those of intimate terrorists (46.2%). These numbers do not amount to a stark contrast between the two groups. Nevertheless, they do demonstrate that the intimate terrorists in this study appeared more resistant to positive change than did the situationally violent abusers. And looking at individual cases, the differences between the two are telling. For instance, the intimate terrorist group included two men, Adam and Doug, who failed to report any plan for self-governance (versus one, Brett, in the situationally violent group) and three men, Eric, Frank, and Nic, whose programs of freeing the self were not credible. While Eric and Nic both hinted that they anticipated future relationships in which they would exercise more power over partners, Frank's ambiguous description of his partner's termination of their relationship contradicted his vision of an independent self. In sum, the intimate terrorists in this study were less likely to see the need for change in their selves and were less able to express programs of independence. This suggests that the subjective orientations that make intimate terrorists more lethal abusers in intimate relationships—heightened attachment to and control over partners—also made them more resistant to change following contact with legal authorities.

These findings complicate what has been an otherwise negative assessment of mandatory arrest and no-drop prosecution. Although the respondents in this study do not take responsibility for their violence and see themselves as victims of an unjust criminal legal system, some do exhibit deterred violent subjectivities. Additional research would, of course, be needed that included the past and present partners of these abusers, to verify their pursuit of these strategies and to report on their performance. Nevertheless, the findings evidence that aggressive criminal legal interventions against domestic violence do achieve change in the violent orientations of abusers.

Discussion

Punishment carries greater consequences for domestic violence suspects than previously noted. These include not only the loss of jobs and trust in marriages, which affect those with "high stakes in conformity," but also the loss of the assurance that their abuse will be kept private by their partners. Public exposure of private violence costs batterers their social recognition as normal, nonviolent citizens and intimate partners, a stigmatization that affects various aspects of their lives, from the ability to secure employment to the ability to realize intimacy with new partners. To mitigate these costs, batterers attempt to reprivatize their violence by keeping their abusive histories secret and defining their selves as nonviolent. The consequences of their violent pasts continue to weigh on them as they discuss their futures. Most express a will to avoid contact with the criminal justice system. In addition, they describe particular plans for governing the self in order to realize this goal. Involving different configurations between the self, intimate

TABLE 19—Deterred Violent Subjectivities by Abuser Type

Abuser Type	Deterred	Nondeterred
Situationally Violent	66.6% (8/12)	33.3% (4/12)
Intimate Terrorist	46.2% (6/13)	53.8% (7/13)

other, and social forces such as religion and employment, these programs of self-governance carry different implications for abusers' careers in intimate abuse. While some evidence deterred batterer subjectivities, others carry little hope for change in their performance of violence.

Foretelling Failure: The Challenges of Long-Term Deterrence. The self-governance projects detailed in this chapter represent important contributions to our understanding of the impact of mandatory arrest and no-drop prosecution. At the theoretical level, they reinforce the point, demonstrated in chapter 4, that individuals actively participate in the outcomes they experience from legal encounters. Prevailing thinking on the efficacy of aggressive arrest and prosecution is heavily structuralist. The logic of the "stakes in conformity" thesis (Maxwell et al. 2002) is that jobs, when mixed with punishment, will compel batterers to avoid violence in the future. Conversely, the absence of these structural forces predicts renewed violence. However, this chapter has shown also that abusers define for themselves different programs for enacting personal change to avoid contact with the criminal justice system. And these plans hold different implications for future performances of violence.

Part and parcel of this insight is a reinterpretation of the "stakes in conformity" thesis itself. To date, criminologists have claimed that those with "low stakes in conformity" are not deterred by arrest because they simply have nothing to lose by getting arrested again. However, the narratives of batterers contradict this claim. Unemployed (and unmarried) batterers still have much to lose. Most centrally, they lose social recognition as normal, nonviolent people, which affects future prospects of employment and intimacy as well as their self-worth. The efforts of respondents in this study to present themselves as normal and nonviolent belies the notion that they are in want of something to lose.

So, then, how does employment matter? On the one hand, it provides resources needed to control situations of violence. It is well known that domestic violence victims with more access to economic resources are better able to manage their situations of violence (Kurz 1998:204–5). As a result, women from higher socioeconomic groups report experiencing less domestic violence than their less wealthy counterparts (Rennison & Welchans 2000:10). And while it has been assumed that domestic violence offenders, by virtue of being batterers, possess the goal of controlling their partners and preventing them from leaving relationships, past research as well as the narratives of the men in this study demonstrate that not all batterers are alike. For those sincerely wanting to leave relationships, a lack of resources may result in failed strategies of self-governance. Chris, for instance, planned to move away from his partner, who called the police to report his abuse. He recognized that this plan was contingent on finding a place to live as well as a job to support himself. Of course, the job prospects for an unskilled, unemployed, middle-aged black man like Chris are not great. Nor are the prospects of finding affordable housing, since prior drug convictions preclude his receiving state housing assistance. If he is unable to secure the resources he needs to be independent, he might be expected to return to intimate relationships with female partners who, in addition to providing intimacy, provide housing and sources of income.

It should be noted that resources seem to matter for plans of self-control as well. Tom noted that he was now able to walk way from conflicts because he had his own car. Those without access to such resources might, conversely, be unable to realize their plans of controlling the self. Again, more research is needed to explore these ideas. However, it is through such dynamics that those with "less stake in conformity" might experience higher rates of recidivism. It is not that they have nothing to lose so much as they don't have enough to get by on.

These points on the importance of resources foretell difficulties that respondents will experience in trying to realize their programs of change. To close, I want to review three other problems with these programs of self-governance that are likely to complicate the plans of deterred violent subjects from realizing lives outside of intimate abuse.

First, deterrence is not necessarily enough. In the simplest of terms, deterrence means that punished offenders do not repeat the actions for which they have been punished. And while this is certainly an important consideration in evaluating the success of interventions against domestic batterers, it is not the only one, since domestic violence victims suffer from a range of abusive tactics (Stark 2007). In this vein, past research has demonstrated that the quality of life and sense of well-being deteriorate for many victims of violence following their partners' contact with the criminal justice system (Dobash et al. 2000:138). Following their punishment, abusers may avoid physical violence, a sign of being deterred, in favor of psychological forms of control. For instance, Tom, who noted that he and his girlfriend were "closer" since his arrest, explained that he and his girlfriend frequently would kid about the incident now. "We sit back here and joke about it," he said, "how I was in the handcuffs, and how she was looking out the window, looking at me, and I was looking at her with the evil eye. And I'm like, 'I wouldn't have [had] to go through that if you wouldn't have called in the first place.' She be like, 'I know, I know, quit making me feel bad about it.' She like, 'I know, I know.'" Although Tom made their joking about the incident seem innocent, the joke ended with her expressing remorse for having called the police rather than with him expressing remorse for hitting her.

Second, batterers' ability to control their selves might be weak, making self-governance a poor form of domestic violence governance. In discussing his future, Bob recognized that "I got to stop drinking" to realize his goal of doing "the right thing" and staying out of trouble. But he also acknowledged that his plans of self-control were likely to fail if he perceived a partner being untruthful to him. He said, "If you find one and she only going to bullshit you, right, there is the heat." The ability of Bob's self to manage the boundaries between violence and nonviolence appears slight. He offered no insight into the mechanisms, beyond quitting drinking, by which he might control his self. And he had already excused his violence before the fact should he find his self drunk. As such, these amateur programs of self-governance may not be skilled enough to keep abusers out of violence.

These comments in turn suggest the importance of therapeutic interventions in instilling abusers with socially, rather than personally, relevant definitions of abuse as well as techniques for managing their selves. However, the comments of respondents who had attended some partner abuse classes hint at potential problems in the administration of counseling. This is the third potential problem facing deterred batterers' careers outside violence. For one, participation in treatment groups involves financial costs and time demands that respondents found straining. Aaron described the classes he would have to take, "I got take this family life class and I got to pay $120 before they even enroll you. How am I going to have $120 to pay these people? If I'm going to pay them, I'm going to be homeless." As well, men may resist the therapy itself for what they perceive to be efforts to label them as bad people. Carl noted in attending his first classes, "A lot of questions that I have, they just say the same thing. They say, 'Do you have low self-esteem?' Does that mean that I'm a wife beater?" As noted before, definitions of the self as nonviolent were central to batterers' responses to criminal justice interventions. To the extent that counseling challenges this definition of the self, participants may resist participating in the programs, feeding the high drop-out rates that these programs suffer (Cadsky et al. 1996).

Peering into the future, it is apparent that the outcomes that deterred domestic violence subjects ultimately experience will be shaped through the interaction of their programs of self-governance, their violent selves, and the efforts of state authorities to shape them, as well as their ability to tie their programs of change to individual economies that can support them. While certain failures can be foretold, we need not be fatalistic about the potential of society to change batterers' behavior. Rather, this knowledge invites us to refine our responses to intimate partner abuse.

Conclusion

Governing Domestic Violence as a Crime, and the Limits of Legal Power

Mandatory arrest and no-drop prosecution policies count as the clearest manifestations of the sea change in society's response to intimate partner abuse. Once a private matter to be managed by women individually in the secluded space of their homes, abuse now counts as a public offense that state authorities vow to combat through the criminal justice apparatus. In criminalizing domestic violence and mandating state interventions, mandatory policies count as a further example of "governing through crime," the process of society coming to define social problems as crimes to be administered by criminal legal strategies (Simon 2007).

Part and parcel of this expansion in the governmentality of crime in contemporary society is a reconceptualization of the criminal justice system itself. As other studies highlighting the criminalization of social problems—such as drug abuse (Nolan 2001), juvenile delinquency (Kupchik 2004), mental health (Goldkamp & Irons-Guynn 2000), and domestic violence (Mirchandani 2005)—make clear, the legal system has come to be viewed in contemporary times not simply as an institution dedicated to social control and maintaining the status quo, but one embracing social change as well. Courts' traditional technocratic focus on procedural issues is giving way to a new therapeutic orientation emphasizing offender treatment and change, reflected both in the language of the court's officers and its interventions with deviant and criminal subjects (see Mirchandani 2005 and Nolan 2001 for contrasting appraisals of this process).

Using mandatory interventions against intimate partner abuse as a case study, this book has sought to examine how this transformation of criminal justice plays out in practice and whether the criminal legal system can fulfill the none-too-modest potential of serving as an agent for positive social change. In the end, it offers a mixed balance sheet. On the one hand, the policies have brought fundamental change in the way that the police and criminal courts handle intimate abuse cases. As the first chapter described, officers in the Plainsville Police Department adjust their practice of policing in order to accommodate the mandatory arrest policy and disrupt abusive relationships. Isolating batterers from their spaces and relations of abuse, the police deploy different tactics that extend the exercise of public power and law over them. In so doing, they disrupt rather than reinforce traditional notions of public and private space. The second chapter demonstrated that the exercise of public power over abusers continues in the court setting. Each of the different actors in the Centralia County Court adjusts her interactions with abusers to accommodate the no-drop policy, with the state's attorney's office in particular using no-contact orders, aggressive charging strategies, and jail time to compel those intending to try their cases to plead guilty.

These findings confirm those of past research on domestic violence courts. As Mirchandani (2005) has reported, judges, prosecutors, and defense attorneys in these courts adhere to a feminist perspective on the patriarchal nature of intimate partner violence and adapt their exchanges with abusers—judges admonish offenders in court while lawyers on both sides of the aisle have defendants plead guilty—to promote offender accountability. Such changes in court practice, as well as those in police practice, can be read to enhance victim safety and independence by immediately disrupting abusive relationships and placing abusers under the supervision of the state.

On the other hand, this research has shown that mandatory arrest and no-drop prosecution carry unintended consequences that can prove harmful for victims. As offenders' own narratives demonstrate, they pressure victims to go to the state to have charges dropped. They break off relationships and deprive partners (who are also the mothers of their children) valuable financial and emotional resources. They turn to psychological forms of control that predispose partners to not call the police again. And they look to locate new intimate partners who they believe will be willing to accept their abuse. What's more, intimate terrorists, the most dangerous type of abusers, prove the most resistant to change. By failing to affect the violent subjectivities of most abusers, then, these policies allow many batterers to continue their abuse.

Criminalization and the power of the law as a force for social change might thus be more limited than hoped. In Centralia County, the state is able to gain custodial authority over intimate abusers. It is able to detain them, impose no-contact orders against them, convict them, and sentence them to counseling. But it is unable to have them take responsibility for their actions. Put another way, while mandatory arrest and no-drop prosecution extend the grip of domestic violence governance upon intimate abusers, thus redrawing the boundaries between public and private space, they do not erase those boundaries. The policies ultimately encounter their limits within batterers themselves, who act to define their selves as nonviolent and thus resist the imposition of contaminated abuser identities upon them.

One is reminded here of Foucault's (1979) distinction between "juridico-discursive" power, in which authorities inform subjects of what they can or cannot do (Foucault 1979:82–85), and "strategical" power, which operates through a "multiplicity of force relations" that shape and transform the subjectivities of those whom authorities target (Foucault 1979:92–93). In Centralia County, the state, within the framework of mandatory policies and through the various tactics it employs to condition suspects' compliance with authority, is able to gain and exercise juridical power over intimate abusers. Law enforcement and court officers can make suspects talk, place them in detention, have them appear before court, compel them give up their right to contest charges and sign their guilt, and sentence them to therapy. But the state is unable to establish strategical power, or what might better be referred to as "subjectifying power," over them. That is, the same legal authorities cannot "govern the souls" (Rose 1999) of abusers to transform the abusive subjectivities from which their violence is thought to emerge.

In addition to sketching the boundaries of law's power, this work has thematized the different forces that work to oppose the law. Here we return to the three main themes that began the book.

The power of the law to affect the subjectivities of batterers is in the first instance resisted by the *agency of abusers*. As this study has shown, intimate abusers are not passive in the face of police and court interventions. Instead, they continually resist their advance through different expressions of agency. The fourth chapter described how abusers express their agency in lying to law enforcement officers to avoid arrest, fraternizing in jail to formulate legal strategies to resist prosecution, pressuring defense attorneys to represent them in the manner they desire, violating no-contact orders, requesting family members to intervene on their behalf, and changing their patterns of interaction with their partners to maintain control and influence over them. The fifth chapter explained how abusers define their violence in specific ways—through denials, excuses, minimizations, justifications, and claims of self-defense—that shield them from culpability, with intimate terrorists tending to stick to one story and situationally violent abusers using multiple accounts. The sixth chapter demonstrated how abusers engage in self-governance projects, through which they seek to define on their own terms the course of their future lives. While most projects envisioned futures free from police and court contact, many, especially those of intimate terrorists, failed to promise futures free of intimate abuse.

Taken together, these instances of abuser agency belie the image, present in past domestic violence research such as the influential arrest studies, of batterers as mere rational actors who can be punished out of their patterns of abuse. Batterers are, of course, rational. They are quite calculating when defying no-contact orders. And they do not wish to experience the pains of arrest and prosecution again. But fear of punishment does not impact all abusers the same way. And they devise diverse schemes that allow them to balance the risks of future detection with their continued desire to conduct intimate relationships upon their own terms.

The power of the law to change abusers is in the second instance repelled by the *intersection of social structures* that pattern and define individuals' experience of the social world. While mandatory arrest and no-drop prosecution are designed to reshape specific patterns of gendered interactions in society, they are not easily separated from other patterns of structured inequality. As chapter 4 demonstrated, although intended to have abusers focus on the wrongness of their actions, arrest and prosecution are frequently understood in terms of race and class. African American offenders in Centralia County often took their punishments as unjust sanctions motivated by the race biases of the predominantly white local legal establishment. And the group of batterers participating in this study, who predominantly toiled away in low-income, service-sector jobs, commonly believed that the state was punishing them to enrich itself. Given the interconnectivity of race, class, and gender, the meaning-making capacity of domestic violence law is limited.

This point reinforces the message of past research emphasizing the disproportionate impact of domestic violence policies on low-income, minority populations (Maguigan 2003; Coker 2001). But the connection is not as obvious as it may first seem. While Coker (2001:811) reasons that "law and policy . . . developed from the experiences of a generic category 'battered women,' is likely to reflect the needs and experiences of more economically advantaged women and white women," various studies suggest that minority men and women actually benefit from mandatory policies. In brief, "research suggests that mandates reduced [race] bias in arrest, increased the willingness of black women to call the police and had a dramatic protective effect for black men," who have experienced decreasing rates of partner assault homicides (Stark 2005:152).[1] These benefits are far from the minds of the participants in this study, however, and whatever gains minorities receive directly from mandatory policies are likely diminished by the intense policing they experience in other aspects of their lives. Thus, the lesson to be taken from this study is the difficulty of pursuing a progressive agenda through institutions and organizations that have engendered such negative consequences for so many in this country. In Centralia County, which like many areas of the country is marked by deep racial and class divisions, it is not easy to deliver punishments expressing social disapproval of abusive gender relations without also arousing the experiences of racial and class inequalities that underlie their delivery.

The most surprising source of opposition to the power of the law is the practice of legal power itself. That is, *the tactics* through which the police and courts come to exercise control over domestic violence suspects simultaneously produce meanings that undercut the message of mandatory policies. As chapter 1 described, the police use both theme-building and verbal-judo tactics that mirror abusers' own accounts of violence during arrest procedures ("you didn't touch her at all," "it's not up to me, the law mandates an arrest"). As chapter 2 detailed, defense attorneys use similar tactics to realize client control ("I would agree with you that it's ridiculous"), while the court silences abusers during its efforts to efficiently process large numbers of plea bargains. Although these tactics are critical in ceasing the immediate violence of abusers, their power draws precisely from the fact that they reinforce, or otherwise leave unchallenged, abusers' view of the world and their behavior.

This is the most novel finding of the research, as few previous domestic violence studies have emphasized the manner in which power is exercised as critical to the outcomes it produces.[2] Invoked here is the concept of "procedural justice" popularized by Tom Tyler (1990), the idea that offenders' perceptions of how fairly criminal punishments are meted out will affect their future rates of compliance with the law. In this study, we have seen how the various actors of the criminal justice system, when administering mandatory arrests and prosecutions, rely on tactics that color offenders' perception of domestic violence law as well as their own behavior.

This finding in turn further accentuates the difficulties in aligning the struggle for ending domestic violence through the apparatus of the criminal justice system. If members of the criminal justice community come to embrace a feminist understanding of the problem of intimate partner abuse (Mirchandani 2005), the organizations in which they work possess their own operational logic, which can undermine the goals of domestic violence law. At the most basic level, the police look to accomplish arrests with as little resistance from suspects as possible, a goal that tactics such as theme-building and verbal judo help realize. Burdened by heavy dockets, the courts seek to realize convictions with as little participation from defendants as possible, an aim that plea bargains accommodate. But both operations discount the possibility of having the abuser's views of violence expressed and challenged. The dissonance between the goals of the anti-violence movement and the practice of criminal law bolsters the voices of those calling to reform the current approach to fighting domestic violence.

Important as these three themes are, I am under no illusion that this research represents the final or definitive word on the power of mandatory arrest and no-drop prosecution against intimate abusers. This project has carried with it various limitations which need to be highlighted for the sake of future evaluations. Most importantly, though a study on the efficacy of criminal legal interventions, it does not provide any indicator of whether the persons interviewed for the research actually reoffended. This deficit owes principally to the absence of victim interviews, which represent the only reliable measure of intimate abusers' behavior. Restrictions in time and resources made this option unfeasible.

This limitation could have been mitigated by conducting a second interview with participants. A second interview, set some months into the future, would have provided the opportunity to gauge changes in abusers' relation to violence and projects of self-governance. Originally, I had sought to carry out this longitudinal research design. However, a lack of resources again made this an impractical option.

Another shortcoming of this evaluation is that it fails to account for the efficacy of batterer intervention programs, the primary site for state interventions to rework abusers' violent subjectivities (Merry 1995). I had originally intended to include treatment programs as part of this research. However, detailing the operations of power present in therapy groups as well as the outcomes in abusers' subjectivities would have doubled the length of the current study. In other words, such a project is needed to complement the present one, but it deserves its own book-length investment of time and resources.

In addition to these limitations, the reliability of batterers as sources of data is another area of concern. As has been noted at various points, these persons are notoriously unreliable sources of data on their own behavior. In general, this study has overcome this challenge by following a research design that does not require taking respondents at their word. That is, rather than using abusers' narratives to understand what happens in the criminal justice system and whether they are violent again, this work has used these stories, together with observations of police and court practice, to understand how batterers construct their interactions and experiences with the criminal justice system and how these experiences influence their relation to past and future violence. This research design has for the most part proven successful, and it has allowed me to analyze abusers' stories for inconsistencies, such as the case of a stalker (Frank) who misrepresented the termination of his intimate relationship. Still, without the participation of respondents' intimate partners, it is impossible to know whether statements about controlling the self and freeing the self are sincere or simply efforts to depict a responsible, nonviolent self to the interviewer.

Debating Domestic Violence Law and the Path Forward

Bearing these limitations in mind, the findings from this study still represent key contributions that inform the debates surrounding the use of the criminal justice system to combat intimate partner abuse. As noted in the introduction to the book, activists and scholars are divided on the value of mandatory arrest and no-drop prosecution policies in ensuring victim safety, ending abusive relationships, and changing offenders. These debates invoke different streams of feminist activism and different visions of progressive change. On the one hand, liberal feminists value the policies as essential resources in protecting women from abuse and ensuring that criminal legal authorities handle intimate violence cases in the same manner they handle stranger violence cases (Flemming 2003). On the other hand, radical feminists, social justice feminists, and conservatives criticize the policies for removing decision making from women, exposing poor and minority women to increased surveillance by state agencies such as child welfare services, and neglecting to provide women other resources in addition to personal safety, such as housing, child care, and employment assistance, that would allow them to better manage their situations of abuse (Dasgupta 2003; Roberts 2001; Coker 2001; Schneider 2000; Mills 1999; Merry 1995).

At this level of debate, the findings from this research lend support to the position that mandatory policies do not do enough in the fight against domestic violence. While mandatory arrest and prosecution do disrupt abusive intimate relationships and result in convictions of most suspects, they do not affect the violent subjectivities of most intimate abusers. The policies fail to disrupt abusers' evasions of responsibility for violence and mostly fail to deter. Additionally, the majority of batterers use their encounters with the police, jail, and courts to affirm themselves as victims of an unjust criminal justice system. Finally, intimate terrorists are the most resistant to change.

It is fair to ask whether this assessment of mandatory arrest and no-drop prosecution is too demanding. That is, perhaps promoting change in the violent subjectivities of abusers is too much to ask of these policies, and all that can be reasonably hoped for is that the policies disrupt offenders' abuse and provide victims and service providers the opportunity to manage these situations more effectively. And to the extent that these policies result in increased arrests and permanent disruptions of abusive relationships, they are performing an irreplaceable function in the fight against intimate violence.

The security function of presumptive arrest is clearly an essential benefit of aggressive arrest and prosecution policies. However, as this study demonstrates, this security function is not easily separated from other outcomes that add negatively to the account of aggressive arrest and prosecution policies. In resisting the approach of state power upon them, abusers adjust their behaviors in different ways—pressuring victims to go to the state, terminating relationships, turning to psychological forms of abuse, looking for the "right" partner—that negatively impact women. Clearly, then, the "security" of arrest and prosecution is not enough. Change in abusers' subjectivities needs to remain a central goal of state interventions against intimate violence.

To this, one could also charge that the responsibility for changing the violent subjectivities of batterers lies with batterer intervention programs rather than arrest and prosecution policies. However, many abusers—those who are found not guilty and those whose cases are dismissed, which accounts for 25% of the men arrested for domestic violence in Centralia County—drop out of the criminal justice system before they reach this stage. What's more, attendance in programs is notoriously poor (Bennett & Williams 2005). Nancy, the victim's advocate in the state's attorney's office, estimated that "4 out of 14" is a normal program completion rate for participants attending partner abuse classes in Centralia County. Drop-outs are subject to new criminal prosecution for failure to complete sentencing. But renewed court attention to these cases does little to address the concern that these men are not changing. Finally, questions of attendance aside, there is little evidence that these programs actually work (Jackson et al. 2003). In a study evaluating the performance of two abusers programs, Dobash et al. (2000) do show that therapy groups are more effective than other criminal legal interventions in changing the abusive attitudes and behaviors of batterers. However, the numbers are somewhat misleading, since their study examined only the outcomes of persons who had actually completed the programs. More recently, Labriola et al. (2005) find that batterer programs prove no more effective in reducing rearrests than do simple forms of judicial monitoring. In sum, then, partner abuse programs offer no assurance that batterers will change as they move deeper into the criminal legal apparatus. Considering this, the need for improvements in the police's and courts' handling of abusers becomes more urgent.

How to improve society's response to domestic violence is also the subject of much debate. Even liberal feminists who believe in criminalization consider reform necessary. This view is best expressed by Evan Stark, who argues that the current criminal legal approach falls short because it is premised upon a flawed understanding of abuse. Current interventions are based on a vision of abuse as a discrete act—similar to common fights and assaults—which threatens the physical safety of victims. But victims of "coercive control" "experience abuse as continuous or ongoing," making such abuse more akin to course-of-conduct crimes like harassment or stalking (Stark 2007:99). Also, what is threatened in coercive control is not only or even necessarily physical safety, but the liberty and autonomy of victims. Thus, the criminal justice system needs to adjust its focus away from "fights" and to "coercive control," since "the current terms for abuse subsume large numbers of men and women whose behaviors do not merit public sanction . . . and effectively exclude whole classes of victims whose survival depends on public recognition" (Stark 2007:370).

This is a fascinating proposal that deserves serious consideration. Most importantly, it, unlike current policy, is founded upon an understanding of intimate partner abuse as a constellation of abusive acts. Also, in calling for authorities to target the most severe type of abuse (coercive control) and de-prioritize the least severe (fights), this proposal envisions focusing resources to those who require them the most. The proposal succeeds pragmatically as well, since it would not necessarily require any new funds from the state, which are increasingly difficult to secure given current budget deficits and spending priorities, but simply a reallocation of existing resources.

At the same time, various questions remain. First is how the system would prosecute cases of coercive control, which again do not necessarily involve physical violence. In Centralia County, juries were very reluctant to convict without evidence of serious physical injury, which is why the state relies on plea bargains for securing convictions. Thus, if a redefinition of abuse were to happen, to gain convictions the state would likely still rely on plea bargains, which do little to challenge the abusive subjectivities of offenders. Second is how the system would deal with victims who, having experienced coercive control, feel disempowered and disinclined to testify against their abusers. The partners of the abusers participating in this study often cooperated with the state, but others, pressured by abusers' family and friends, did not. How do state's attorneys prosecute such cases without doing further harm to victims' sense of self? Third, if this study has done nothing else, it has shown that criminal legal organizations possess their own institutional logics and cultures, which influence how they handle offenders and apply the law. This is the central law and society lesson. Given this, it is difficult to be optimistic about the ability of the system to differentiate between different types of violence and enact domestic violence law in the way envisioned by advocates. More than reforming how the criminal justice system *sees* domestic violence, effort is required to reform how it *practices* domestic violence law.

At the other end of the advocacy spectrum are radical feminists, who view the state as inherently "masculinist" (Brown 1995:166–96). According to this view, rather than liberating women, "the state increasingly takes over and transforms the project of male dominance" (Brown 1995:193). As such, even the protections that the state offers women against the intimate violence of men, which are simply extensions of men's traditional custodial powers over women, come at a price. These not only include the high number of women and minority men arrested for domestic violence, but increased state surveillance by child welfare agencies over households with children exposed to violence. As a consequence, radical feminists look to reform the social response to intimate violence by bypassing the state altogether. In its place, they back grassroots activism intended to respond to domestic violence in inventive ways informed by the lived experiences of women at the local level. A vision of such activism is embodied in IN-CITE!, a nationwide network of activists dedicated to sponsoring local-level efforts to address different social problems in underprivileged, overpoliced communities (INCITE!, 2005). INCITE!'s domestic violence program is built around principles of community-level consciousness raising and developing approaches to conflict resolution that do not involve calls to the police (INCITE!, 2005).

This proposal too possesses considerable merit. Significantly, it places both victim and community empowerment at the center of the discussion. In doing so, it fully recognizes the intersection of different forms of structural inequality in individual women's lives. Reasoning that those women and those communities who are most harmed by state interventions can never be empowered by criminal justice sanctions, this proposal devises a method for empowerment by keeping ownership and responsibility for managing conflicts in the hands of local communities and victims.

Of course, the major problem with this approach is that in Western industrialized countries the state alone possesses the legal privilege to violence. And short of the state's cooperation, it is difficult to imagine how society could effectively disrupt abusive relationships. Thus, it seems irresponsible to abandon the state as an ally in the fight against domestic violence. Without an adequate security alternative to replace the police, abandoning the state is tantamount to abandoning women to endure intimate violence alone. This is clearly not a step forward. In addition, the radical feminist position that the state is essentially masculinist or patriarchal too seems misguided. The very history of the battered women's movement seems to contradict the notion that the state is inherently anything. Prior to the adoption of mandatory arrest and no-drop prosecution, there was debate about whether the state could ever be brought to follow such radical, pro-feminist policies (Ferraro & Pope 1993). However, this page in the history of the feminist movement proved the state to be malleable and open to change. Whereas the police did not arrest abusers at one time, they now do. And whereas state's attorney's offices were once loath to prosecute abusers, they now do.

The concerns of radical feminists have been voiced by social justice feminists as well. This camp, however, considers the hard-fought gains that antiviolence activists won from the state too important to give up. As Dasgupta (2003) reasons, "centralizing the ownership for ending violence against women within communities is not the same as absolving government of its obligations to protect women" (19). Along the same lines, many women, especially those looking for immediate relief from violence when calling the police, express high rates of satisfaction with the criminal justice system (Hester 2006). From another angle, aggressive state action, in addition to the security it provides women, sends a strong message to society as a whole that "domestic violence is morally wrong" (Coker 2004:1349). Finally, because the state holds vital resources for survivors of violence, including income, housing, and child care assistance as well as legal resources such as orders of protection, a retreat from the state is not in order.

Social justice feminists, then, while critical of criminalization, suggest refining the current regime of domestic violence governance in a way that would "further public control of police and prosecutor response without simultaneously increasing state control of women" (Coker 2004:1335). This includes increasing state expenditures on welfare services that allow women to better manage their abuse (Merry 1995; Schneider 2000) as well as Lawrence Sherman's (1992) proposal to replace mandatory arrest policies with mandatory action policies that would require law enforcement officers to take an action, whether transporting the suspect to a detoxification center or transporting the victim to a shelter, when responding to domestic violence calls (255–56; see Coker 2004:1335). Mandatory action would ensure victim safety, while staving off the onset of the criminal legal apparatus, which proves deleterious to many victims and counterproductive in changing abusers.

Part of the list of alternatives is offering victims the *choice* of "restorative justice and other alternative adjudicatory processes" in place of traditional criminal prosecution (Coker 2004:1335). Restorative justice (Braithwaite 1989) is an alternative approach to dispute resolution that aims to repair the harm caused by criminal behavior rather than simply punishing the guilty. Support for its use in domestic violence cases has been growing, in large part because its principles and processes respond to the shortcomings of the current adversarial justice approach. For instance, in the community conferencing model of restorative justice, which Hopkins et al. (2004) view as the model most appropriate to domestic violence cases, "family members and supporters for the victim and offender" are brought together "in a professionally facilitated meeting to address the wrong done and the harm that resulted from that wrong . . . and to identify what the offender is going to do to make right the wrong" (4). In contrast with the current adversarial justice approach, which places action in the hands of the state, the community conference model is victim-centered. Supported by her family and friends, the victim is empowered by being able to confront her abuser in the company of trusted friends and to name the harm caused by his actions. Restorative justice also allows victims to identify reparations, such as material resources, that better serve their immediate interests and needs (Coker 2004:1345). Thus, if set within a "feminist/critical race feminist" framework, restorative justice could function as a "transformative" process leading to the empowerment of women (Coker 2002:143–49).

To be sure, this is an idealized vision of domestic violence governance. However, studies show that conferencing models prove effective for handling family and sexual violence. Studying the use of conferences in handling "400 sexual-offense youth justice cases" in South Australia, Daly et al. (2003) found that "conferences outperform court in measures that matter to victims. Offenders through conferences admitted to their offending, whereas one half the court cases were dismissed; and for penalties, . . . offenders through conference did more for victims (apology and acknowledgement), more for the community (through community service), and more for themselves (involvement in a therapeutic service) than offenders whose cases went to court" (see Curtis-Fawley & Daly 2005:610–11). Similarly, in their handling of 32 family violence cases through "family group conferencing," Pennell and Burford (2002) find that conferencing helped realize "a reduction in indicators of child maltreatment and domestic violence," "an advancement in children's development," and "an extension of social supports" (110).

This vision of change is not without its critics. Stark, for one, problematizes the notion of choice at the heart of this approach. He writes, "Much criticism of state intervention is grounded in a variant of the clinical conceit, the view that individual agency and 'choice' are the foundation of 'empowerment' and, therefore, that interventions are properly assessed by whether they respect women's choices and ameliorate suffering." But he continues: "Choices are not made in a social vacuum. By abstracting individual volition from the structural context that constrains both the capacity to choose and the options available, the clinical conceit privileges private solutions through which persons become 'reconciled' to their reality over collective political or justice strategies designed to expand available options" (Stark 2005:150).

Stark is right to question the supposed connection between choice and individual empowerment, especially since choice continues to function as a neoliberal trope masking the operation of power in various contexts. However, the promise of restorative justice does not lie in its trumpeting choice. Rather, it lies in its administration of justice. In contrast to the type of justice currently administered and described in this work—where the police and courts are central and victims and abusers are peripheral (and silent)—restorative justice works to have victims actively define the justice outcomes that will best serve their needs, and offenders confront the true nature of their actions. Ultimately, I think this strategy of altering *the way justice is practiced* carries the greatest potential for defeating domestic violence. In an effort to build upon this approach, then, I want to finish by reviewing the policy implications of this book and suggesting different types of changes that could be enacted to strengthen the social response to partner abuse.

Practicing Change and the Promise of Procedural Justice

The findings from this work suggest two general strategies for improving the criminal justice system's handling of intimate abusers. These vary in scale. The first is to build upon the positive changes that already result from mandatory arrest and no-drop prosecution. This research has shown, for instance, that some offenders express plans to change by submitting their selves before God, controlling their selves, and freeing their selves. Many of these plans, if sustained, can lead to nonabuse. Thus, a first policy recommendation would be to recognize these plans for change by deterred abusers and work to help abusers realize them.

One way to do this would be to modify the court's sentencing practices on domestic violence cases. Currently, the Centralia County State's Attorney's Office seeks plea bargains that will result in sentences of "probation" or "conditional discharge." "Conditional discharge" is a probation-like sentence, but does not require the person to meet with a probation officer. Both of these sentences leave convicts with criminal records, allowing the state to charge future domestic violence offenses as felonies. In addition, as a condition of most domestic violence sentences, the state's attorney's office has the offender attend partner abuse classes. As noted in chapter 6, classes add financial burdens and can generate defiance among participants.

To support the positive changes of deterred abusers, the state could offer the option of forgoing partner abuse classes, whose program of change conflicts with that of deterred subjects. As an added incentive for change, the state could also offer these subjects "court supervision" sentences, which do not leave a criminal record if the person successfully completes his sentence. Thus, the person would have the opportunity to prove his claim of a nonviolent self and erase the stigma of a domestic violence conviction by not being abusive again. In addition, rather than simply turning these offenders loose, the state could also require them to meet with probation officers to review their plans for avoiding violence. These sessions could include state referrals to employment centers and housing assistance. Offenders could also be made to provide the names of community contacts, such as priests or pastors in cases of submitting the self, whom the state could contact to help ensure compliance with plans of self-governance.

To be taken seriously, this strategy could not be offered to each and every abuser professing a plan of positive self-government. Rather, victim interviews would need to be conducted to determine the type of batterer the criminal justice system is dealing with. Repeat offenders and first-time intimate terrorists with demonstrated patterns of controlling and violent behavior might not be trusted with such an option. However, for first-time, situationally violent offenders with a plan for change, this sentencing framework would build upon the deterrent momentum of arrest and prosecution in a way that would promote their programs of change.

The second strategy for reform is to modify current criminal justice practice to produce a greater number of positive outcomes in the first place. Current research on "procedural justice" asserts that the manner in which legal authorities treat people affects the outcomes resulting from legal encounters. In his research on citizens' compliance with the law, Tom Tyler (1990) finds that people's compliance with the law is most strongly connected to their perceptions of "the actions and motives of the decisionmaker" (Huo & Tyler 2000:7). Strikingly, "perceptions of fair treatment" by legal authorities matter more to people than "receiving favorable outcomes" from their legal encounters. As a consequence, people's compliance with the law can be enhanced by having legal authorities use procedurally just tactics that citizens perceive to be fair, neutral, respectful, and participatory. "When people feel that they have been treated fairly . . . , they are more likely to comply with the authority's wishes, even when following the directive is not in their immediate interest" (Huo & Tyler 2000:8).

This study has demonstrated that abusers view their interactions with the police, jail, and court as procedurally unjust. By altering the practices that batterers view as unjust, legal interventions against them could prove more effective. The following is a list of "practicable" changes at each level of criminal justice bureaucracy that promise greater change in the violent subjectivities of intimate abusers.

Policing. As noted above, Lawrence Sherman (1992), one of the chief architects of the National Institute of Justice arrest studies, has proposed to replace mandatory arrest policies with mandatory action policies (255–56). This is an intriguing idea, since it would provide victims security while offering offenders alternative treatments, such as alcohol counseling, that they could benefit from. However, a few concerns remain. For example, one wonders what message this would send both offenders and society. For those abusers who excuse their behavior by attributing it to alcohol, being transported to a detoxification center would simply reinforce their evasions of responsibility. As well, it does not address the concern that police interactions with offenders often collude with the latter's abusive attitudes and beliefs. Finally, by not punishing offenders, and transporting victims to a shelter instead, mandatory action policies could endanger the message that domestic violence is morally wrong (Coker 2004:1349). This criticism is not to dismiss the idea of mandatory action policies, but to simply note key reservations about them.

Instead of simply replacing mandatory arrest policies, they could be enhanced in a few ways. For one, better police investigations are needed. The Centralia County state's attorney's office noted this, explaining how the lack of taped victim statements and photographs of injuries restricts its ability to try cases. And offenders cited this, revealing how differences in the amount of time spent with each party as well as the lack of photographs and follow-up interviews lead them to distrust officers' actions. By addressing these concerns, the police would not only strengthen cases that the state could then bring to trial, but would also foster abusers' perception of fairness in the system.

In addition to this, law enforcement officers should provide arrested suspects clear, legally grounded explanations of what they did wrong. As this study has shown, displacing responsibility for arrest to domestic violence laws is counterproductive. Explaining the rationale for an arrest would increase abusers' perception of fairness by heightening the transparency of the process and giving suspects fewer reasons to guess at the police's motivations for arresting them. By the same measure, the police could also explain to arrestees why the state takes intimate abuse cases seriously. Policing policies on domestic violence cases are clearly unique. And rather than using that distinctiveness as a way to deflect criticism, officers could take the lead in the construction of meaning in domestic violence arrests by explaining that domestic violence is a unique type of crime and that society no longer condones it.

Such changes do not, of course, address the racial tensions and distrust that characterize police–citizen encounters in communities like Centralia County and that lead to perceptions of racial bias and victimization. However, Tyler's (2000) research also finds that procedural justice is important across racial and ethnic categories. As such, greater attention to procedurally just policing tactics, tactics that increase the participation of abusers in the process as well as their perceptions of fairness, could mitigate these feelings of distrust.

Jail. It is clear that better facilities are required for the incarceration of abusers. The goal is not to make suspected batterers comfortable, as one could expect critics of such a proposal to claim. Rather, it is to treat all criminal suspects with a basic level of human respect and dignity that will increase their perceptions of being treated fairly and prevent them from creating victim identities based on their jail experiences. Improving facilities means increasing cell space in order to avoid overcrowding holding cells. For those suspects not able to bond out, daily activities are needed, as well as adequate food. Gaining convictions through material and temporal deprivation is simply incompatible with having persons take responsibility for their actions.

The role of the holding cell and jail as spaces of meaning making needs also be recognized. To the extent that meaning making is an inherent part of suspects' jail experience, administrators, like police officers, could take the lead in molding the meanings of these encounters. Additional jail space would allow administrators to house domestic violence suspects separately and disrupt their discussion of cases. More productively, authorities could hold meetings with inmates explaining the rationale behind the state's aggressive approach to domestic violence cases. Finally, administrators need to exercise greater control over jail guards' comments about domestic violence cases. While these comments might be seen to lighten the mood of the jail, they are factually wrong (the person who calls the police first is not the person who avoids arrest, and the law does not mandate arrests whenever a domestic violence call is received) and counterproductive when parroted by suspects as reasons for their detention.

Courts. The greatest potential for change in the current regime of domestic violence governance lies in the adjudication of cases. Unlike the police and jail, which serve key functions in providing victims security from their abusers, the criminal court does not directly impact victim safety. As such, there is greater leeway for change at this level of criminal justice bureaucracy.

For one, the court's handling of domestic violence cases could be enhanced. One way to do this would be to eliminate its reliance on plea bargains. Plea bargains lessen the impact of convictions on abusers, who come to see the court as a closed community that pressures them to accept negotiated convictions. This leads to greater distrust of the system as well as further distancing from one's own actions. Securing convictions by trial, conversely, would lessen the opportunities for abusers to evade responsibility for violence by more clearly linking their convictions to the evidence of their abuse. Of course, the ability to take cases to trial requires the state to strengthen its cases, which further prioritizes the need for improved police investigations.

Even if criminal courts eliminated plea bargaining, there still exist important questions concerning the appropriateness of adversarial justice for deciding domestic violence cases. For instance, the criminal legal system endows the batterer with the constitutional right to remain silent as well as have a lawyer represent him in the court. While these rights hardly work to the benefit of most criminal suspects, they do shield them from having to discuss their actions. In allowing batterers this, criminal courts fail to disrupt their stories of evasion. For this reason, alternative models of adjudication, such as restorative justice, prove appealing.

The community conferencing model of restorative justice mentioned above is a particularly promising model for affecting the violent subjectivities of men. First, it places the victim rather than the state at the center of the adjudication process and empowers her to name the harm she has suffered. This is positive in a few ways. For one, it precludes batterers from dismissing the case as the concern of only the state. Also, it allows a broader definition of harm to enter the adjudication process than that captured in the criminal statutes. The state, as Stark (2007) explains, tends to read harm in terms of physical violence alone. Additionally, batterers would be made to listen to their victims tell them the harm they have caused, not just in a single incident, but in a wider variety of contexts and through different types of behavior.

Second, the community conferencing model would help fight abusers' evasions of responsibility for violence. It would eliminate the defense attorney from the equation and make the offender speak for himself. And while evasions of responsibility are still likely, the network of friends and family gathered around the victim would provide a support system for challenging these evasions, thereby lessening the opportunities for offenders to deny, justify, minimize, and excuse their behavior. Thus, "offenders are more likely to be held accountable in a meaningful way than is true in ordinary criminal justice processing" (Coker 2004:1345).

Third, community conferencing would reduce the costs of adjudication for participants. Instead of having to attend multiple court dates to have attorneys resolve cases, the parties to the case could resolve it in a single session. While some might see this as a retreat from a central punitive aspect of the current approach (the process is the punishment), it would also diminish the view that the process is more concerned with enriching the state than it is about addressing the harms caused by domestic abuse. Reducing the costs of adjudication for batterers would also translate into additional money that they could be made to pay victims as part of settlement agreements (Coker 2004:1345).

Fourth, community conferencing would reduce the pronounced racial disparities characterizing the current system. At the Centralia County Court, most attorneys and all the judges are white, while a disproportionate number of the defendants are African American. Community conferencing could alter this by ensuring that the number of community and family participants outnumbers the professionals taking part (Pennell & Burford 2002:109–10). By making the adjudication process more reflective of the persons and communities involved in the dispute, participants would feel they have a greater stake in the process (Coker 2002:145–47). In addition, they would be less likely to read its results in racial terms.

Finally, community conferencing offers the promise of reintegrative shaming (Braithwaite 1989). This research makes clear that being identified as a batterer has a stigmatizing effect on abusers. Rather than having this stigma result in future efforts to avoid detection, the community conference can outline a course of action, dictated by the victim, that the offender would complete to be accepted back into the community. The inclusion of community and family members into the process also strengthens their stakes in the monitoring process to ensure that the offender complies with the terms of the agreement.

Community conferencing, like the above suggestion for greater flexibility in sentencing, should not be thought of as a universal approach for adjudicating domestic violence cases. Again, victims should have the option to choose which type of adjudication they want. In addition, for severe cases of abuse, where it is clearly in the best interest of both the victim and society to detain batterers, traditional criminal justice mechanisms should be used to ensure that these high-risk offenders are placed in jail and prison. As such, restorative justice would not be a replacement of the current criminal justice system, but a complement to it (Strang & Braithwaite 2002:19).

These policy proposals, to make sentencing arrangements more flexible to support individual abusers' programs of change and to make broad changes in the practice of domestic violence law at the policing, jailing, and adjudication levels, will not solve all the problems associated with the legal system's handling of intimate abusers. Nor do I harbor any illusions that they could. Racial and class disparities in this society exist outside criminal justice administration. Thus, the policy changes would ultimately do little to affect the life opportunities of persons living in disadvantaged communities. These disparities heighten the risk of domestic violence and also complicate victims' ability to survive abuse. Nevertheless, they do offer practicable means for enhancing the potential and power of common legal interventions to positively affect the violent subjectivities of intimate abusers.

Finally, in the interest of realizing more effective social interventions against intimate partner abuse, we must also be cognizant of the changing political terrain upon which these battles are waged. The construction of the current regime of domestic violence governance, achieved through the hard work of feminist activists and others, coincided with a particular period of American economic prosperity and national-level political support for such measures. Indeed, the implementation of mandatory arrest and no-drop prosecution in Centralia County has been possible only through federal and state funds made available from the budget surpluses of the 1990s. As political leaders prioritize a global war on terror whose end cannot be foreseen and respond to economic uncertainties that threaten the funding of domestic programs, outside forces could very well decide the fate of legal measures such as mandatory arrest and no-drop prosecution. It is in this sense, then, that the promise to transform abusive men falls together with the ability of activists and researchers to keep violence against women on the national agenda and to develop new interventions at the local level that rely less on federal monies. Through such efforts, we can help ensure that society does not reprivatize abuse for women to endure alone.

Appendix A

Description of Research Methods

Broadly speaking, this study investigates how mandatory arrest and no-drop prosecution impact intimate abusers. Answering this question required addressing more specific questions regarding the police (what happens to intimate abusers when they are arrested under mandatory arrest policies?), courts (what happens to intimate abusers when they are prosecuted under no-drop prosecution policies?), and abusers (how do mandatory arrest and no-drop prosecution affect them?) and an ambitious research design for collecting data from these sources. This appendix describes the methods I used to complete this task.

Police. To study *what happens to intimate abusers when they are arrested under mandatory policies*, I conducted field research with the Plainsville Police Department. Plainsville is one of the three cities in Centralia County. This field research consisted of 25 ride-alongs completed over nine months with Plainsville officers. Each ride-along lasted approximately four hours.

Ride-alongs offered the chance to observe mandatory arrest policing in time. During a single four-hour ride-along, I would accompany officers to three or four calls for service. This number increased on weekends, when people were more likely to be out and more likely to be consuming alcohol. Thus, while I did not keep records of each call for service that we responded to, I estimate that my 25 ride-alongs resulted in at least 75 calls for service. From these calls for service, 18 involved domestic disturbances, of which 10 qualified as domestic disputes between intimate partners.

As a method of data collection, ride-alongs also offered the opportunity to discuss domestic violence policing with officers. These conversations usually brought forth scripted answers concerning the importance of recognizing domestic violence as a social problem and the need for a proactive policy. To direct our conversations to the actual handling of batterers, I questioned officers about the specific tactics and strategies they use in policing domestic violence cases.

To augment the data from ride-alongs, I sat in on a two-day domestic violence seminar for recruits at the university's police training center. I attended the training session with 60 police academy cadets. I also interviewed the chief of the Plainsville Police Department and studied policing literature for information on new policing tactics and strategies. To complete my investigation of mandatory arrest practice, I collected observations over two nights at the Centralia County Jail, where all domestic violence suspects are transported following their arrests. As with my field research with the police, I focused my observations on the different tactics and procedures that jail guards use to interact with suspects.

Court. To study *what happens to intimate abusers when they are prosecuted under no-drop prosecution policies,* I conducted field observations at the Centralia County Court, sitting in at the courtroom to observe arraignment, pretrial, plea bargain, and trial proceedings. I observed each type of proceeding, adhering to the field research rule of thumb to collect observations until the phenomena under investigation become familiar or predictable (Gilgun 2001). I attended 15 arraignment hearings, observing over 50 cases of domestic violence offenses. I observed a larger number of pretrial hearings, as I used these proceedings to recruit suspects for interviews. In all, I made over 1,000 observations of pretrial hearings involving hundreds of different domestic violence cases. Pretrial hearings would often conclude with cases allotted for plea bargains. In addition, cases heard at pretrial were often scheduled for separate plea sessions. From these separate proceedings, I was able to observe 30 cases concluded through plea bargains. Observing trials involving misdemeanor domestic battery charges proved much more difficult, given the rarity of such trials. As a result, I observed only two criminal trials involving domestic battery cases.

Criminal defendants' contact with the criminal court setting extends outside the courtroom as well. In Centralia County, criminal defendants are prepared for arraignment at a prearraignment intake meeting with public defenders held at the county jail. Through arrangements with the public defender's office and the county jail, I was able to accompany defense lawyers on 10 occasions to observe their prearraignment meetings with arrestees charged with criminal conduct. I observed 147 suspects go through such prearraignment meetings, which included 33 persons arrested on domestic violence charges.

Field observation of the court setting did have its limits. I was not able to observe attorney–client meetings, a central element of batterers' contact with the criminal legal setting. Private attorneys did not permit me to observe their client meetings, and the public defender's office allowed me to observe only upon the informed consent of their clients, which was requested following a warning that my notes could be subpoenaed by the state. This warning deterred potential participants. To compensate for this, I conducted interviews with local defense attorneys to reconstruct their interactions with clients. I interviewed 10 attorneys, which included four public defenders handling misdemeanor domestic battery cases, five private defense attorneys handling a steady number of domestic battery cases, and a defense attorney working with the university's student legal services who handles the majority of the office's criminal cases. Each interview lasted approximately one hour.

Finally, I rounded out my research on the courts by interviewing members of the state's attorney's office. I interviewed the two assistant state's attorneys responsible for prosecuting domestic battery cases in the county as well as the office's domestic violence victims advocate, who was largely responsible for the implementation and operation of the no-drop prosecution policy. Each of these interviews also lasted approximately an hour.

Intimate Abusers. To study *how presumptive arrest and no-drop prosecution affect the abuse of violent subjects,* I conducted interviews with 30 domestic violence suspects and/or convicts. Recruiting participants proved difficult. The first challenge was motivating men to talk about shameful behavior. I was fortunate to receive a dissertation improvement grant from the National Science Foundation's Law and Social Science Program, which allowed me to offer suspects financial compensation for their participation. I initially paid participants $25 per interview. Given the low initial response rate, I increased the amount to $40. While the funds helped recruitment, they did serve to generate a predominantly lower-class and lower-middle-class pool of participants.

Another challenge in terms of recruitment was locating men to participate. Researchers in the past (Eisikovits & Buchbinder 2000; Dobash et al. 2000; Hearn 1998; Ptacek 1988) have recruited batterers through batterer intervention programs (BIPs). I decided to forego this option, since BIPs comprise another site of governmentality whose specific purpose is to change men. Using men from BIPs would have therefore contaminated the subjects participating in my research. In addition, it would have biased the selection of participants to those actually found guilty of domestic violence offenses.

I initially planned to recruit batterers through the Centralia County Jail. I made arrangements with the head of the jail to have recruitment letters provided to arrestees upon their release. Thirteen suspects contacted me for interviews, including two women. While this strategy did prove effective in enrolling participants in the study, these respondents were disproportionately poor persons with prior criminal offenses. In addition, because these persons had cases pending, this recruitment technique left open the possibility that the state could subpoena my notes to use in prosecuting their cases.

To diversify the types of respondents and lessen the risk to their participation, I next recruited men at the conclusion of their cases. To do this, I attended pretrial hearings and plea bargain sessions and approached persons for interviews following the termination of the proceedings. This strategy resulted in six interviews. While this strategy helped me diversify my pool of participants, it proved extremely time-consuming, especially given the frequency with which courts reschedule hearings.

To increase the efficiency of my recruiting efforts, I finally decided to track domestic battery cases through the county court's Web site and mail letters of invitation to suspects whose cases had recently ended. This final strategy proved the most satisfactory. I conducted 11 interviews with persons to whom I had mailed letters.

Interviewing these respondents proved challenging, because, as past research notes, batterers are evasive in their talk about their violent behavior. Additionally, as Schwalbe and Wolkomir (2001) explain, masculine subjects in general are likely to view the interview as a threatening interaction that requires them to give up control of the conversation. Men can be expected to react to this threat by minimizing their participation in the interview, remaining silent, or exaggerating their rationality, autonomy, and control when describing their experiences (Schwalbe & Wolkomir 2001).

Anticipating these responses from my interview subjects, I could not approach my interviews as simple fact-finding conversations, in which I would ask men if their violent behavior or attitudes had changed since their interactions with the police and courts. Instead, I sought to put men in charge of data production by having them construct narratives (Riessman 1993) concerning their experiences with the criminal justice system. I had respondents construct three distinct narratives, to explore different dimensions of the efficacy of mandatory arrest and no-drop prosecution upon them.

First, to connect the practices of mandatory arrest and no-drop prosecution that I observed during my field work with abusers' experiences of the criminal justice system, I asked respondents to describe their interactions with the police and the courts. To avoid clichéd answers and/or minimized responses ("they were OK"), and to access respondents' experiences with the practices of the police and court, I used such "grand tour questions" (Goodman 2001; Miller & Crabtree 2004) as "What happened when the police arrived?" and "What happened at the jail?" or said, "Tell me about your first meeting with your defense attorney." I conducted a content analysis

(Lieblich et al. 1998:112–41) of these narratives, paying particular attention to the mention of particular police and court practices that I had observed in my ethnographic research as well as the meanings that these legal encounters held for abusers.

Second, to understand whether being arrested and prosecuted for domestic violence affected respondents' accountability for their violence, I first asked them to narrate the events that led to their arrest. I again used a grand tour question—"What happened on the day you were arrested?"—to prompt the men to talk about their experiences. I then compared these narratives of "what happened" with the stories they told police at the time of their arrest, which I accessed through police reports.

While the two narratives could not be expected to be similar in detail, given the substantial differences in the "social organization" (Ewick & Silbey 1995) of their telling (a criminal investigation versus a paid interview with a doctoral student), I focused on the "core narratives" (Gilgun 2001:348) or "emplotment" (Lawler 2002:245; Freeman 2004:65) of the stories. Core narratives with no fundamental change provided an indication that the person had not changed. Alternatively, stories that changed in terms of who committed the violence, who was responsible for the violence, and so forth indicated a change in the person's relation to violence. I studied these differences between core narratives to understand the different types of changes men experience in relation to their violence.

Third, to understand whether being arrested and prosecuted changed respondents' lives at all, I had respondents answer the question, "How has this experience affected your life?" I used "probes" (Goodman 2001:314) to have men specifically discuss whether they were still with their partners and whether they expected to still have disputes with their current and/or future partners. I conducted a "content analysis" (Lieblich et al. 1998:112–41) of these stories, looking to identify common experiences and trends.

Appendix B
Classification of Research Participants

Name	Violence Type	Summary of Recent Incident(s)
1. Ann	Situational	*Criminal History:* Prior domestic violence arrests *Recent Incident:* Retrieving bike from ex-boyfriend; fight ensues *Victim Statement:* No reported controlling behavior *Participant Statement:* Various conflicts with sister; no reported controlling behavior
2. Betty	Situational	*Criminal History:* Prior domestic violence arrests *Recent Incident:* Argument with ex-boyfriend over her coming home late *Victim Statement:* Dispute over phone; no reported controlling behavior *Participant Statement:* Reports violent resistance to partner's violence, reported controlling behavior on his part (he's upset with her for being out late); reports conflicts are alcohol-related; no reported controlling behavior on her part
3. Adam	Intimate Terrorism	*Criminal History:* No prior domestic violence arrests *Recent Incident:* Wife does not pick him up from work because kids are asleep. He comes home, throws things at wife, and threatens her with knife. *Victim Statement:* Reported controlling behavior (threats to cut her for not obeying him, jealous of attention given to her kids, increased aggression since marriage) *Participant Statement:* No reported controlling behavior; reported frustration with children

Name	Violence Type	Summary of Recent Incident(s)
4. Bobby	Situational	*Criminal History*: No prior domestic violence arrests *Recent Incident*: He gets out of jail and comes to stay at girlfriend's apartment. Argument follows when she tells him to leave. *Victim Statement*: No reported controlling behavior or prior violence *Participant Statement*: No reported violence or controlling behavior in past; highly misogynist
5. Chris	Situational	*Criminal History*: Prior domestic violence arrests *Recent Incident*: Argument over him playing the stereo loud *Victim Statement*: No reported controlling behavior; dispute over his loud radio *Participant Statement*: No reported controlling behavior; dispute over his loud radio; past incidents involving disputes with daughter's boyfriend and with girlfriend following a call from ex-boyfriend looking to speak with him
6. Dave	Intimate Terrorism	*Criminal History:* Prior domestic violence arrests *Recent Incident:* Ex-girlfriend goes to Dave's residence to pick up their son. Before she leaves, Dave argues with her about money that she owes him and grabs her by the back of the neck. *Victim Statement:* Multiple prior violent episodes; reported choking; afraid to prosecute; reported controlling behavior (harassing phone calls following breakup, stalking her house despite OP, threats to kill her if he goes back to jail, pressure to drop charges, and continuing harassment) *Participant Statement:* No reported controlling behavior; reported prior violence related to alcohol and substance abuse
7. Eric	Intimate Terrorism	*Criminal History:* Prior domestic violence arrests *Recent Incident:* He gets upset she did not come home previous night and attempts to touch her crotch and initiate sex against her will. He then grabs her by neck. *Victim Statement:* Reported controlling behavior (he's upset she did not come home previous night, he attempts to touch her crotch and initiate sex against her will); reported choking; prior incident of threats to "take her somewhere so no one could ever find her" *Participant Statement:* Reports frequent arguments, violence against partner

Name	Violence Type	Summary of Recent Incident(s)
8. Frank	Intimate Terrorism	*Criminal History:* Prior domestic violence arrests *Recent Incident:* He is stalking ex-girlfriend after relationship has ended and eventually kidnaps her. *Victim Statement:* Reported controlling behavior (various types including kidnapping, stalking); reported suicidal behavior on his part following separation *Participant Statement:* Reported controlling behavior (stalking and efforts to isolate partner)
9. Gary	Intimate Terrorism	*Criminal History:* Prior domestic violence arrests *Recent Incident:* He chokes ex-girlfriend after she refuses to have sex. He disconnects the phone line and takes away her cellular phone as she tries to call the police. *Victim Statement:* Reported choking and loss of consciousness; reported controlling behavior (gaining access to apartment and refusing to leave after breakup, attempts to force sex, threats to kill her upon her refusal) *Participant Statement:* Reported frequent physical violence; reported controlling behavior (regulating what she purchases)
10. Henry	—	*Criminal History:* No prior domestic violence arrests *Recent Incident:* Case involves brother. He accuses brother of stealing Social Security check and threatens him with a knife. *Victim Statement:* No reported controlling behavior *Participant Statement:* No reported violence or controlling behavior
11. Isaac	Situational	*Criminal History:* Prior criminal sexual assault conviction; prior domestic violence arrests *Recent Incident:* At a party, he accuses girlfriend of sleeping with a woman. Argument ensues and he batters her, forces her into a vehicle, and continues to batter her while bringing her to her home. *Victim Statement:* Reported violent and controlling behavior following argument at party (he forces her into vehicle and continues battering her at home); "only a verbal argument" (her children had been taken away due to police contact at residence); no prior violence and controlling behavior reported; appears frightened when police arrive on report of violation of order of protection *Participant Statement:* No reported violent or controlling behavior in past

Name	Violence Type	Summary of Recent Incident(s)
12. John	—	*Criminal History:* No prior domestic violence cases *Recent Incident:* Argument with girlfriend over his care of their baby *Victim Statement:* N/A *Participant Statement:* Reports arguments about parenting and annoyance with one another's families; no reports of controlling behavior
13. Kevin	Situational	*Criminal History:* No prior domestic violence cases *Recent Incident:* Argument with girlfriend over a cigarette. She tries to make him leave the apartment. He refuses, knocks her to the ground, and bites her. *Victim Statement:* Reports argument over cigarette; no prior violent or controlling behavior reported *Participant Statement:* No reported violent or controlling behavior
14. Larry	Intimate Terrorism	*Criminal History:* Prior domestic violence and general violence cases *Recent Incident:* He strikes girlfriend in the head multiple times and threatens to kill her if she calls the police. *Victim Statement:* Controlling: does not let her sleep. *Participant Statement:* Reports abusing partner for fun; reports frequent, severe violence with frequent injuries; reports violence related to alcohol
15. Mike	Situational	*Criminal History:* No prior domestic violence cases *Recent Incident:* He gets in argument with girlfriend after not being allowed into local bar. Back home, he grabs her by legs and drags her in order to leave residence. *Victim Statement:* No reported violent or controlling behavior in past; abuse followed argument at bar; reported grabbing of legs *Participant Statement:* No reported violent or controlling behavior in past
16. Nic	Intimate Terrorism	*Criminal History:* No prior domestic violence arrests *Recent Incident:* Wife comes home and Nic and she get into argument about watching children. He starts to leave and she asks him to stay and talk. He grabs her away from front door, throws her to the floor, and kicks her twice.

Name	Violence Type	Summary of Recent Incident(s)
		Victim Statement: Reports physical abuse once a week during last two months; reported getting kicked; gives victim statement *Participant Statement:* Reported mutual controlling behavior (checking each other's phone call log)
17. Oscar	Intimate Terrorism	*Criminal History:* No prior domestic violence arrests *Recent Incident:* He gets into verbal argument with wife about not being able to afford a home. He grabs her, throws her to the ground, drags her by the hair, and stomps on her with his feet. *Victim Statement:* Reported controlling behavior (he locks her out of house for the night following incident and kicks her out of house the next day); reported being grabbed by hair and dragged on the floor *Participant Statement:* Controlling behavior (kicks her out of house after argument); anticipates continuing the relationship into the future
18. Pete	—	—
19. Quinn	—	—
20. Ralph	—	—
21. Steve	Situational	*Criminal History:* Prior domestic battery arrest *Recent Incident:* He asks girlfriend to show him where her current boyfriend lives. She does and he calls her a "bitch" and a "whore." She spits at him. He stops and pulls her out of car by the hair. *Victim Statement:* Reported controlling behavior (ex-boyfriend wants her to take him to see new boy friend's residence; he calls her a "bitch" and a "whore" for having new boyfriend); reported being pulled by hair and dragged on the ground; no reported violent or controlling behavior in past *Participant Statement:* Reports violent behavior following argument with girlfriend; no reported controlling behavior
22. Tom	Situational	*Criminal History:* No prior domestic battery arrests *Recent Incident:* He gets into argument with girlfriend at her house after she takes car from him while he is at work. He pushes her against the wall. *Victim Statement:* No reported violent or controlling behavior in past; abuse follows argument over use of car; reported being pushed against the wall *Participant Statement:* No reported violent or controlling behavior in past

Name	Violence Type	Summary of Recent Incident(s)
23. Victor	Intimate Terrorism	*Criminal History:* Prior domestic violence arrests; prior criminal sexual assault arrest *Recent Incidents:* 1. Verbal argument on highway and witness reports that he strikes girlfriend; 2. She reports that Victor made numerous attempts to contact her by phone, violating no-contact order. *Victim Statement:* No reports of violent or controlling behavior in present or past; she is fearful in talking to police *Participant Statement:* Reported frequent conflicts with partner; reported mild violence but no controlling behavior
24. Walter	Situational	*Criminal History:* No prior domestic violence arrests *Recent Incident:* Girlfriend states that Walter hit her in the face and head with his fists and with the telephone during an argument. *Victim Statement:* No reported violent or controlling behavior in past; abuse follows his accusations that she is having affair; reported being hit in head with his fists and with telephone *Participant Statement:* Denies any abuse; no reported violent or controlling behavior in past
25. Aaron	Intimate Terrorism	*Criminal History:* No prior domestic violence arrests *Recent Incident:* He suspects girlfriend is having affair on him while he is out of town, and he stalks her to find out. He confronts her, grabs hold of her arms, and slams her into the wall of the hallway, causing her head to hit the wall. Keeps entering her apartment without permission *Victim Statement:* No reported controlling behavior; reported "mistreatment" in past *Participant Statement:* No reported violent behavior in past; reported controlling behavior (stalking victim in order to verify suspicions that she is cheating on him)
26. Brett	Intimate Terrorism	*Criminal History:* Prior domestic violence arrest 10 years prior *Recent Incident:* Girlfriend comes home and he accuses her of "cheating" on him. She asks him to leave and he refuses. She picks up cell phone to call the police. He grabs it from her, throws it in corner, and then chokes her on the couch.

Name	Violence Type	Summary of Recent Incident(s)
		Victim Statement: No reports of violent or controlling behavior in past; abuse follows dispute about her going out for evening and her mothering responsibilities *Participant Statement:* Reported controlling behavior (checking what cars at her new residence)
27. Carl	Intimate Terrorism	*Criminal History:* No prior domestic violence arrests *Recent Incident:* She is asleep when Carl comes into room and starts yelling about money and suspected boyfriends. He removes the covers from her, lifts up her skirt, and yells about her "sleeping around." She pushes him away and he strikes her across the left side of her face. *Victim Statement:* Reported controlling behavior (he comes to her apartment after termination of relationship, unannounced, inspects her clothing while she is sleeping, and insults her); no reported violent or controlling behavior in past *Participant Statement:* Reported controlling behavior (he comes to her apartment after termination of relationship, unannounced, and inspects her clothing while she is sleeping); no reported violent or controlling behavior in past
28. Doug	Intimate Terrorism	*Criminal History:* Prior domestic violence arrests *Recent Incident:* Argument in his truck about her having another boyfriend. She picks up his cellular phone, and he goes "ballistic." He grabs her by the neck and tells her that he is going to kill her. *Victim Statement:* Reported controlling behavior (he stuck large knife in her favorite stuffed animal) *Participant Statement:* Reported multiple violent events in past; reports experiencing delusions during interview
29. Ed	Situational	*Criminal History:* No prior domestic violence arrest; prior criminal sexual assaults *Recent Incident:* A male and female with past sexual relationship get into argument over money owed to him. He pushes her into a closet. *Victim Statement:* No reported violent or controlling behavior in past *Participant Statement:* No reported violent or controlling behavior in past

Name	Violence Type	Summary of Recent Incident(s)
30. Carrie	Situational	*Criminal History:* No prior domestics violence arrest *Recent Incident:* Female scratches male after learning he is not watching their baby and has been in contact with an ex-girlfriend. *Victim Statement:* No reported violent or controlling behavior in past *Participant Statement:* Cuts him with box cutter; reported multiple violent events in past; no reported controlling behavior by her or partner

Notes

Introduction

1. In this book, I use the terms *intimate partner abuse, intimate partner violence,* and *domestic violence* interchangeably to refer to abuse occurring within intimate relationships. This includes abuse between persons who are or have ever been married or dating, regardless of cohabitation. While intimate partner abuse clearly includes lesbian and gay couples (Letellier 1994; Ristock 2002), my research focuses exclusively on abuse in heterosexual relationships. I also differentiate intimate partner abuse from family violence and gender violence. While intimate partner abuse does constitute part of these categories, family violence and gender violence refer to a wider range of abusive practices than those I study. Family violence, for instance, includes child abuse, while gender violence includes rape, sexual assault, sexual harassment, and hate crimes. Given that the social response to these abusive practices is different from the social response to intimate partner abuse, I find separating these categories appropriate for this study.

2. These measures are sometimes referred to as *presumptive arrest.* The difference in terminology owes to the language of the policies themselves. Mandatory arrest policies dictate that officers "must" or "shall" arrest when probable cause exists, while presumptive arrest polices dictate that they "should" arrest. The departments where I collected data utilized both wordings in their arrest policies. I primarily use the term *mandatory arrest* in this work, since it is the more widely circulated term.

3. These policies are also referred to as *evidence-based* or *mandatory prosecution.* The terms *no-drop* and *mandatory* are misnomers to an extent, since state's attorneys still maintain discretion to not prosecute a case. *Evidence-based,* meanwhile, indicates the strategy to build cases based on types of evidence other than victim statements. This term too is somewhat unwieldy, as it suggests victim statements as something other than evidence. These shortcomings aside, I primarily use the term *no-drop prosecution* in this work, since it is the more widely used term.

4. There is a good deal of debate on the question of whether mandatory policies intensify the racial inequalities witnessed in the criminal justice system more generally. Looking at the percentages of persons arrested and prosecuted, it is clear that African Americans make up a disproportionate number of arrestees relative to their numbers in the general population. However, evidence also indicates that mandatory policies, by standardizing officers' response to domestic violence cases, actually reduce the racial disparities in arrest statistics, even if African Americans remain disproportionately represented (see Stark 2007:151–53). While I return to this topic later in the book, my

point here is that racial discrimination is not to be understood only in raw numbers, but also in offenders' experiences of the law.

5. How one refers to persons arrested and prosecuted on domestic violence charges is a delicate question. Most of the people participating in this study were reported to have been violent by their partners. It makes sense, then, to refer to them as *intimate abusers*, *batterers*, and *abusive partners*, terms that acknowledge their violence. However, some of these respondents were ultimately not found guilty by the criminal justice system. Thus, from a legal perspective, calling these persons abusers is unjustified. In this work, I refer to the participants using the terms *abusers*, *batterers*, and *abusive partners*, as well as *suspects*. In using the term *suspects*, I do not look to diminish their actions or silence the voices of their partners. Indeed, Appendix B of the book reports the range and severity of violent acts that these respondents are reported to have committed.

6. This is not to say that domestic violence was never treated as a criminal offense by police, or that arrests never occurred. However, as a whole, arrest was not embraced as the appropriate response to domestic violence calls (Martin 1976; Dobash & Dobash 1979).

7. The earliest shelters appeared in Denmark, the United Kingdom, the United States, Canada, Australia, and the Netherlands. Interestingly, while feminist groups often organized these efforts, in the United States, "domestic violence programs were as likely to be organized by the YWCA, the Salvation Army, or unaffiliated individuals" (see Stark 2007:28–30).

8. The National Institute of Justice sponsored a series of studies in the mid-1980s on the effects of arrest on domestic batterers. The original study was the well-publicized Minneapolis experiment of Sherman and Berk (1984). Following the project, the NIJ funded five studies to replicate its findings. The five replication studies were conducted in Colorado Springs, CO (Berk et al. 1992); Omaha, NE (Dunford et al.1990); Charlotte, NC (Hirschel and Hutchinson 1992); Miami-Dade County, FL (Pate & Hamilton 1992); and Milwaukee, WI (Sherman et al. 1992a).

9. In statistical analyses of the replication studies, the "stake in conformity" hypothesis holds most strongly for the category of employment. Arrest made unemployed suspects more likely to commit future violence in three of the experiments. Conversely, arrest made unmarried suspects more likely to commit future violence in one out of two experiments with data on the category (Sherman 1992:185).

10. Sherman (1992), who designed the arrest experiments, refers to this as a "black box problem," that the experiments reported "the connection between arrest and violence, but did not explain *why* that connection was found" (89).

11. This name is fictitious. The names of places and persons in this research have been changed to protect participants' anonymity.

12. In this study, I will use the term *domestic violence cases* to refer to different types of criminal behaviors that are considered domestic violence offenses. These include domestic battery, violation of an order of protection, stalking, and interference with the reporting of domestic battery, among others. The majority of the cases mentioned in my research involve either domestic battery or violations of orders of protection.

13. A more detailed description of this study's research methods can be found in Appendix A.

1—The Practice of Mandatory Arrest

1. Later research demonstrated, however, that these figures were inflated and based on misinterpretations of the FBI data (Garner & Clemmer 1986). Other studies likewise worked to dispel the myth of domestic violence calls as especially dangerous by showing previous estimates of officer deaths and injuries sustained in policing these calls to be exaggerated (Margarita 1980; Hirschel et al. 1994). However, as the

brief description of police training in this chapter attests, the statistical assurance that domestic violence calls are not that dangerous has not eliminated police officers' belief that they are.

2. The department's policy reads as follows: "In cases involving domestic violence, an officer shall make an arrest without a warrant when probable cause exists under the following circumstances: (a) When a felony has been committed; (b) When any weapon has been used to inflict injury or to intimidate or threaten the victim; (c) When an offense is committed in the presence of the officer; (d) When an officer has confirmed that a valid Order of Protection is in effect, that the offender has been served or has knowledge of the order, and a police enforceable condition of the order has been violated by the offender; (e) It has been determined that the automatic 72 hour no-contact provision of a bond is in effect; or that the no contact provision of a pending case is in effect. In all other cases an arrest should be made if probable cause exists that an offender has committed an act of domestic violence, constituting a criminal offense." Meanwhile, the state's domestic violence law, written in 1986, defines domestic battery as the following: "A person commits domestic battery if he intentionally or knowingly without legal justification by any means: (1) Causes bodily harm to any family or household member . . . (2) Makes physical contact of an insulting or provoking nature with any family or household member."

3. Jailing in this study refers to custodial holding, not criminal sentencing. In a more recent study, Hester (2006) finds that only 4 out of 869 domestic violence incidents, or 0.5%, recorded by the police resulted in custodial convictions.

4. Sykes and Brent (1983) group verbal tactics into three distinct types: definitional (questioning), imperative (commands), and coercive (the threat or actual use of physical coercion). Of these tactics, the most commonly used is definitional. "The officer takes charge in most encounters by merely asking a question. In asking a question, the officer not only immediately starts to accomplish one essential task, but also forces the attention of the civilian on the task at hand" (Sykes & Brent 1983:62–63).

5. Rubinstein's (1973) rich ethnography of policing displays a sensitivity to the importance of space to policing. Specifically, he notes that the "positioning and distance of a patrolman in relation to the person he is seeking to control are absolutely critical" (Rubinstein 1973:305). Bayley and Bittner (1984) do as well, in explaining that when officers knock at residences where violence is suspected, they do not stand in front of the doors, for fear that someone inside might have a gun and fire a shot through the door (37).

6. Bayley and Garofalo (1989) find "presence" to be the most influential policing tactic. Describing the police's response to violence in general, the authors note, "Most conflict stops as soon as the police arrive, attacks on the police are rare, and the force used by police is usually slight" (20).

7. The distinction between "control" and "supportive" actions is Sun's (2003:27–28). The identification of their application in domestic violence policing is mine.

8. The misspelling of the word "be" is present on the form itself. The misspelling, and the otherwise ragged appearance of the copies of the form that the officers provide victims, could be seen to communicate their own messages about the department's handling of domestic violence cases.

9. DCFS stands for the Department of Child and Family Services. The police are required to contact DCFS any time a child is reported to have been abused or witness to abuse.

10. While I have been couching much of the description of the police encounter in Foucauldian terms to this point, I find Goffman's (1961) description of asylums more instructive for understanding the tactics used in the Centralia County Jail than Foucault's (1977) fêted description of the prison. The primary reason for this is that the county jail does not possess the disciplinary, reformative mission of Foucault's prison. In its function as a short-term detention facility, it simply looks to hold criminal

suspects rather than shape them into new subjects. This fact lends its practice of power a different flavor.

11. Most recently, Hirschel and Buzawa (2002) found that women represented 30.8%, 17.4%, and 28% of domestic battery arrests in the states of Connecticut, Rhode Island, and Arizona, respectively (1456).

2—The Practice of No-Drop Prosecution

1. The office instituted the program after receiving a federal Domestic Violence Prosecution Grant made possible by the 1994 Violence Against Women Act (VAWA).

2. Hence, as noted in the introduction, no-drop prosecution is also often referred to as "evidence-based" prosecution.

3. In pursuing pleas, the state aims for "on the nose" pleas (Flemming 1990:44) to the charge of domestic battery, a predicate offense, which means that future violations will automatically be charged as felonies. In addition, the state nearly always requires partner abuse classes or treatment for alcohol or substance abuse, as a condition of the plea agreement.

4. I was unable to learn the story-gathering approach of one of the ten attorneys I interviewed.

5. While these pressures were noted by the public defenders I spoke with, it needs also be said that many clients actively look to plead or are relieved when they learn a plea deal is available. The process is indeed the punishment for many defendants (Feeley 1979:30; Heumann 1978:69). Nevertheless, public defenders approach most clients with an eye to gaining their trust and moving their cases along.

6. "Hun" is short for "honey."

7. Persons convicted of misdemeanor or felony domestic violence charges are prohibited from possessing a firearms ownership card.

8. Matt, the state's attorney, noted that he had tried, and lost, two domestic battery cases in his six months on the job. Marge, the public defender, who had spent four years handling domestic battery cases, said that she had tried probably four cases in that time. To put that number in perspective, Marge estimated she handled 300 domestic battery cases per year.

9. As noted in chapter 1, this percentage does exceed numbers reported in previous research.

10. Matt, the assistant state's attorney, estimated that in "the vast majority of our cases, 80–90% of them, the victim is not cooperative." I have no figures to corroborate this estimate, which is higher than past studies have shown. For instance, Dawson and Dinovitzer's (2001) study of victim cooperation in a specialized domestic violence court found that 45% of victims did not cooperate with the prosecution of their cases.

3—Research Participants and Their Violence

1. For a fuller description of the methods used in this study, including recruitment and interview procedures, please see Appendix A at the end of the book.

2. Johnson and Stark differ slightly with regard to the gendered nature of the most serious forms of abuse. While Johnson (2006:1011) has found a small number of cases of "mutual violent control," in which women as well as men are violent and controlling, Stark (2006:1024) has not encountered a case of women exercising "coercive control" over men.

3. As noted in the previous two chapters, women comprise a sizable percentage of the persons arrested for domestic violence in Centralia County. In Plainsville, women represented 37% of domestic violence arrests in 2001.

4. Cases of "violent resistance" and "mutual violent control" do not appear in this sample. This probably owes in part to the fact that most participants were men. In "violent resistance," the individual, usually a woman, is violent, but the partner is controlling and violent. While three women took part in this study, I have no evidence that their partners were controlling and violent. And only in one case (Betty) did a participant claim to have been abused by her partner. Absent evidence of patterns of controlling behavior, however, her case resembled "situational couple violence." Meanwhile, none of the male research participants claimed to be the victims of controlling behavior by their partners, which would be characteristic of "mutual violent control." However, as later chapters describe, many men did come to see themselves as victims in other senses.

5. More specifically, Stark's typology would require one to differentiate between "fights," "assaults," and "coercive control." Since most of my participants were accused of being violent, most would fall into Stark's categories of fights and assaults. Yet many also displayed the control tactics described by Stark as constitutive of "coercive control." In the end, then, I found "SCV" and "IT" the more harmonious terms.

6. I conducted shorter interviews with three of these men (Pete, Quinn, Ralph) immediately following their appearances in court and did not have the opportunity to record their personal information. These shortened interviews focused primarily on their experiences with the criminal justice system. In the fourth case (John), I was unable to locate a police report for his case.

7. Given the fact that the typology of batterers described by Johnson has not yet been widely applied in domestic violence research, there is not yet a reliable way of knowing whether 13 cases of intimate terrorism out of a sample of 25 domestic violence cases is either high or low. Johnson (2006a) himself supposes that most domestic violence is SCV (fn.11). However, most domestic violence for which women seek help is IT (68% of a court sample, 79% of a shelter sample) (Johnson 2006a:1011). Compared to this, 13 intimate terrorists out of a sample of 25 batterers who have gone to court would be lower than expected.

8. "VR" refers to "violent resistance."

9. Stark (2007) convincingly demonstrates that "the risk of severe or fatal injury increases with separation" and that "a majority of partner assaults occur while partners are separated" (115).

4—Abusers' Experiences with Mandatory Arrest and No-Drop Prosecution

1. This evidentiary principle is, of course, not limited to domestic violence cases. As Deborah Tuerkheimer (2004) notes, courts exclude evidence of prior acts in most cases due to concerns that "evidence of a criminal defendant's prior bad acts . . . could lead jurors to convict in the absence of proof beyond a reasonable doubt, or to engage in prohibited 'propensity reasoning'—that is, to assume that if the defendant is the type of person who has engaged in particular conduct in the past, he is more likely to have done so on the occasion in question" (989). As a consequence, "the rules of evidence mute stories of battering" (990). Exceptions to these evidentiary rules are encoded in statutes against stalking, which criminalize patterns of behavior. In addition, judges do hold the discretion to allow evidence of patterned abuse in individual domestic violence cases. However, most courts continue to treat domestic violence as a transactional offense rather than as a pattern of criminal conduct (see Tuerkheimer 2004:989–1014).

2. Ten of the thirty persons interviewed for this research had not had their cases adjudicated at the time of our interview. The interviews were completed in the time between the arraignment and disposition of their cases. Of these cases, one was dismissed and seven ended in plea bargain convictions, a fact that reinforces the centrality of plea

bargains in prosecuting domestic violence cases in Centralia County. I was unable to determine the disposition of the other two cases. These cases represent a limitation in the data, since these respondents as a group did not have as full an experience of no-drop prosecution as did the others. Nevertheless, six of the ten did have prior domestic violence convictions. Further, all of these respondents were in the midst of defending themselves from criminal prosecution. As a result, each was able to provide meaningful insight into the experience of being prosecuted for domestic violence.

3. It bears mentioning that in 2005, three prisoners at the Centralia County Jail committed suicide by hanging. One of the suspects killed himself shortly after his detention, while the other two killed themselves after spending over four months incarcerated. The Centralia County Sheriff's Department responded by promising increased psychological evaluations of inmates and increased room checks to ensure that inmates are not attempting suicide.

4. Police-officer-perpetrated domestic violence is a significant, but understudied, phenomenon. Johnson (1991) finds that the rate of domestic violence among police officers far exceeds that of the general population, though the research methods used in this study have been critiqued (see Kappelar 1999). I thank an anonymous reviewer for bringing the Kappelar article to my attention.

5. "V of OP" and "VOP" stand for "violation of order of protection."

6. Lundy Bancroft (2002) notes a similar viewpoint in the men he has worked with in counseling. "My clients support laws that prohibit domestic abuse," he writes, "as long as they are applied to other men. Each one has a mental image of what a 'real abuser' is like, and it isn't him" (296). The interesting, if subtle, point to be discerned in the three quotes above is that these men support domestic violence laws on the basis of women's inequality (they are weaker than men and need to be protected) rather than their equality (they are the same as men and deserve the same treatment).

5—Abusers' Relation to Violence

1. Because this chapter focuses on the effects of arrest and prosecution on abusive men's relation to violence, I focus specifically on the interviews I completed with men.

2. These categories are not mutually exclusive. Respondents frequently offered multiple types of stories to depict their violence.

3. Bancroft's (2002) book relating his experiences working with intimate abusers in batterer intervention programs also makes mention of self-defense stories. However, the men he writes about never found their partners' actions threatening. He notes, "they admit that they were not frightened or injured by their partners" (299). The self-defense stories described here differ in that the men do present themselves as having felt threatened by their partners.

4. As noted before, I was unable to locate criminal cases for three of the respondents. In addition, two respondents, Walter and Ed, did not make a statement to the police.

5. It is difficult, of course, to corroborate individual allegations of state coercion. Such claims were common among respondents, however, and the state's attorney noted as well that his office subpoenas victims to testify against their abusers.

6—Change in the Lives of Abusers

1. Analyses of the arrest experiments originally demonstrated a deterrent effect both for men who were employed and for men who were married, with a slightly stronger effect associated with the former (Pate & Hamilton 1992; Sherman 1992; Sherman et al. 1992a; Sherman et al. 1992b). However, as noted in the introduction to the book, Maxwell et al.'s (2002) reexamination of the arrest experiment data, which used the

victim reports that the arrest experiments collected but were unable to analyze due to gaps in the data, found that marriage did not promote deterrence (68). The deterrent effect remained for employment.

2. One respondent, Henry, was violent against his brother. He is excluded from this accounting.

3. I borrow the term *self-governance* from Valverde (1998), who in her study of alcoholism describes Alcoholics Anonymous as "an approach to ethical governance" "relying primarily on self-governance rather than on advice or exhortation" (120). Here, I develop the term in a different manner. Rather than referring to institutionalized programs of action, the projects of self-governance described in this section are personalized programs of action, developed by individual subjects to realize change in their lives.

4. Interestingly, and importantly, Stark (2007) explains that this narrow conception of domestic violence owes primarily to the women's antiviolence movement, which has publicized intimate partner abuse through images of severe physical injury and vulnerable victims. While these terms have proven effective in heightening public awareness of domestic violence, they also "effectively exclude whole classes of victims whose survival depends on public recognition." As a result, "relabeling" of intimate partner abuse is required that recognizes "the psychological or emotional dimensions" of "coercive control" (370).

Conclusion

1. It is reasoned that the greater availability of victims services, in the form of shelters and aggressive legal interventions, have provided black women alternatives to the use of fatal violence for managing abusive relationships.

2. One notable exception is a study by Paternoster et al. (1997), which in reanalyzing the Milwaukee Domestic Violence Experiment data found that "the use of fair procedures" suppressed "subsequent violence." Noteworthy as well is a recent study by Labriola et al. (2005) on the efficacy of batterer intervention programs and judicial monitoring on abuser rearrests. Finding no significant differences between batterer programs and judicial monitoring in rates of rearrest, the authors explain that their "findings are qualified . . . by the nature of judicial monitoring. . . . The feedback conveyed by the judicial hearing officer during monitoring appearances was generally brief, matter-of-fact, and often couched in legal terminology that some offenders may not have understood" (ix). Like this study, then, these authors point to the influence of how punishments are delivered on what outcomes punishments produce.

Works Cited

Alpert, Geoffrey, & Robert Dunham (1997) *Policing Urban America*. 3rd ed. Prospect Heights, IL: Waveland.

Alschuler, Albert (1976) "The Trial Judge's Role in Plea Bargaining," 76 *Columbia Law Rev.*, 1059–1154.

——— (1975) "The Defense Attorney's Role in Plea Bargaining," 84 *Yale Law J.*, 1179–1314.

——— (1968) "The Prosecutor's Role in Plea Bargaining," 36 *University of Chicago Law Rev.*, 50–112.

Anderson, Kristin, & Debra Umberson (2001) "Gendering Violence: Masculinity and Power in Men's Accounts of Domestic Violence," 15 *Gender and Society*, 358–80.

Avakame, Edem, & James Fyfe (2001) "Differential Police Treatment of Male-on-Female Spousal Violence: Additional Evidence on the Leniency Thesis," 7 *Violence against Women*, 22–45.

Ballesteros, Octavio (1979) *Behind Jail Bars*. New York: Philosophical Library.

Bancroft, Lundy (2002) *Why Does He Do That? Inside the Minds of Angry and Controlling Men*. New York: Berkley Publishing.

Bard, Morton (1970) *Training Police as Specialists in Family Crisis Intervention*. Washington D.C.: U.S. Department of Justice.

Bayley, David, & Egon Bittner (1984) "Learning the Skills of Policing," 47 *Law and Contemporary Social Problems*, 35–60 (4).

Bayley, David, & James Garofalo (1989) "The Management of Violence by Police Patrol Officers," 27 *Criminology*, 1–25.

Bennett, Larry, & Oliver Williams (2005) "Controversies and Recent Studies of Batterer Intervention Program Effectiveness," available on-line at: [www.vawnet.org] (accessed January 15, 2009).

Berg, Bruce (1999) *Policing in Modern Society*. Boston: Butterworth Heinemann.

Berk, Richard, et al. (1992) "A Bayesian Analysis of the Colorado Springs Spouse Abuse Experiment,"83 *J. of Criminal Law and Criminology*, 137–69.

Berk, Sarah F., & Donileen R. Loseke (1980–81) "'Handling' Family Violence: Situational Determinants of Police Arrest in Domestic Disturbances," 15 *Law and Society Rev.*, 317–46.

Binder, Arnold, & James Meeker (1992) "The Development of Social Attitudes toward Spousal Abuse," in E. Buzawa and C. Buzawa, eds., *Domestic Violence: The Changing Criminal Justice Response*. Westport, CT: Greenwood.

Bittner, Egon (1970) *The Functions of the Police in Modern Society*. Chevy Chase, MD: National Institute of Mental Health.

Black, Donald (1980) *The Manners and Customs of the Police.* New York: Academic Press.

Blumberg, Abraham (1967) "The Practice of Law as a Confidence Game," 1 *Law and Society Rev.,* 15–39.

Braithwaite, John (1989) *Crime, Shame, and Reintegration.* Cambridge: Cambridge University Press.

Brennan, Patricia (1989) "A 'Cry for Help' Went Unheeded," *Washington Post,* 2 October.

Brooks, Richard, & Haekyung Jeon-Slaughter (2001) "Race, Income, and Perceptions of the U.S. Court System," 19 *Behavioral Sciences and the Law,* 249–64.

Brown, Michael (1981) *Working the Street: Police Discretion and the Dilemmas of Reform.* New York: Russell Sage Foundation.

Brown, Wendy (1995) *States of Injury.* Princeton, NJ: Princeton University Press.

Brzozowski, Jodi-Anne (2004) *Family Violence in Canada: A Statistical Profile.* Ottawa: Statistics Canada.

Buel, Sarah Mausolff (1988) "Mandatory Arrest for Domestic Violence," 11 *Harvard Women's Law J.,* 213–26.

Burchell, Graham, et al., eds. (1991) *The Foucault Effect: Studies in Governmentality.* Hemel Hempstead: Harvester Wheatsheaf.

Butler, Judith (1989) *Gender Trouble: Feminism and the Subversion of Identity.* New York: Routledge.

Buzawa, Eve, & Carl Buzawa (2003) *Domestic Violence: The Criminal Justice Response,* 3rd ed. Thousand Oaks, CA: Sage.

—— (1996a) *Domestic Violence: The Criminal Justice Response, 2nd ed.* Thousand Oaks, CA: Sage.

——, eds. (1996b) *Do Arrests and Restraining Orders Work?* Thousand Oaks, CA: Sage.

Buzawa, Eve, et al. (1996) "The Role of Arrest in Domestic versus Stranger Assault: Is There a Difference?" in E. Buzawa and C. Buzawa, eds., *Do Arrests and Restraining Orders Work?* Thousand Oaks, CA: Sage.

Buzawa, Eve, et al. (1999) *Response to Domestic Violence in a Pro-Active Court Setting, Executive Summary.* Washington D.C.: National Institute of Justice.

Cadsky, Oto, et al. (1996) "Attrition from a Male Batterer Treatment Program: Client–Treatment Congruence and Lifestyle Instability," 11 *Violence and Victims,* 51–64.

Cahn, Naomi (2000) "Policing Women: Moral Arguments and the Dilemmas of Criminalization," 49 *DePaul Law Rev.,* 817, 819–820.

Cahn, Naomi, & Lisa Lerman (1991) "Prosecuting Woman Abuse," in M. Steinman, ed., *Woman Battering: Policy Responses.* Cincinnati: Anderson.

Carlson, Christopher, & Frank Nidey (1995) "Mandatory Penalties, Victim Cooperation, and the Judicial Processing of Domestic Abuse Assault Cases," 41 *Crime and Delinquency,* 132–49.

Casper, Jonathan (1972) *American Criminal Justice: The Defendant's Perspective.* Englewood Cliffs, NJ: Prentice-Hall.

Cate, Rodney, & Sally Lloyd (1992) *Courtship.* Newbury Park, CA: Sage.

Chaudhuri, Molly, & Kathleen Daly (1992) "Do Restraining Orders Help? Battered Women's Experience with Male Violence and Legal Process," in E. Buzawa and C. Buzawa, eds., *Domestic Violence: The Changing Criminal Justice Response.* Westport, CT: Auburn House.

Coker, Donna (2004) "Race, Poverty, and the Crime-Centered Response to Domestic Violence: A Comment on Linda Mills's *Insult to Injury: Rethinking Our Response to Intimate Abuse,*" 10 *Violence against Women,* 1331–53.

—— (2002) "Transformative Justice: Anti-Subordination Processes in Domestic Violence Cases," in H. Strang & J. Braithwaite, eds., *Restorative Justice and Family Violence.* Cambridge: Cambridge University Press.

—— (2001) "Crime Control and Feminist Law Reform in Domestic Violence Law," 4 *Buffalo Criminal Law Rev.,* 801–60.

Conley, John, & William O'Barr (1990) *Rules versus Relationships: The Ethnography of Legal Discourse*. Chicago: University of Chicago Press.

Connell, R. W. (2000) *The Men and the Boys*. Berkeley: University of California Press.

Coulter, Martha, et al. (1999) "Police-Reporting Behavior and Victim–Police Interactions as Described by Women in a Domestic Violence Shelter," 14 *J. of Interpersonal Violence*, 1290–98.

Curtis-Fawley, Sarah, & Kathleen Daly (2005) "Gendered Violence and Restorative Justice," 11 *Violence against Women*, 603–38.

Daly, Kathleen, et al. (2003) *Sexual Offence Cases Finalised in Court, by Conference, and by Formal Caution in South Australia for Young Offenders, 1995–2001: Final Report, August 2003*. Brisbane, Australia: School of Criminology and Criminal Justice, Griffith University.

Dasgupta, Shamita Das (2003) *Safety & Justice for All: Examining the Relationship between the Women's Anti-Violence Movement and the Criminal Legal System*. New York: Ms. Foundation. Available on-line at http://www.ms.foundation.org/user-assets/PDF/Program/safety_justice.pdf (accessed July 2, 2008).

Davies, Jill, et al. (1998) *Safety Planning with Battered Women: Complex Lives/Difficult Choices*. Thousand Oaks, CA: Sage.

Davis, Robert, et al. (2003) "Increasing the Proportion of Domestic Violence Arrests That Are Prosecuted: A Natural Experiment in Milwaukee," 2 *Criminology and Public Policy*, 263–82.

Dawson, Myrna (2004) "Rethinking the Boundaries of Intimacy at the End of the Century: The Role of Victim–Defendant Relationship in Criminal Justice Decision-making over Time," 38 *Law and Society Rev.*, 105–38.

Dawson, Myrna, & Ronit Dinovitzer (2001) "Victim Cooperation and the Prosecution of Domestic Violence in a Specialized Court," 18 *Justice Quarterly*, 593–622.

Dean, Mitchell (1999) *Governmentality: Power and Rule in Modern Society*. London: Sage.

_____ (1994) *Critical and Effective Histories: Foucault's Methods and Historical Sociology*. London: Routledge.

Dean, Mitchell, & Barry Hindess, eds. (1998) *Governing Australia: Studies in Contemporary Rationalities of Government*. Cambridge: Cambridge University Press.

Dobash, Rebecca, & Russell Dobash (2000) "Evaluating Criminal Justice Interventions for Domestic Violence," 46 *Crime and Delinquency*, 252–70.

—— (1998) "Violent Men and Violent Contexts," in R. Dobash & R. Dobash, eds., *Rethinking Violence against Women*. Thousand Oaks, CA: Sage.

—— (1979) *Violence against Wives: A Case against Patriarchy*. New York: Free Press.

Dobash, R. Emerson, et al. (2000) *Changing Violent Men*. Thousand Oaks, CA: Sage.

Dugan, Laura (2003) "Domestic Violence Legislation: Exploring Its Impact on the Likelihood of Domestic Violence, Police Involvement, and Arrest," in 2 *Criminology and Public Policy*, 283–312.

Dugan, Laura, et al. (2003) "Exposure Reduction or Retaliation? The Effects of Domestic Violence Resources on Intimate-Partner Homicide," 37 *Law and Society Rev.*, 169–98.

Dunford, Franklyn, et al. (1990) "The Role of Arrest in Domestic Assault: The Omaha Police Experiment," 2 *Criminology*, 283–312.

Dutton, Donald (1998) *The Abusive Personality: Violence and Control in Intimate Relationships*. New York: Guilford Press.

Edin, Kathryn (2000) "Few Good Men: Why Low-Income Single Mothers Don't Get Married," 11 *American Prospect*, 26–31.

Edin, Kathryn, & Laura Lein (1997) *Making Ends Meet: How Single Mothers Survive Welfare and Low-Wage Work*. New York: Russell Sage Foundation.

Eisenstein, James, & Herbert Jacob (1977) *Felony Justice: An Organizational Analysis of Criminal Courts*. Boston: Little, Brown.

Eisikovits, Zvi, & Eli Buchbinder (2000) *Locked in a Violent Embrace: Understanding and Intervening in Domestic Violence*. Thousand Oaks, CA: Sage.

Emerson, Robert (1969) *Judging Delinquents: Context and Process in Juvenile Court*. Chicago: Aldine.

Epstein, Deborah (1999) "Effective Intervention in Domestic Violence Cases: Rethinking the Roles of Prosecutors, Judges, and the Court System," 11 *Yale Journal of Law and Feminism*, 3–39.

Ewick, Patricia, & Susan Silbey (1998) *The Common Place of Law: Stories from Everyday Life*. Chicago: University of Chicago Press.

—— (1995) "Subversive Stories and Hegemonic Tales: Toward a Sociology of Narrative," 29 *Law and Society Rev.*, 197–226.

Fagan, Jeffrey (1996) *The Criminalization of Domestic Violence: Promises and Limits*. NIJ Research Report. National Criminal Justice Reference Service, http://www.ncjrs.gov/pdffiles/crimdom.pdf (accessed December 2, 2008).

Federal Bureau of Investigation (2003) *Law Enforcement Officers Killed and Assaulted*. Washington, DC: U.S. Department of Justice.

—— (2002) "Ten-Year Arrest Trends: 1993–2002," available at: fbi.gov/ucr/cius_02/html/web/arrested/04–table32.html.

—— (1995) *Law Enforcement Officers Killed and Assaulted*. Washington, DC: U.S. Department of Justice.

—— (1977) *Law Enforcement Officers Killed*. Washington, DC: U.S. Department of Justice.

—— (1975) *Law Enforcement Officers Killed*. Washington, DC: U.S. Department of Justice.

Feeley, Malcom (1979) *The Process Is the Punishment: Handling Cases in a Lower Criminal Court*. New York: Russell Sage Foundation.

Felson, Richard, et al. (1999) "The Victim-Offender Relationship and Calling the Police in Assaults," 37 *Criminology*, 931–47.

Felstiner, William (1998) "Justice, Power, and Lawyers," in B. Garth and A. Sarat, eds., *Justice and Power in Sociolegal Studies*. Evanston, IL: Northwestern University Press.

Ferraro, Kathleen, & Tascha Boychuk (1992) "The Court's Response to Interpersonal Violence: A Comparison of Intimate and Nonintimate Assault," in E. Buzawa and C. Buzawa, eds., *Domestic Violence: The Changing Criminal Justice Response*. Westport, CT: Auburn House.

Ferraro, Kathleen, & Lucille Pope (1993) "Irreconcilable Differences: Battered Women, Police, and the Law," in N. Zoe Hilton, ed., *Legal Responses to Wife Assault: Current Trends and Evaluation*. Newbury Park, CA: Sage.

Finn, Mary, & Loretta Stalans (1995) "Police Referrals to Shelters and Mental Health Treatment: Examining Their Decisions in Domestic Assault Cases," in 41 *Crime and Delinquency*, 467–80.

Flemming, Barbara (2003) "Equal Protection for Victims of Domestic Violence," 18 *J. of Interpersonal Violence*, 685–92.

Flemming, Roy (1990) "The Political Styles and Organizational Strategies of American Prosecutors: Examples from Nine Courthouse Communities," 12 *Law and Policy*, 25–50.

—— (1986) "Client Games: Defense Attorney Perspectives on Their Relations with Criminal Clients," in 11 *American Bar Foundation Research J.*, 253–72 (spring).

Fleury, Ruth (2002) "Missing Voices: Patterns of Battered Women's Satisfaction with the Criminal Legal System," 8 *Violence against Women*, 181–205.

Ford, David (2003) "Coercing Victim Participation in Domestic Violence Prosecutions," 18 *J. of Interpersonal Violence*, 69–84.

——— (1991) "Prosecution as a Victim Power Resource: A Note on Empowering Women in Violent Conjugal Relationships," 25 *Law and Society Rev.,* 313–34.

Ford, David, & Mary Jean Regoli (1993) "The Criminal Prosecution of Wife Assaulters," in N. Zoe Hilton, ed., *Legal Responses to Wife Assault: Current Trends and Evaluation.* Newbury Park, CA: Sage.

——— et al. (1996) "Future Directions for Criminal Justice Policy on Domestic Violence," in E. Buzawa and C. Buzawa, eds., *Do Arrests and Restraining Orders Work?* Thousand Oaks, CA: Sage.

Foucault, Michel (1979) *The History of Sexuality,* vol. 1. London: Allen Lane.

——— (1977) *Discipline and Punish: The Birth of the Prison.* London: Allen Lane.

——— (1965) *Madness and Civilization: A History of Insanity in the Age of Reason.* London: Tavistock.

Freeman, Mark (2004) "Data Are Everywhere: Narrative Criticism in the Literature of Experience," in C. Daiute and C. Lightfoot, eds., *Narrative Analysis: Studying the Development of Individuals in Society.* Thousand Oaks, CA: Sage.

Fritzler, Randal, & Leonore Simon (2000) "Creating a Domestic Violence Court: Combat in the Trenches," in 37 *Court Rev.,* 28–39 (spring).

Frohmann, Lisa (1997) "Convictability and Discordant Locales: Reproducing Race, Class, and Gender Ideologies in Prosecutorial Decision-Making," 31 *Law and Society Rev.,* 531–55.

Garner, Joel, & Elizabeth Clemmer (1986) *Danger to Police in Domestic Disturbances: A New Look, Research in Brief.* Washington, DC: U.S. Department of Justice, National Institute of Justice, 1986.

George, Suja (1998) "The Construction of Domestic Violence among Police Officers." Ph.D. diss., Department of Human and Community Development, University of Illinois, Urbana.

Gilgun, Jane (2001) "Grounded Theory and Other Inductive Research Methods," in Bruce Thyer, ed., *The Handbook of Social Work Research Methods.* Thousand Oaks, CA: Sage.

Goffman, Erving (1965) *Stigma: Notes on the Management of Spoiled Identity.* Englewood Cliffs, NJ: Prentice-Hall.

——— (1961) *Asylums: Essays on the Social Situation of Mental Patients and Other Inmates.* Chicago: Aldine.

Goldkamp, John, & Cheryl Irons-Guynn (2000) *Emerging Judicial Strategies for the Mentally Ill in the Criminal Caseload: Mental Health Courts in Fort Lauderdale, Seattle, San Bernardino, and Anchorage.* Washington, DC: Bureau of Justice Assistance.

Goodman, Harriet (2001) "In-Depth Interviews," in Bruce Thyer, ed., *The Handbook of Social Work Research Methods.* Thousand Oaks, CA: Sage.

Goodman, Lisa, et al. (1999) "Obstacles to Domestic Violence Victims' Cooperation with the Criminal Prosecution of Their Abusers: The Role of Social Support," 14 *Violence and Victims,* 427–44.

Hagan, John, & Celesta Albonetti (1982) "Race, Class, and the Perception of Criminal Injustice in America," 88 *American J. of Sociology,* 329–55.

Hanna, Cheryl (1996) "No Right to Choose: Mandated Victim Participation in Domestic Violence Prosecutions," 109 *Harvard Law Rev.,* 1850–1910.

Hart, Barbara (1996) "Battered Women and the Criminal Justice System," in E. Buzawa and C. Buzawa, eds., *Do Arrests and Restraining Orders Work?* Thousand Oaks, CA: Sage.

Hartley, Carolyn Copps (2003) "A Therapeutic Jurisprudence Approach to the Trial Process in Domestic Violence Felony Trials," 9 *Violence against Women,* 410–37.

Hearn, Jeff (1998) *The Violences of Men: How Men Talk about and How Agencies Respond to Men's Violence against Women.* Thousand Oaks, CA: Sage.

Hendricks, James, & Jerome McKean (1995) *Crisis Intervention: Contemporary Issues for On-Site Interveners*. 2nd ed. Springfield, IL: Charles C. Thomas.

Herrell, Stephen, & Meredith Hofford (1990) *Family Violence: Improving Court Practice*. Reno, NV: Family Violence Project, National Council on Juvenile and Family Court Judges.

Hester, Marianne (2006) "Making It through the Criminal Justice System: Attrition and Domestic Violence," 5 *Social Policy and Society*, 79–90.

Heumann, Milton (1978) *Plea Bargaining*. Chicago: University of Chicago Press.

Hirschel, David, & Eve Buzawa (2002) "Understanding the Context of Dual Arrest with Directions for Future Research," 8 *Violence against Women*, 1449–73.

Hirschel, J. David, & Ira W. Hutchinson (2003) "The Voices of Domestic Violence Victims: Predictors of Victim Preference for Arrest and the Relationship between Preference for Arrest and Revictimization," 49 *Crime and Delinquency*, 313–36.

——— (1992) "Female Spouse Abuse and the Police Response: The Charlotte, North Carolina Experiment," 83 *J. of Criminal Law & Criminology*, 73–119.

Hirschel, David, et al. (1994) "The Relative Contribution of Domestic Violence to Assault and Injury of Police Officers," 11 *Justice Quarterly*, 99–117.

Hobart, Margaret (2000) "The Legal Consciousness and Legal Mobilization of Battered Women in Phoenix, Arizona and Seattle, Washington." Presented at the annual meeting of the Law and Society Association, Miami (May).

Holtzworth-Munroe, Amy, & Gregory Stuart (1994) "Typologies of Male Batterers: Three Subtypes and the Differences among Them," 116 *Psychological Bulletin*, 476–97.

Hopkins, C. Quince, et al. (2004) "Applying Restorative Justice to Ongoing Intimate Violence: Problems and Possibilities," in 23 *Saint Louis University Public Law Rev.*, 289–311.

Hosticka, Carl (1979) "We Don't Care about What Happened, We Only Care about What Is Going to Happen," 26 *Social Problems*, 599–610.

Hoyle, Carolyn (1998) *Negotiating Domestic Violence: Police, Criminal Justice and Victims*. Oxford: Oxford University Press.

Hoyle, Carolyn, & Andrew Sanders (2000) "Police Response to Domestic Violence: From Victim Choice to Victim Empowerment?" 40 *British Journal of Criminology*, 14–36.

Huo, Yuen, & Tom Tyler (2000) *How Different Ethnic Groups React to Legal Authority*. San Francisco: Public Policy Institute of California.

INCITE! Women of Color Against Violence (2005) *About Incite!*, http://www.incite-national.org/index.php?s=35 (accessed June 22, 2005).

International Association of Chiefs of Police (1989) *IACP Model Domestic Violence Policy*. Alexandria, VA: IACP.

Jackson, Shelly, et al. (2003) *Batterer Intervention Programs: Where Do We Go from Here?* National Institute of Justice Special Report. Washington, DC: U.S. Department of Justice.

Jaffe, Peter, et al. (1993) "The Impact of Police Laying Charges," in Hilton, N. Zoe, ed., *Legal Responses to Wife Assault: Current Trends and Evaluation*, Newbury Park, CA: Sage.

Johnson, Leanor Boulin (1991) *On the Front Lines: Police Stress and Family Well-Being: Hearing before the Select Committee on Children, Youth, and Families House of Representatives*. 102nd Cong., 1st sess., May 20. Washington, DC: U.S. Government Printing Office.

Johnson, Michael (2006a) "Conflict and Control: Gender Symmetry and Asymmetry in Domestic Violence," 12 *Violence Aaainst Women*, 1003–18.

——— (2006b) "Violence and Abuse in Personal Relationships: Conflict, Terror, and Resistance in Intimate Partnerships," in A. Vangelista & D. Perlman, eds., *The Cambridge Handbook of Personal Relationships*, New York: Cambridge University Press.

———— (1995) "Patriarchal Terrorism and Common Couple Violence: Two Forms of Violence against Women in U.S. Families," 57 *J. of Marriage and the Family*, 283–94.

Jones, Dana, & Joanne Belknap (1999) "Police Responses to Battering in a Progressive Pro-Arrest Jurisdiction," 16 *Justice Quarterly*, 249–73.

Kimmel, Michael (1996) *Manhood in America: A Cultural History*. New York: Free Press.

Klein, Andrew (1996) "Re-Abuse in a Population of Court-Restrained Male Batterers: Why Restraining Orders Don't Work," in E. Buzawa and C. Buzawa, eds., *Do Arrests and Restraining Orders Work?* Thousand Oaks, CA: Sage.

Klinger, David (1995) "Policing Spousal Assault," 32 *J. of Research in Crime and Delinquency* 308–24.

Kupchik, Aaron (2004) Youthfulness, Responsibility and Punishment: Admonishing Adolescents in Criminal Court, 6 *Punishment and Society* 149–73.

Kurz, Demie (1998) "Old Problems and New Directions in the Study of Violence against Women," in R. Bergen, ed., *Issues in Intimate Violence*. Thousand Oaks, CA: Sage.

Labriola, Melissa, et al. (2005) *Testing the Effectiveness of Batterer Programs and Judicial Monitoring: Results from a Randomized Trial at the Bronx Misdemeanor Domestic Violence Court*. Washington, DC: National Institute of Justice.

LaFave, Wayne (1965) *Arrest: The Decision to Take a Suspect into Custody*. Boston: Little, Brown.

Lawler, Steph (2002) "Narrative in Social Research," in T. May, ed., *Qualitative Research in Action*. Thousand Oaks, CA: Sage.

Leo, Richard (1996) "The Impact of *Miranda* Revisited," 86 *J. of Criminal Law and Criminology*, 621–92.

Letellier, Patrick (1994) "Gay and Bisexual Male Domestic Violence Victimization: Challenges to Feminist Theory and Responses to Violence," 9 *Violence and Victims*, 95–106.

Levine, James (1975) "The Impact of 'Gideon': The Performance of Public and Private Criminal Defense Lawyers," 8 *Polity*, 215–40.

Lieblich, Amia, et al. (1998) *Narrative Research: Reading, Analysis, and Interpretation*. Thousand Oaks, CA: Sage.

Lynch, David (1999) "Perceived Judicial Hostility to Criminal Trials: Effects on Public Defenders in General and on Their Relationships with Clients and Prosecutors in Particular," in 26 *Criminal Justice and Behavior*, 217–34.

Lyon, Andrea (1996) "Be Careful What You Wish For: An Examination of Arrest and Prosecution Patterns of Domestic Violence Cases in Two Cities in Michigan," 5 *Michigan Journal of Gender and Law*, 253–98.

Maguigan, Holly (2003) "Symposium: Wading into Professor Schneider's 'Murky Middle Ground' between Acceptance and Rejection of Criminal Justice Responses to Domestic Violence," 11 *J. of Gender, Social Policy, and the Law*, 427–45.

Margarita, Mona (1980) "Killing the Police: Myths and Motives," 452 *Annals of the American Association of Political and Social Science*, 63–71.

Martin, Del (1976) *Battered Wives*. San Francisco: Glide.

Martin, Margaret (1997) "Double Your Trouble: Dual Arrest in Family Violence," 12 *J. of Family Violence*, 139–57.

Massing, Michael (2000) *The Fix*. Berkeley: University of California Press.

Mastrofski, Stephen, et al. (2000) "The Helping Hand of the Law: Police Control of Citizens on Request," 38 *Criminology*, 307–42.

Mather, Lynn (1979) *Plea Bargaining or Trial? The Process of Criminal-Case Disposition*. Lexington, MA: D.C. Heath.

Matoesian, Gregory (1993) *Reproducing Rape: Domination through Talk in the Courtroom*. Chicago: University of Chicago Press.

Maxwell, Christopher, et al. (2002) "The Preventive Effects of Arrest on Intimate Partner

Violence: Research, Policy, and Theory," in 2 *Criminology and Public Policy,* 51–80.

Merry, Sally Engle (2002) "Governmentality and Gender Violence in Hawai'i in Historical Perspective," 11 *Social and Legal Studies,* 81–111.

—— (2001) "Spatial Governmentality and the New Urban Social Order: Controlling Gender Violence through Law," in 103 *American Anthropologist,* 16–29.

—— (1995) "Wife Battering and the Ambiguities of Rights," in A. Sarat & T. Kearns, eds., *Identities, Politics, and Rights.* Ann Arbor, MI: University of Michigan Press.

Mileski, Maureen (1974) "Courtroom Encounters: An Observation Study of a Lower Criminal Court," in J. Robertson, ed., *Rough Justice: Perspectives on Lower Criminal Courts.* Boston: Little, Brown.

Miller, Susan (2001) "The Paradox of Women Arrested for Domestic Violence: Criminal Justice Professionals and Service Providers Respond," 7 *Violence against Women,* 1339–76.

Miller, William, & Benjamin Crabtree (2004) "Depth Interviewing," in S. Hesse-Biber and P. Leavy, eds., *Approaches to Qualitative Research: A Reader on Theory and Practice.* Oxford: Oxford University Press.

Mills, Linda (2003) *Insult to Injury: Rethinking Our Responses to Intimate Abuse.* Princeton, NJ: Princeton University Press.

—— (1999) "Killing Her Softly: Intimate Abuse and the Violence of State Intervention," 113 *Harvard Law Rev.,* 550–613.

Mirchandani, Rekha (2005) "What's So Special about Specialized Courts? The State and Social Change in Salt Lake City's Domestic Violence Court," 39 *Law and Society Rev.,* 379–418.

Morgan, David (2005) "Class and Masculinity," in R. W. Connell, et al., eds., *Handbook of Studies on Men and Masculinities.* Thousand Oaks, CA: Sage.

Muir, William Jr. (1977) *Police: Streetcorner Politicians.* Chicago: University of Chicago Press.

Murphy, Christopher, et al. (1998) "Coordinated Community Intervention for Domestic Abusers: Intervention System Involvement and Criminal Recidivism," 13 *J. of Family Violence,* 263–84.

Nardulli, Peter (1986) "'Insider' Justice: Defense Attorneys and the Handling of Felony Cases," 77 *J. of Criminal Law and Criminology,* 379–417.

Newbold, Greg (2003) "Rehabilitating Criminals: It Ain't That Easy," in J. Ross and S. Richards, eds., *Convict Criminology.* Belmont, CA: Wadsworth/Thompson Learning.

Nolan, James (2001) *Reinventing Justice: The American Drug Court Movement.* Princeton, NJ: Princeton University Press.

Packer, Herbert (1968) *The Limits of the Criminal Sanction.* Stanford, CA: Stanford University Press.

Pate, Anthony, & Edwin Hamilton (1992) "Formal and Informal Deterrents to Domestic Violence: The Dade County Spouse Assault Experiment," 57 *American Sociological Review,* 691–97.

Paternoster, Raymond, et al. (1997) "Do Fair Procedures Matter? The Effect of Procedural Justice on Spouse Assault," 31 *Law and Society Rev.,* 163–204.

Pennell, Joan, & Gale Burford (2002) "Feminist Praxis: Making Family Group Conferencing Work," in H. Strang and J. Braithwaite, eds., *Restorative Justice and Family Violence.* Cambridge: Cambridge University Press.

Pickering, Andrew (1995) *The Mangle of Practice: Time, Agency, and Science.* Chicago: University of Chicago Press.

Pleck, Elizabeth (1987) *Domestic Tyranny: The Making of Social Policy against Family Violence from Colonial Times to Present.* Oxford: Oxford University Press.

Ptacek, James (1999) *Battered Women in the Courtroom: The Power of Judicial Responses.* Boston: Northeastern University Press.

—— (1988) "Why Do Men Batter Their Wives?" in K. Yllo and M. Bograd, eds., *Feminist Perspectives on Wife Abuse.* Newbury Park, CA: Sage.

Rapping, Elayne (2000) "The Politics of Representation: Genre, Gender Violence and Justice," *Genders* (32). Available online at http://www.genders.org.

Reiss, Albert (1971) *The Police and the Public.* New Haven: Yale University Press.

Rennison, Callie Marie, & Sarah Welchans (2000) *Intimate Partner Violence.*" Bureau of Justice Statistics Special Report. Washington, DC: U.S. Department of Justice.

Riessman, Catherine Kohler (1993) *Narrative Analysis.* Newbury Park, CA: Sage.

Ristock, Janice (2002) *No More Secrets: Violence in Lesbian Relationships.* London: Routledge.

Rose, Nikolas (1999) *Powers of Freedom: Reframing Political Thought.* New York: Cambridge University Press.

—— (1996) *Inventing Our Selves: Psychology, Power, and Personhood.* New York: Cambridge University Press.

Rottman, David, & Pamela Casey (1999) "Therapeutic Jurisprudence and the Emergence of Problem-Solving Courts," in *National Institute of Justice J.,* 12–19 (July).

Roy, Maria, ed. (1977) *Battered Women: A Psychosocial Study of Domestic Violence.* New York: Van Nostrand Reinhold.

Rubinstein, Jonathan (1973) *City Police.* New York: Farrar, Straus, and Giroux.

Ruttenberg, Miriam (1994) "A Feminist Critique of Mandatory Arrest: An Analysis of Race and Gender in Domestic Violence Policy," *J. of Gender, Social Policy & the Law,* 2:171.

Sabo, Don (2005) "The Study of Masculinities and Men's Health: An Overview," in M. Kimmel et al., eds., *Handbook of Studies on Men and Masculinities.* Thousand Oaks, CA: Sage.

Sampson, Robert, & Dawn Jeglum Bartusch (1998) "Legal Cynicism and (Subcultural?) Tolerance of Deviance: The Neighborhood Context of Racial Differences," 32 *Law and Society Rev.,* 777–804.

Sarat, Austin (1990) "'The Law Is All Over': Power, Resistance and the Legal. Consciousness of the Welfare Poor," 2 *Yale J. of Law & Humanities,* 343–79.

Sarat, Austin, & William Felstiner (1995) *Divorce Lawyers and Their Clients: Power and Meaning in the Legal Process.* New York: Oxford University Press.

Schechter, Susan (1982) *Women and Male Violence: The Visions and Struggles of the Battered Women's Movement.* Boston: South End Press.

Schneider, Elizabeth (2000) *Battered Women and Feminist Lawmaking.* New Haven: Yale University Press.

Schwalbe, Michael, & Wolkomir, Michelle (2001) "The Masculine Self as Problem and Resource in Interview Studies of Men," 4 *Men and Masculinities,* 90–103.

Shepard, Melanie, & Ellen Pence, eds. (1999) *Coordinating Community Responses to Domestic Violence: Lessons from Duluth and Beyond.* Thousand Oaks, CA: Sage.

Sherman, Lawrence (1992) *Policing Domestic Violence: Experiments and Dilemmas.* New York: Free Press.

Sherman, Lawrence, & Richard Berk (1984) "The Specific Deterrent Effects of Arrest for Domestic Assault," 49 *American Sociological Review,* 261–72.

Sherman, Lawrence W., et al. (1992a) "The Variable Effects of Arrest on Criminal Careers: The Milwaukee Domestic Violence Experiment," 83 *J. of Criminal Law and Criminology,* 137–69.

Sherman, Lawrence, et al. (1992b) "Crime, Punishment, and Stake in Conformity: Legal and Informal Control of Domestic Violence," 57 *American Sociological Review,* 680–90.

Silbey, Susan S., & Patricia Ewick (2003) "Narrating Social Structure: Stories of Resistance to Legal Authority," 108 *American J. of Sociology,* 1328–72.

Simon, Jonathan (2007) *Governing through Crime: How the War on Crime Transformed American Democracy and Created a Culture of Fear.* New York: Oxford University Press.

Simpson, Mark (2002) "Meet the Metrosexual." Salon.com, July 22 (accessed July 24, 2008).

Skolnick, Jerome (1974) "Social Control in the Adversary System," in J. Robertson, ed., *Rough Justice: Perspectives on Lower Criminal Courts.* Boston: Little, Brown.

Smart, Carol (1995) *Law, Crime, and Sexuality: Essays in Feminism.* Newbury Park, CA: Sage.

Smith, Alisa (2003) "Battered Women on Pro-arrest Laws," in R. Muraskin, ed., *It's a Crime: Women and Justice.* 3rd ed. Upper Saddle River, NJ: Prentice Hall.

Stalans, Loretta, & Mary Finn (1995) "How Novice and Experienced Officers Interpret Wife Assaults: Normative and Efficiency Frames," in 29 *Law and Society Rev.,* 287–321.

Stark, Evan (2007) *Coercive Control: The Entrapment of Women in Personal Life.* New York: Oxford University Press.

—— (2006) "Commentary on Johnson's "Conflict and Control: Gender Symmetry and Asymmetry in Domestic Violence," 12 *Violence against Women,* 1019–25.

—— (2005) "Reconsidering State Intervention in Domestic Violence Cases," 5 *Social Policy and Society,* 149–59.

—— (1996) "Pro-Arrest of Batterers: A Reply to Its Critics," in E. Buzawa and C. Buzawa, eds., *Do Arrests and Restraining Orders Work?* Thousand Oaks, CA: Sage.

Stephens, B. Joyce, & Peter Sinden (2000) "Victims' Voices: Domestic Assault Victims' Perceptions of Police Demeanor," 15 *J. of Interpersonal Violence,* 534–47.

Stets, Jan, & Murray Straus (1989) "The Marriage License as a Hitting License: A Comparison of Assaults in Dating, Cohabitating, and Married Couples," in M. Straus and R. Gelles, eds., *Physical Violence in American Families: Risk Factors and Adaptations to Violence in 8,145 Families.* New Brunswick, NJ: Transaction.

Stover, Robert, & Dennis Eckart (1974–75) "A Systematic Comparison of Public Defenders and Private Attorneys," 3 *American J. of Criminal Law,* 265–300.

Strang, Heather, & John Braithwaite, eds. (2002) *Restorative Justice and Family Violence.* Cambridge: Cambridge University Press.

Straus, Murray, et al. (1980) *Behind Closed Doors: Violence in the American Family.* New York: Doubleday.

Straus, Murray, et al. (1996) "The Revised Tactics Conflict Scales (CTS2)," 17 *J. of Family Issues,* 283–316.

Straus, Murray, & Richard Gelles, eds. (1989) *Physical Violence in American Families: Risk Factors and Adaptations to Violence in 8,145 Families.* New Brunswick, NJ: Transaction.

Sun, Ivan (2003) "A Comparison of Police Field Training Officers' and Nontraining Officers' Conflict Resolution Styles: Controlling versus Supportive Strategies," 6 *Police Quarterly,* 22–50.

Sykes, Richard, & Edward Brent (1983) *Policing: A Social Behaviorist Perspective.* New Brunswick, NJ: Rutgers University Press.

Terrill, William (2003) "Police Use of Force and Suspect Resistance: The Micro Process of the Police–Suspect Encounter," 6 *Police Quarterly,* 51–83.

Thompson, George, & Jerry Jenkins (1993) *Verbal Judo: The Gentle Art of Persuasion.* New York: William Morrow.

Thurman vs. City of Torrington, et al. (1984) Civil No. H-84-120, United States District Court for the District of Connecticut, 595 F. Supp. 1521; 1984 U.S. Dist., October 23, 1984. Available at LexisNexis Academic.

Tuerkheimer, Deborah (2004) "Recognizing and Remedying the Harm of Battering: A Call to Criminalize Domestic Violence," 94 *J. of Criminal Law and Criminology*, 959–1031.

Tyler, Tom (2000) "Multiculturalism and the Willingness of Citizens to Defer to Law and to Legal Authorities," 25 *Law and Social Inquiry*, 983–1019.

——— (1990) *Why People Obey the Law*. New Haven: Yale University Press.

U.S. Attorney General's Task Force on Family Violence (1984) *Final Report*. Washington, D.C.: U.S. Attorney General.

United States Census (2000) *Census 2000*. www.census.gov (accessed December 25, 2008).

Valverde, Marianne (1998) *Diseases of the Will: Alcohol and the Dilemmas of Freedom*. Cambridge: Cambridge University Press.

Waits, Kathleen (1985) "The Criminal Justice System's Response to Battering: Understanding the Problem, Forging the Solutions," 60 *Washington Law Rev.*, 267–329.

Wanless, Marion (1996) "Pro-Arrest: A Step toward Eradicating Domestic Violence, but Is It Enough?" 2 *University of Illinois Law Rev.*, 533–87.

Weitzer, Ronald (2000) "Racialized Policing: Residents' Perceptions in Three Neighborhoods," 34 *Law and Society Rev.*, 129–55.

Welch, Donna (1994) "Mandatory Arrest of Domestic Abusers: Panacea or Perpetuation of the Problem of Abuse?" 43 *DePaul Law Rev.*, 1133–65.

Wilson, James Q. (1968) *Varieties of Police Behavior: The Management of Law and Order in Eight Communities*. Cambridge: Harvard University Press.

Wiseman, Frederick (2001) *Domestic Violence*. VHS. Cambridge, MA: Zipporah Films.

Wortley, Scot, et al. (1997) "Just Des(s)erts? The Racial Polarization of Perceptions of Criminal Injustice," 31 *Law and Society Rev.*, 637–76.

Yngvesson, Barbara (1994) "Making Law at the Doorway: The Clerk, the Court, and the Construction of Community Order in a New England Town," in C. Greenhouse, et al., eds., *Law and Community in Three American Towns*. Ithaca, NY: Cornell University Press.

Zorza, Joan (1994) "Must We Stop Arresting Batterers? Analysis and Policy Implications of New Police Domestic Violence Studies," 28 *New England Law Rev.*, 929–90.

——— (1992) "The Criminal Law of Misdemeanor Domestic Violence, 1970–1990," 83 *J. of Criminal Law and Criminology*, 46–72.

Index